Dimensions of
Madeleine L'Engle

Dimensions of Madeleine L'Engle

New Critical Approaches

Edited by SUZANNE BRAY

McFarland & Company, Inc., Publishers
Jefferson, North Carolina

LIBRARY OF CONGRESS CATALOGUING-IN-PUBLICATION DATA

Names: Bray, Suzanne, 1962– editor.
Title: Dimensions of Madeleine L'Engle : new critical approaches / edited by Suzanne Bray.
Description: Jefferson, North Carolina : McFarland & Company, Inc., Publishers, 2017. | Includes bibliographical references and index.
Identifiers: LCCN 2016055384 | ISBN 9781476664354 (softcover : acid free paper) ∞
Subjects: LCSH: L'Engle, Madeleine—Criticism and interpretation.
Classification: LCC PS3523.E55 Z64 2017 | DDC 813/.54—dc23
LC record available at https://lccn.loc.gov/2016055384

BRITISH LIBRARY CATALOGUING DATA ARE AVAILABLE

ISBN (print) 978-1-4766-6435-4
ISBN (ebook) 978-1-4766-2798-4

© 2017 Suzanne Bray. All rights reserved

No part of this book may be reproduced or transmitted in any form or by any means, electronic or mechanical, including photocopying or recording, or by any information storage and retrieval system, without permission in writing from the publisher.

Front cover image of Madeleine L'Engle (Madeleine L'Engle Papers [SC-3], Special Collections, Buswell Library, Wheaton, Illinois); background image of tree in fall © 2017 ValentinaPhotos/iStock

Printed in the United States of America

McFarland & Company, Inc., Publishers
  Box 611, Jefferson, North Carolina 28640
  www.mcfarlandpub.com

Contents

Preface	1
New Directions in L'Engle Studies? SUZANNE BRAY	3
A Scientific Girl and Two Intuitive Boys: The Unconventional Protagonists of *A Wrinkle in Time* ANNE-FRÉDÉRIQUE MOCHEL-CABALLERO	40
Thinking, Doing and Delaying Insemination in Madeleine L'Engle's *Many Waters* CHANTEL LAVOIE	51
Narration of the Poet as a Young Woman: Intertextuality, Genre and World-Building in L'Engle's Austin Family Novels CAROL S. FRANKO	65
What Madeleine Inherited from Her "Grandfather George": The Influence of George MacDonald on Madeleine L'Engle in Her Children's Fantasy Books SOPHIE DILLINGER	90
Madeleine L'Engle: An Anti-Romantic Romantic? GREGORY G. PEPETONE	111
Discarded Image and Expanding Universe: The (Meta)physics of C.S. Lewis and Madeleine L'Engle NAOMI WOOD	133
A Problematic Sense of Place: Madeleine L'Engle's "White in the Moon the Long Road Lies" GÉRALD PRÉHER	149

Of God and Women: The Evolution of Theology in
  L'Engle's Biblical Reimaginings
    EMILY LOUISE ZIMBRICK-ROGERS   160
"And what should I do in Illyria?": Discovering the
  American South and Its Gods in Madeleine L'Engle's
  The Other Side of the Sun
    SUZANNE BRAY   178

Selected Works   189
About the Contributors   195
Index   197

Preface

Madeleine L'Engle died on September 6, 2007, after a long and successful career as a writer. From 1963, when her best-known novel, *A Wrinkle in Time*, won the Newbery Medal, L'Engle was in the public eye, everything she wrote sold well and she was in constant demand to give speeches, write forewords, and to advise and encourage younger writers. However, in spite of her overwhelming success with the reading public, L'Engle has been largely ignored by academia. Although several biographies have been published, mostly aimed at the young adult reader, as well as many testimonies of her influence as a teacher and spiritual director, very little real literary criticism has been done on any of L'Engle's work except on the first three books of the time quintet, and practically no serious articles have been published on any of her adult fiction. At the present moment, there exists very little academic writing on her religious works, poems or short stories, and there has been little analysis of her theories of writing. On the other hand, L'Engle's works have been strongly criticized by members of the public and, in some cases, banned. It has been said, for example, of *A Wrinkle in Time* that "some people think it's too Christian, while others think it is not Christian enough" (Baldarasso). The novel has also been claimed to promote New Age ideology, Communist sympathies and even Satanism.

This book is an attempt to stimulate intellectual discussion about all of L'Engle's work and to show that the vast majority of her writings, not only the best-known children's books, are worthy of academic study. The first essay suggests, using Madeleine L'Engle's life and geographical attachments as guidelines, different aspects of her work which would repay further study. Critical essays on specific books or stories by L'Engle, by scholars from both sides of the Atlantic, provides a more analytical approach to her writings. Finally, a detailed bibliography provides ideas for further reading.

Some of the essays analyze works that have never been studied in depth before. Gérald Préher, for example, examines one of L'Engle's early short stories that throws light on her always ambiguous relationship with the American South, while Emily Louise Zimbrick Rogers includes an examination of the Genesis trilogy and three other of L'Engle's less well-known biblical works in her highly original article. Gregory G. Pepetone also breaks new ground in his discussion of Madeleine L'Engle's relationship with Romanticism. Gender issues are frequently evoked in these critical essays. Anne-Frédérique Mochel-Caballero examines the way in which L'Engle reverses gender stereotypes in *A Wrinkle in Time*, while Chantel Lavoie analyzes the author's message to male teenagers in *Many Waters*. Gender is also important in Carol S. Franko's study of Vicky's nature and vocation in the Austin family novels and Emily Louise Zimbrick-Rogers' overview of L'Engle's biblical midrash.

Emily Louise Zimbrick-Rogers also tackles another recurrent theme in these essays: L'Engle's theology. Her contribution shows L'Engle's approach to biblical interpretation and how her writings attempt to give a voice to voiceless characters in the narrative, while producing a more complete presentation of the character of God. Sophie Dillinger shows how much L'Engle's theology owes to George MacDonald, while Naomi Wood compares and contrasts the theological message in L'Engle's works with that of her fellow Anglican C.S. Lewis. Lastly, the study of *The Other Side of the Sun* as a conversion story also brings to light several of L'Engle's main theological themes.

If this book gets people thinking and talking about Madeleine L'Engle, as well as reading and studying more of her works, the authors will have succeeded.

New Directions in L'Engle Studies?

Suzanne Bray

It is quite frequent to study Madeleine L'Engle from the point of view of her target audience—as a children's writer or a young adult writer, even occasionally as a Christian writer.

It is considerably rarer to analyze or categorize her works with regard to their setting. And yet, L'Engle's works may easily be divided into groups along these lines. A very large number of her novels are set a in a small New England village where the characters live in a large, rambling house with extensive grounds, rather like Madeleine's own family home, Crosswicks. However, there are also three distinct sub-groups of her work set in potentially more exotic settings: New York, the Deep South and the Alps. In each of these cases, the setting, and L'Engle's attitude towards it, plays an integral part in the works themselves and in the message the author tries to convey. L'Engle's world is not the same when she, or her protagonists, are natives, people who half belong or are exiles, when they feel at home in the culture or alienated from it. As L'Engle's roots and experiences are examined, it is possible to see ways not only to understand L'Engle better, but also to situate her more clearly in the American literary landscape.

In the Beginning: Madeleine L'Engle as a New York Writer

> Frank: You know what, Cam, there's something awfully exciting about New York even if you've been born and brought up in it.
> Camilla: I think it's even more exciting if you've been born and brought up in it [*Camilla* 254].

4   Dimensions of Madeleine L'Engle

Although Madeleine L'Engle was named as a member of the New York Writers Hall of Fame in 2011 ("Literary Landmark") and every year numerous fans come to the Episcopalian cathedral on Morningside Heights to discover more about her, L'Engle is rarely mentioned as a New York writer. *The Cambridge Companion to the Literature of New York* (Patell and Waterman) does not even mention her. Neither do most of the numerous tourism websites encouraging literary pilgrims to visit the city and suggesting they follow Holden Caulfield to the Central Park Zoo carousel, drink champagne with Gatsby at the Plaza Hotel, or copy Holly Golightly by having breakfast at Tiffany's famous store on Fifth Avenue. For those who know L'Engle's writing, this may seem surprising, as so many of her works bring the city alive, and unlike Paul Auster's Quinn, for whom "no matter how well he came to know its neighborhood and streets, [New York] always left him with the feeling of being lost" (3–4), the majority of Madeleine's characters, from the 1920s to the last years of the twentieth century, feel at home in the city and find within it a place where they belong. Moreover, L'Engle brought the Cathedral of St. John the Divine to life and transformed it into both a literary landmark and a beacon of light and hope in the urban darkness.

Madeleine L'Engle Camp was born on what she called "the asphalt island of Manhattan" (*From This Day* 3) on November 29, 1918. This enabled her to identify with one of her favorite literary heroines, Emily from L. M. Montgomery's *Emily of the New Moon*, because "although Manhattan Island and Prince Edward Island are not much alike, they are still islands" (qtd. in Rosenberg 14–15). Her childhood home was a two-bedroom apartment on East 82nd Street, by the intersection with Park Avenue, not far from the Metropolitan Museum of Art, which was her "short cut to Central Park" (*Circle* 147).

In her early childhood, Madeleine's parents lived what Leonard Marcus describes as "an elegant if far from opulent beau monde life" (3) in New York City. Many of their friends were actors, musicians, artists and singers and Madeleine's parents held a supper party for several of them every Sunday evening (Gonzales 17). They also dressed for dinner every day and went out frequently to the theatre or opera house themselves (Marcus 4). For little Madeleine, her parents seemed to live in "a world of parties" (*From This Day* 4). Her own life, however, was made up of her beloved nanny, Mrs. O'Connell, and various governesses, plus "supper on a tray in the nursery, dancing lessons, music lessons, skating lessons, art lessons" (*Summer* 79). It also included many long walks around the city and visits to museums and art galleries. When she was eight, Madeleine's father, Charles Camp, decided she was old enough to go to the opera, but this was not a success as she had not been warned about the tragic ending (Gonzales 18). Young Madeleine also went to various private schools in New York, including the Brearley School (Marcus 45), which she did not like, and Todhunter School (Gonzales 26–27), which she did.

Although the Camps themselves were far from rich, Madeleine mixed with many rich girls at school including her "closest friend," whom she called a "poor little rich girl" and who lived in an "enormous, Italianate mansion" (*Summer* 34). This was almost certainly April Warburg, the daughter of the wealthy New York banker James Paul Warburg, who was also a financial advisor to Franklin D. Roosevelt. Madeleine's short story "Evening of a Governess," written over ten years later, beautifully evokes "the perfumed atmosphere and stifling status-conscious social order" (Marcus 9) of her school friend's household.

Madeleine's New York childhood ended in 1930 when her family moved to France, but Madeleine always referred to the city as "where I belonged" (*From This Day* 12) and felt at home there.

After graduating from Smith College in 1941, Madeleine, in her own words, "headed like a homing pigeon for New York," claiming that not only was it "the place of [her] birth," but also where she would find "music and art, theatre and publishing" (*From This Day* 12). At first, she shared an apartment on Ninth Street in Greenwich Village with "three other girls—two aspiring actresses, an aspiring pianist" (*The Small Rain* vii). The pianist, Frances Burnett from Jacksonville, Florida, who went on to have a successful career, impressed Madeleine with her commitment and self-discipline, "no matter what the rest of us were doing, she practiced eight hours per day" (*Irrational Season* 161). Her experience would be used in future years for Madeleine's many pianist characters, including Julie and Katherine Forrester. Although, as Madeleine later noted, "the glamorous world [her] parents had known during the twenties had been long gone" (*From This Day* 12), New York during the Second World War was still an exciting place to be. It was "a city which was still safe to walk in" (*From This Day* 31) and so Madeleine with her little dog, Touché, explored their surroundings and got to know them well. A favorite walk was "over to Fifth Avenue, past Mark Twain's house, past the Marshall Chess Club, where the windows were still lit" and back via the Ascension Episcopal Church on the corner of Tenth Street and Fifth Avenue (*From This Day* 39). She also enjoyed riding on the Staten Island ferry "to cool off in the breeze from the water" (*From This Day* 37) or riding the bus down Fifth Avenue. Although Madeleine was short of cash and considered, at that time, that the famous Russian Tea Room, where she would later take her grand-daughters (Marcus 186), was "definitely out of [her] pocketbook range" (*From This Day* 21), she was able to enjoy the more expensive amenities of the city when richer relatives visited. A distant cousin, Norman, took her "to dinner at the Plaza, in the elegant Edwardian room" and "listened to the famous Hildegarde sing Noël Coward songs" (*From This Day* 31), finishing the evening with a ride through Central Park in a horse-drawn hansom cab.

Madeleine's main reason for moving to New York was "to live [her] own life and work in the theater, which [she] considered the best possible school for a writer" (*Summer* 132). However, this was easier said than done and to start with, to earn her living, she sold war bonds in the theaters and, as she was good at this, got "sent from theater to theater and ultimately saw everything on Broadway" (*From This Day* 16). She also volunteered at St. Vincent's Hospital on Twelfth Street, where she gained information which would be useful for her fictional doctors like Suzy Davidson (née Austin) and Mimi Oppenheimer in years to come. Later on, she was fortunate enough to get a small part and an understudy's job with Eva Le Gallienne's company for the play *Uncle Harry*. She continued to work with the same team for two further productions.

Distracted from her literary work by their noisy lifestyle, Madeleine left her housemates and, in the summer of 1942, moved, on her own, into a small walk-up apartment on Twelfth Street, where she would have the peace and quiet she needed to write (*From This Day* 19). However, this was not really big enough and did not have a real kitchen, so she was delighted when, in 1944, *Mademoiselle* magazine bought one of her short stories for $200 and enabled her to move into a bigger and nicer apartment on the parlor floor of a brownstone at 32 West Tenth Street, where Leonard Bernstein was an upstairs neighbor. Madeleine's affection for her home here is evident from the number of her pleasant fictional characters who would live in the apartment. Julie Forrester (*Small Rain* 33) rented it, Katherine Forrester (*Severed Wasp* 6) later owned the whole building and lived on the parlor floor, while Chantal Wheaton (*Certain Women* 134) occupied it during the war years. While she was living there, Madeleine also experimented with drama and her New York light comedy, *18 Washington Square South*, was first produced in Northampton, Massachusetts (Baptiste 67) and later published in 1944. Her first novel, *The Small Rain*, which is partly set in New York, came out the following year. Her future husband, Hugh Franklin, was living in a studio apartment with a garden on West 55th Street at the time (*From This Day* 46). Madeleine gave it to her heroine, Emma Wheaton, in *Certain Women*.

Madeleine continued to live on Tenth Street after her marriage to Hugh Franklin until, in 1952, just before the birth of their second child, they moved to Goshen, Connecticut, to escape the exhausting and chaotic life of the New York theatre and thinking it would be a healthier place to bring up their children. Even in Goshen, the Franklins had a group of friends known, according to Frederica Brenneman, as the "New York crowd" (Marcus 162), although this merely meant that they had been born and raised outside Goshen. By 1960, the Franklins were ready to return to New York, and their daughter Josephine found them an 8-room apartment on the fifth floor of a building on the corner of West End Avenue and 105th Street, with a view over the Hudson River. Madeleine continued her dog-walking and got to know the

Upper West Side of the City very well indeed. She continued to live there until the end of her life. Her dinner parties, at least once a week, according to her grand-daughter Léna Roy, gathered "all kinds of people from all walks of life" (Marcus 189). Léna mentions "mathematicians and scientists" (Marcus 189), while her father, Alan Jones, evoking an earlier period, speaks of "stray bishops from England," "theatre people and writers" and even "Lincoln Kirstein, the founder of the City ballet" (Marcus 180). The apartment was also a base from which she could take her children, grandchildren and visitors to discover the city. Léna Roy mentions being taken to the Hayden Planetarium, the Frick Museum, the Metropolitan Museum, the Russian Tea Room and an annual ballet performance of *The Nutcracker* (Marcus 186).

Madeleine loved New York. Sometimes the city nourished her theological thinking, as when she found evidence of the Incarnation in what she observed, "In New York, I find it in the sight of a spindly, naked, dead-looking tree in the barren island on Broadway near our apartment, the bare branches suddenly bursting forth with magnolia blossoms in spring! I find it in snow (even deadly snow) falling past the lamps in Riverside Park when we walk the dogs at night" (*Circle* 165). However, she was well aware of New York's problems, admitting that "the glory of the incarnate world [...] is too frequently obscured in the city because of what we human beings have done to it" (*Irrational Season* 12). But although the glory was hidden, discerning it in New York was an important challenge for her: "If I cannot see God's love here on the Upper West Side of New York where we have done everything possible to destroy the beauty of creation, it is going to do me little good to rejoice in beauty in the uncluttered world of the country" (*Irrational Season* 13). And find it she did in "the quick generosity of all the shopkeepers on the block" (*Irrational Season* 84) or walking her dog at night on the upper level of Riverside Park (*Irrational Season* 150) or, even more particularly, in the Cathedral of St. John the Divine on Morningside Heights.

When Hugh and Madeleine returned to New York in 1960, in their opinion "the public school in the neighborhood [...] was one of the worst in New York" (*Circle* 238). For this reason, they sent their children to the nearby St. Hilda's and St. Hugh's Episcopal School, run by the nuns of the Community of the Holy Spirit. This led to Madeleine's discovery of the Cathedral, a second home, where she would become librarian, writer-in-residence and a committed member of the worshipping community—so much so that the Bishop would sometimes come to her apartment for Christmas dinner (Magnus 278). Katharine Weber sees Madeleine's relationship with the Cathedral as significant for her whole life and work: "There must be some great big metaphor you can drag in relating to the fact that it's a building that is perpetually under construction. I feel as if she had some sort of kinship with that space. It stood apart from the city for her, as a sanctuary" (Marcus 52). Madeleine herself spoke of "a place of trees and grass and beauty, and within this place a gracious, book-filled room where I am free to write" (*Irrational Season* 85). She not only wrote her books there, but also received visitors, sometimes individuals, sometimes school groups, who would come to speak to her.

New York in L'Engle's Fiction

New York plays a significant part in five of L'Engle's novels and in three short stories. It is mentioned in several others. For example, although the action in the semi-autobiographical "Evening of a Governess" does take place in New York, this is irrelevant to the plot and it could equally well have been set in any major East Coast city. Two other early stories, however, "Please Wear your Rubbers," the one bought by *Mademoiselle* in 1944, and "The Birthday," both have a definite New York setting. The former focuses on the despairing protagonist's decision to stay for two nights in the Algonquin Hotel, "where she'd always dreamed of going on her honeymoon" (190). The luxurious hotel represents the ultimate object of desire and a symbol of the happy, comfortable life from which the protagonist is excluded. At the same time, the contrast between the struggles and suffering of unsuccessful aspiring actresses and the glamorous life of those who do succeed is subtly portrayed.

"The Birthday" on the other hand, is a tale of childhood told from the child's point of view. The protagonist, Cecily, like Madeleine herself, is a New York only child, raised in the world of Central Park, museums, the Egyptian tombs (4), the Fifth Avenue bus and the Statue of Liberty (31). As a small girl, Madeleine, living in a city apartment block, surrounded by anonymous strangers, had looked out of her bedroom window onto a courtyard "where the stories of other city dwellers were sometimes enacted [...] behind unshaded windows" (*From This Day* 3–4), causing her to ask questions about the separateness of all human beings and her own identity. Cecily too looks out at these unknown people and is shocked to realize, for the first time, that "people thought when they were getting ready for bed and they didn't think about her" ("The Birthday" 2), causing her to understand that she is not the center of the universe, except to herself. Although "The Birthday" is an early L'Engle story and lacks some of the subtlety of her later work, Cecily is convincing as a city child and her existential crises are those which only make sense if you live in a crowded place, surrounded by people with whom you have no real relationship. Her mother's hospitalization and the absence of her parents on her birthday morning is far more traumatic than it would be for a girl living in a friendly village where she knows everyone, because Cecily feels abandoned by two of the few people with whom she has genuine personal contact.

The final New York short story, "Transfiguration" (1992), dates from a much later period and fits into the context of the novel *A Severed Wasp*. The protagonist, Sister Egg of the Community of the Epiphany,[1] shares Madeleine L'Engle's own ambivalence about the Upper West Side of New York City, swaying between hope and doubt as to whether redemption is possible. On the one hand, she deplores the fact that there are "thousands homeless and hungry in the city" (25) and that a poor woman should spend Christmas "wrapped in an inadequate blanket, sitting on a bare island on upper Broadway" (26), and yet she rejoices in these same islands, "radiant with magnolia blossoms in the spring, followed by tulips and delicately leafing trees" (26). She also loves the cosmopolitan neighborhood and celebrates "the Taiwanese shopkeeper from whom she always bought garlic because he had the best garlic in the city" (25), the cheerful homeless woman and her dog, the Korean shopkeeper who charges her half price for oranges and the loving child from the Episcopal school. Perhaps unsurprisingly, it is in the cathedral that Sister Egg finds the vision and the words she needs, in a painting of the Transfiguration in one of the bays which line the nave, where, by some trick of the light, the face of Christ appears momentarily to resemble that of the ragged thief who is trying to steal her money. The play of light in the cathedral transfigures all it touches, even the foil-wrapped chocolate kisses in her pocket, and, looking at the painting, for one instant Sister Egg cannot "see the cross, only the glory" (32), which gives her the renewal she needs to continue with her work. If Sister Egg's experience is unique and fictional, her New York is both depressingly and encouragingly real. The suffering and needy are truly and regrettably there, but when the light shifts, the glory is also visible and, for L'Engle, that is real too.

Among L'Engle's novels, *Camilla* (1951) is certainly the one which makes the most use of the author's childhood experience of New York. One reviewer has referred to it as "a New York City story" (Rosenberg 85) and others liken it to Salinger's *Catcher in the Rye*, which was published one month earlier (Smith 18–19). Camilla Dickinson, like Holden Caulfield, is a teenager from the affluent Park Avenue area of New York and, although she has "more innate strength and stability" (Smith 18–19) than Salinger's protagonist, she is, like him, at a key moment in her personal development. She will also be helped to grow up by the city itself. As Margaret Willey writes, *Camilla* is like a 20th century fairy tale where the reader wonders "how will the princess escape supervision long enough to exit the tower, descend into the forest and head for the village?" However, in this tale, the village is Greenwich Village, where Camilla's best friend Luisa lives on Ninth Street with her highly informal and Bohemian family. The whole novel explores the heroine's statement that "Greenwich Village is almost a different world from Park Avenue" (*Camilla* 14) and presents the culture shock which inevitably occurs when the two worlds meet. Park Avenue Camilla, living a wealthy, white, middle class existence with maids and cooks, in an apartment block with a doorman and elevator boy, is fascinated by the ethnically mixed, arty world of the Village, where children seem to mature more quickly than in her protected environment. For Camilla, even Washington Square "had always seemed [...] a much more grown-up park than Central Park" (58).

The limited nature of the Dickinson family's existence is also illustrated by Camilla's frustrated father, Rafferty. A brilliant architect, Rafferty dreams of building a New York apartment block with "sunlight in every room, and space to breathe and a feeling of the city as you looked out of the window" (109), but economic considerations must come first, and superiors without his vision take over the plans and make them "distorted and cramped" (110), like the family's traditional, affluent life. However, walking around the city, as much as meeting Luisa and her family, enables Camilla to find a form of freedom. As a child, this meant getting her nurse to take her through the Metropolitan Museum of Art, where she could see the Egyptian tombs and "the great halls hung with embroidered flags and shields and swords and filled with coats of armor" (38), which transported her into another, imaginary, world. During the critical three weeks narrated in the novel, Camilla walks round the city first with her father, then with Luisa and finally with Luisa's brother Frank, with whom she falls in love. Yet, as Camilla gets to know Frank better, they discover the city together and this helps Camilla define what she believes. In a key scene on the Staten Island ferry, touchingly portrayed in Cornelia Duryée Moore's film of the novel, the two young people realize they "could see nothing ahead" (248) of themselves, neither physically, because of the fog, nor with regard to their uncertain futures. Yet, as they look back at the skyline of New York, it seems "like a mirage or a city in a fairy tale put under a spell and disappearing forever into the mist" (248). This elusive view reflects the reality of their situation—within a few days both of them will leave the city to start a new life elsewhere and their time together, like New York itself, will seem like an enchanted memory.

Fourteen years separate Madeleine L'Engle's two cathedral-based novels, *The Young Unicorns* (1968) and *A Severed Wasp* (1982), and yet, in both stories the cathedral itself dominates the action and the city. Already in the late sixties, Morningside Heights was losing its "old academic elegance" (*Irrational* 12) and the Upper West Side was no longer the "solid, respectable, moneyed" (12) neighborhood it had once been. L'Engle describes it a few years later as "white, black, yellow, tan; where one hears English in a multitude of accents, as well as Spanish, German, Creole, Taiwanese, Chinese, Japanese, Korean, Hindustani, Yiddish, Hebrew, French" (12), a dynamic, cosmopolitan area, but one with problems of poverty, drugs and violence. At the time *The Young Unicorns* was being written, the cathedral was largely neglected. There had been no dean there since John Butler's retirement in 1966 (Marcus 224) and

Madeleine's close friend Canon Edward Nason West was more or less in charge, among his many other responsibilities. In 1972, Bishop Paul Moore would refer to it as "an empty cathedral [...] as dead as a dog" (Marcus 223), although it is only fair to say that L'Engle, at the same period, was encouraged by the fact that "half the congregation at the Cathedral on Sunday [was] under thirty" and that "lots of them [were] long-haired and barefooted" (*Circle* 171), which implies that the building was not completely empty. William Alexander Johnson, a canon of the cathedral from 1973, refers to the period from the late sixties to the end of the eighties as one of "terrible decline" (Marcus 220) and writes of people who would "come into the cathedral and steal things" or "throw rocks at the stained-glass windows" or "get mugged in the Peace Fountain" (220). In Johnson's opinion, "Madeleine knew that the neighborhood was becoming increasingly poor and drug-ridden and dangerous" (220) and her writings reflect this reality. If the city had changed since *West Side Story* (1957), on account of the urban clearance for the Lincoln Center, many of the problems of that period remained and *The Young Unicorns*' New York is still recognizably that of David Wilkerson's *The Cross and the Switchblade* (1962) with its gangs, violence and addiction.

New York in *The Young Unicorns* is seen mainly through the eyes of the Austin family, who have recently moved there from rural Connecticut, and those of Dave (Josiah Davidson), who has always lived there without really noticing his surroundings. One reviewer praised L'Engle for the vivid "feelings of uncertainty and foreboding" she evokes "in her descriptions of the New York City Streets, overrun by drugs and gangs" (Fitzgerald) and her "bleak and disconcerting picture of 1960s New York City." It is made clear that "the Upper West Side of New York City is not a safe place for little kids to wander about in" (*Unicorns* 12) and the Bishop recalls "the riots and rebellion that tore our streets this past summer, and indeed for many summers past" (79). Dave is a former gang member and remembers joining in with "gangs running through the shocked streets, looting and throwing broken bottles" (79–80). When the characters stop talking they can hear "the uneasy breathing of the city" (171). The narrator describes the scene: "an ambulance wailed. There was a sound that might have been gunfire, or a car's muffler backfiring. Horns honked. Brakes screeched. Tires screamed. There was a distant wail of a child" (171). In this ominous atmosphere everyone agrees with the admirable Dr. Gregory that "the city is crying for redemption" (243), even if there is disagreement as to how that redemption may be obtained.

In the midst of this dangerous and sometimes frightening city, as Nancy Adams points out, L'Engle's Cathedral is "a pervasive and numinous presence, at once life-giving and glowing with light, but at other times eerie and unsettling, with rather Gothic overtones." It is both a place of hope and the criminals' headquarters, the focal point of a community of faith and an immense labyrinth of secret passages, hidden nooks and crannies. It is also a place of care and compassion and, as in reality, poor New Yorkers who "could not bring themselves to enter the Cathedral itself came to the Cathedral offices for money, for food, for help with a greedy landlord or extortioner, or simply for a word of kindness or encouragement" (*Unicorns* 203–204). Mari Ness observes that L'Engle's "love and knowledge of that part of New York City shines through" ("Intrigue and Lasers"), which enhances the vivid clarity of the setting. The principal protagonist is Dave, who has "been around the cathedral most of his life" (55), so much so that its "beauty was so everyday a part of his comings and goings that he seldom noticed or acknowledged it" (55). However, from the very start of the novel, Dave regularly looks uphill towards the Cathedral, sees how it dominates the area and observes "its multicolored Octagon of stone and glass glowing brilliantly against the rain-filled sky" (3). In spite of his rebellious attitude, this vision continues to attract him and the fact that he possesses a set of keys to the cathedral provides him with a sense of security and reassurance.

Dave corresponds to a later L'Engle character's descriptions of a typical, self-absorbed New Yorker, "trained not see" and "able to slither through a mob on Broadway so quickly you're almost invisible, but you don't see anybody. They're just bodies" (*Certain Women* 319). Dave too is "so accustomed to the conglomerate and colorful crowd on the Upper West Side of the City that it would have taken someone beyond the bounds of the merely unusual to make him pause and take notice" (5). For this reason, his friendship with blind Emily, who cannot physically see the neighborhood or the Cathedral at all, and country-raised Vicky, who is still observing and discovering her new surroundings, helps open his eyes to the beauty and wonder he has missed. As Donald Hettinga remarks, when Dave "surveys life in the urban landscape of New York City, [he] sees only evil" (*Presenting* 63) and, in one way, "his vision […] is largely correct" (64), for there is much evil in the city. However, it is not the whole story. Although Dave tells her: "You can't go around trusting people […] Not anybody. Not in New York City. Not today" (*Unicorns* 53), Vicky sees beyond the evil and is able to discern between the trustworthy and the unreliable, between light and darkness. Vicky is an observer and as she watches "the lights across in New Jersey, a barge crawling up the river, cars streaming north and south on the West Side Highway" or "the lights of the park baring the dark branches of the trees" (41), she comes to see that the whole city is like the view in front of her, as the wind moves the branches of the trees on Riverside Drive across the street lamps "so that light and shadow mingled and intermingled" (42). As a result, in spite of Dave's warnings, even in the swirling fog where she can hardly see at all, Vicky knows she can trust Canon Tallis, just as much as she knows she should not trust the leather-jacketed Alphabats. Towards the end of the story, when

Dave, Emily and many others have walked into danger, Vicky, with her awareness of light and darkness in the city, draws the Dean and Canon Tallis to the rescue by lighting all the candles in the Cathedral's seven chapels, thus creating a half circle of light, which can be seen by all those who look uphill to Morningside Heights. The Cathedral thus shines in the darkness as a beacon in an evil world. And after the evil has been defeated, the music of the requiem mass rises up to the lancet windows of the central octagon, "cleansing, redeeming" (243) both the Cathedral and the city and setting Dave free to meet his destiny as an adult.

The Cathedral plays in a similar role in L'Engle's much later novel, *A Severed Wasp*. Although the book was actually written fourteen years after *The Young Unicorns*, it is about thirty years later in fictional time as Suzy Austin, age 12 in the earlier novel, is now in her early forties. If teenage gangs are less visibly present in the Upper West Side of the city than in *The Young Unicorns*, there are still drugs and drug dealers, including the Bishop of New York's cook's husband, and violent crime, including the gratuitous murder of a suffragan bishop. In spite of urban renewal schemes and social programs, including work by a former bishop and the Cathedral staff "cleaning up the slums around the Cathedral, and training and employing local kids" (*Wasp* 80), there are still numerous social problems. On Amsterdam, the protagonist notices "gutters and sidewalks were littered with papers, broken bottles, dog turds (in disregard of signs), general filth" (20). There are also piles of garbage in the street (20), slightly muddy water (32), frequent power cuts (43), "buildings with boarded-up windows" (116) and filthy tenements up on Washington Heights (55). Washington Square has become "just another Needle Park" (192) for addicts, there is no safe way to cross 110th Street (14) and the Mother Superior of the Community of the Epiphany has to accept "that a solitary woman driver is no longer safe after dark" (292), even if she is a nun. In the mid-summer intense heat, L'Engle's New York is "a city of fear" (332) and her characters have to fight to resist contagion.

Three bishops on from *The Young Unicorns*, Dave is now the Dean of the Cathedral and has been married to Suzy Austin for over twenty years. Although the Cathedral still dominates the district, its "vast nave sweeping the full length of a city block" (3) and "soft light shimmer[ing] against the columns so that they shine like mother-of-pearl" (3), security has to be tighter than before and, as Dave's elder daughter points out, "all the chapels here have to be kept locked" (69) and "the gold candles and crucifixes have been removed" (69). In spite of this, Dave is said to have once found "a dead chicken at the foot of the high altar" (69) and Katherine Forrester, the protagonist, finds a priest smoking pot there, although she is informed that "pot in cathedrals is nothing new" (118). In spite of all this, the Cathedral is presented as "a happy place [...] in an often unhappy city" (9) and as Katherine is slowly integrated into "the Cathedral family" (388), she comes to love it and to accept its role as a place of refuge and redemption to those around it.

If half of Madeleine's group of friends and contacts in New York came from what she called her "community at St. John's Cathedral" (*Irrational* 180), the other half came from her husband's work in the theatre. These people also included those that she herself had worked with in the theatrical world in the 1940s. Over fifty years of contact with the New York theatre inevitably found its way into her books, from her first novel *The Small Rain* to much later works like *Certain Women* (1992). In her introduction to the 1984 edition of *The Small Rain*, the author admits that much of Katherine Forrester's experience in the novel was based on her own experiences while "sharing an apartment in the Village with three other girls" (vii) during the Second World War. It was a time when "the streets of New York were full of soldiers and sailors" (ix) and yet the arty, alternative lifestyle of the Village attracted many. Reviewer Edward Weeks congratulated L'Engle for successfully portraying bohemian New York, a realm which, in his opinion "can so easily be cheapened, sentimentalized or exaggerated" (125), yet it is fair to say that the author, like her protagonist, loved New York but did not like Bohemianism (*Rain* 361). Katherine's enthusiasm for "West Eleventh Street with its gingko and ailanthus trees, its quietness, its old-world flavor" (305) is endearing, as is her affection for the "jelly lady up on Ninth Avenue where they bought lemon butter and gooseberry jam" (294) or the "old women selling corsages of gardenias and violets" (346) outside the movie theatres. At the same time, her unease with the clientele at Pete's favorite café, The Purple Pigeon, where "heavily painted older women, most of them disappointed leading ladies or out-grown ingénues" (264) try to lure her to join their crowd, is also palpable. L'Engle also effectively evokes naïve Katherine's dismay at the little tavern below Washington Square with its "dirty crooked steps," "heavy stench," ashtrays full of half-smoked cigarettes, as well as a dancing transvestite and an old woman who "lay sleeping, drunkenly sprawled across her table" (311–312). While this negative reaction may, today, seem unduly moralistic, it certainly portrays the very real reaction of many girls from sheltered backgrounds plunged into the seamy side of big city life.

Writing in retrospect about her first novel, Madeleine L'Engle expressed a paradox: "*The Small Rain* is not autobiographical, but my theater experience is on the first page. I am not Katherine, though we share much in common" (*Small Rain* ix). One of those shared elements is theatrical New York. The same ambiguity exists in *Certain Women*. The novel uses "her own memories of her acting career on Broadway in the 1940s" (*Circle of Friends* 19) and Emma Wheaton's personality is not unlike Madeleine's. At the same time, as Cornelia Duryée Moore has pointed out, Emma is "a young actress in Manhattan with long red hair, grey eyes and many eerily-familiar attributes" (*Cir-*

cle of Friends 19), strongly resembling Cornelia herself. For Emma, New York is home (*Certain Women* 271). Like Madeleine, she likes to go to "the Russian Tea Room or the Village Vanguard for supper" (134), while her father David is enthusiastic about Joe's Saloon on Ninth Street, just down the street from the apartment Madeleine shared with her friends, because, unlike several more classy establishments, "theater people went there to talk and not to be seen" (21). The whole Wheaton tribe live all over Madeleine's New York— Edith and then Sophie live with David on Riverside Drive (33), Emma lives on 55th Street (124), Chantal in Greenwich Village (134), Adair in Brooklyn Heights (136), Myrlo and Billy on Park Avenue (24)—and between them they take possession of the city and make it their own.

In all her New York writings, it is the detail that makes L'Engle's city live, from "the unmistakable stench of the New York subway system" (74) or the woman on Broadway "singing *The Old Rugged Cross*, exhorting the city to reform, hiccupping, almost falling and bursting into a string of oaths" (19) in *The Young Unicorns*, to the "young woman walk[ing] down the middle of 105th Street with a very large Great Dane" (*Irrational Season* 1) or the "grinding and gnashing at five o'clock every morning" (*From This Day* 29) of Manhattan's garbage trucks. Yet, the author's own ambiguity with regard to her beloved city also leaves its mark. On the one hand, walking through the streets of the Upper West Side makes her "own little gestures of love in this angry world seem inadequate" (*Circle* 182), while at the same time, she remains convinced that the city is a powerful magnet, attracting whom and what it needs to itself. As L'Engle told Gardner McCall, "New York needs good people and it always draws good people back" (Marcus 339). Within this multifacetted center of population, only the Cathedral remains what Dean James Morton Parks wanted it to be, "a holy place for the whole city" (Marcus 224), a home from home and a shining light for all around to see by. In recognition of this, the Cathedral was officially named a "literary landmark" in Madeleine L'Engle's honor in November 2012, creating a permanent link between her fiction and the real world (Staino).

Madeleine L'Engle as a Southern Writer

Although Madeleine L'Engle's links to New York are regularly acknowledged, it is much less frequently mentioned that she also had deep roots in the American South. Her mother, Madeleine Hall Barnett, was a Southern belle from Jacksonville, Florida. From the author's earliest childhood she regularly visited her grandmother and a tribe of numerous cousins, most of whom were typical Southerners. The L'Engle family had Franco-Swiss, mainly Huguenot, origins and settled in South Carolina, not far from Charleston, and in Florida at the beginning of the 18th century. By the time Madeleine was born, it was a huge network of kin, relatively wealthy, and well-known in regional society. Madeleine's mother would tell her daughter tales about family history and events from her own childhood, helping the author to see herself in the Southern context and to imagine the region's past. Later on, Madeleine was also able to consult both her great-grandmother Mado's letters and diaries, given to her by her mother (*Summer* 175), and the published memoirs of her great-great-grandmother, Susan Fatio L'Engle, which she referred to as "a delightful treasure" (*Rock* 91) and which went back to the first quarter of the 19th century.

Madeleine herself only came to live in the South after her family's return from Europe in the fall of 1933. She remained there, going to school at Ashley Hall in Charleston and spending her vacations in Jacksonville, until she left for Smith College in 1937. Cynthia Zarin writes that, although she enjoyed her school, Madeleine "found Florida stultifying and surreal" (63) and, according to her cousin Mary, "was just completely out of place at that time and in that part of the world" (Marcus 30). As an ambitious young woman, intending to go to college and have a career, Madeleine felt ill-at-ease in an atmosphere where most of her Southern girl cousins had a "highly cultivated charm" (*Summer* 124), but were mainly interested in coming-out balls, looking beautiful and finding their place in society, which meant husband-hunting. Even worse, many of her Southern relatives expected Madeleine "to stay home and take care of [her] delicate mother" (*Summer* 131). Fortunately her mother had no such unrealistic expectations.

However, one advantage L'Engle had in understanding the South and its problems came from her own dual identity. As she wrote several decades later: "My mother was a Southerner and my father was a 'damnyankee,' and I got two totally differently versions of 'the wa-ah,' as my mother called it [...] it's two very different wars, depending on the point of view" (*Rock* 90). Even when, as an adult and a professional writer, Madeleine settled permanently in the North, her mother continued to live in Jacksonville with Dinah, her invaluable African American companion and maid, and provided for many years a living link to Southern culture and the extended family.

Two of Madeleine L'Engle's novels, *Ilsa* (1946) and *The Other Side of the Sun* (1971) are set in the South, as are two short stories, "White in the Moon, the Long Road Lies" (1939) and "Poor Little Saturday" (1956). Three other novels, *Dragons in the Waters* (1976), *A House Like a Lotus* (1984) and *A Live Coal in the Sea* (1996) contain fairly substantial Southern elements. However, the works written before L'Engle's return to the Christian faith in the 1960s clearly show her dislike of many elements of Southern culture and give a negative portrait of the area. The later works are more nuanced. Although L'Engle remains critical of many aspects of Southern life, including the restricted role allowed to women, racial segregation and the misrepresentation by many of the nature of God, she also presents examples of the Southern tradition at its best, with its honorable, cultured gentlemen and ladies who care for others and try hard to live good lives.

"White in the Moon, the Long Road Lies," an early short story written and published while Madeleine was still at college, relies heavily on the author's own experience as a semi-outsider in the South. The protagonist, Selina, about to leave for the North, considers why she is leaving and questions her own identity. On the one hand, she declares that "it's stagnant and old and narrow-minded" (2) in the South and that "no one has survived the Civil War except [...] one or two people" (2), statements far blunter than anything Madeleine would have felt comfortable publishing in her own name. On the other hand, leaving the South means "tearing [her]self apart" (2) and "breaking [her]self off at the roots" (2), "leaving part of herself behind" (3). The story shows that while Selina, and probably Madeleine too, is uncomfortable with Southern people in Southern society, she loves the landscape and feels at home in it. Selina goes to say goodbye to "the ocean and the great stretch of silver beach, the white dunes and leaping wind" (3) and feels in the sand, waves, wind and sky "something that would always be with her" (3). She thinks too, with affection, of the flora and fauna of the region, "sandpipers strutting up and down the beach in early morning, and the sleek black of the porpoises' leap; the flower of Spanish Bayonettes in early spring, and broken shells upon the beach after a storm" (3–4). Although there is no clear plot, the charm of the story is found in the powerful evocation of the Florida coast in late summer, where even the stifling heat and the "buzz of mosquitoes" (1) have their place. The only attractive people are Melly, the caring African-American maid and Bill, Selina's brother who, like Madeleine's best Florida friend Pat, is a doctor and stays in the South for professional reasons. Bill can, rightly, see that Selina has never really belonged in the South, and that she does not "really fit" (2) even with her own family, while Peter, Selina's supposed love, betrays his lack of knowledge of her as he cannot envisage her in the North and sees her as only belonging "in the sun, with the wind and the waves" (3) where he has always seen her.

After Madeleine's first book, *The Small Rain*, had "caused a sensation" ("Cheerful Tragedy" 3) in 1945, the author decided to write a novel set in the South, in a town which strongly resembles Jacksonville. *Ilsa* is in many ways a depressing story—the protagonist was described, justifiably, by one reviewer as "a sapless youth of the Old South," inflicting on readers "the tedium of his perpetual unspoken devotion" (Holsaert 14). However, it is a remarkable evocation of the American South in the first half of the 20th century. The Jacksonville L'Engle describes is the town her mother knew as a child, "a small town where everybody knew each other and almost everybody was kin" (*Sum-*

mer 197). Even when Madeleine and Hugh Franklin were first married, "more than half the congregation" in St. John's Episcopal Church, where Mrs. Camp worshipped, were related to her. Various historians of the South have also stressed this kin-based, genteel society and pointed out that "close-knit marital alliances [...] restricted the circle of gentility to the very wealthiest and well-born families" (Wyatt-Brown 41), creating an almost incestuous community.

The depiction of this small-town life, with its limited social circle, is, as Robert Pick has noted, one of the strengths of the novel. In a review entitled "Three Families, One Town," Pick praises "the galaxy [...] of those Porchers, Woolfs and Silvertons of all ages," which "creates an absorbing atmosphere of authenticity" (30). In addition, the novel starts with a vivid portrayal of the great fire of 1901, which burnt the entire city of Jacksonville. Reproducing her mother's and grandmother's memories of this tragic episode and their own hurried escape from the conflagration, Madeleine uses it to reveal the social divisions of the time. Her 20-year-old mother's clear memories were inserted into her fictional narrative, such as that of "the streets [...] full of terrified people, black and white, draped in sheets to meet the end of the world, waving flaming torches and crying 'Jedgement Day! Jedgement Day!'" (*Summer* 214 and *Ilsa* 23). Just as Madeleine's grandfather "managed to get horses, carriages, wagons, across the river where they were safe from the flames" (*Summer* 214), John Brandes, her heroine's father, saves the Porcher family and their belongings from destruction. However, this does not create a link between the families. Cecilia Porcher claims she would have rather seen her children "being carried downstairs in their coffins" (*Ilsa* 44), than have them ride away and spend the night in the house of a socially inferior Northerner, who had previously dared aspire to the hand in marriage of one of her kin.

One possible reason why *Ilsa* was "published to distinguished reviews but very modest sales" (*From This Day* 130) may come from its too accurate depiction of many of the negative elements of Southern society at the time and the too close resemblance between some of the characters and members of Madeleine's own family. Even the protagonist's surname, Porcher, is from Madeleine's family—for example, her Aunt Nadia's father's name was Peter Porcher L'Engle. The author's unease with the South is apparent throughout the book. Henry Porcher, the protagonist, is a sensitive young man, with a certain talent for the violin. He never even tries to earn his own living as he "always had enough money, and enough time in which to be sorry for [him]self" (*Ilsa* 276). He also spends several years in France, supposedly studying music, but actually just leading a bohemian lifestyle at his father's expense. This is not unlike the situation of two of Madeleine's maternal uncles. Bion Barnett Jnr was a moderately talented artist, who never actually earned his own living, but spent a lot of time studying art in France and, as a cousin remarked, "his banker father paid his bills" (Marcus 33). Bion Jr.'s twin brother, William, embarrassed the family by marrying a French unmarried mother at the end of the First World War and, like his twin, showed no interest in banking, business or making money in any other way. Madeleine, who earned her own living from the day she left college, clearly felt uncomfortable with this way of life. This unease was typical of Northerners who, as Nina Silber explains, from the Civil War onwards, "attacked white Southern men and women for their apparent disregard for any and every form of honorable labor, for their devotion to a system which rested on idleness and slothfulness" (9).

If, as Diane Roberts claims, Southern gentlemen "come in two flavors, contemplative or active, Hamlet or Hotspur" (86), in *Ilsa*, Monty Woolf provides a pugnacious contrast to his ineffectual cousin Henry. Noticeable for his "kind of unsteady gentleman-of-the-old-South manner" (*Ilsa* 168), Monty fulfils all the negative stereotypes by always "showing off and talking big" (213), hunting, drinking too much and ill-treating, deceiving or neglecting his wife, Ilsa, while insisting she lives like a traditional Southern lady. He also lets his father's law practice collapse and "resents having to work," being "firmly convinced he ought to be subsidized for life" (*Ilsa* 178) and finally dies young from drinking too much bad gin.

Madeleine L'Engle's own dislike of *Ilsa* meant that she never allowed it to be reprinted, which is regrettable as its portrayal of the South, although perhaps overly negative, vividly captures the atmosphere of a period. The author even maintained her negative attitude to her protagonist nearly forty years later, when she described Henry as coming from "one of those inbred Southern families" and having "late in life married a distant cousin in Paris, a singer" (*Lotus* 249)—presumably Telcide, who appears in *Ilsa*. This marriage leads to Henry's grandson, Henri, inheriting "a latent strain of insanity, violent insanity" (249) from the Porchers and being confined in a psychiatric hospital.

L'Engle's next Southern work, the short story "Poor Little Saturday" (1956), has an equally negative attitude to the American South. However, its fast-moving plot and pleasant teenage protagonist make it a far less depressing read than *Ilsa*. The nameless narrator/protagonist lives in a "nosy little town in South Georgia" (227) where everyone knows everyone else's business. Just out of town is "a deserted, boarded-up plantation house" (227), which no one has lived in since the Civil War when the owner, Colonel Londermaine, was killed in action and his beautiful wife, Alexandra, committed suicide. The narrator is fascinated by the abandoned property and its decayed grandeur from a bygone age. He also goes there because the neglected, overgrown gardens are shady and cool, providing respite from the scorching summer heat.

The action takes place during a boiling hot September, which the narrator describes as "our hottest month" (228). The heat and its influence on the action is accentuated: it "lay coiled and shimmering on the road" (228) and burned through the narrator's calloused feet. In his simple home the walls and floors are hot to touch and, even in his bedroom, there were "flies buzzing around [his] face" (228). To make matters worse, the narrator has bad spells of malaria, shivers and sweats from the fever and has an aching head. Although it is never spelled out explicitly, the text makes it clear that the narrator is poor, but white and literate. His first encounter with the beautiful witch woman and young Alex occurs when he is in the middle of a particularly bad malaria attack. There is at least some doubt as to whether he really meets them or whether he is delirious. Alex is a typical Southern girl in her mid-teens, dressed, Pollyanna-style, in a "blue and white gingham" dress with "a white ruffled petticoat underneath it" (229), her dark-brown hair parted in the middle and worn in "two heavy braids" (229). She also bears a remarkable resemblance to the portrait of Alexandra Londermaine in the plantation house drawing-room. Apart from the fact that the witch woman has a great quantity of mahogany-colored hair and wears a deep purple velvet robe, no precise details are given about her appearance. The narrator feels "she must be immensely tall" and that "she must be very beautiful" (231), although he admits "she would never have fulfilled any of the standards of beauty set by our town," implying perhaps that she was too dynamic, dominant and imposing to please the small Southern town's ideas of what was fitting for women. She also appears to have intellectual interests, studying pharmacy, chemistry and physics as well as reading numerous books and keeping various wild animals.

The narrator lives in peace with his two new friends until the day he is found to have round his neck the sapphire and diamond ring Alexandra Londermaine was wearing for her portrait and which had disappeared the night she hung herself. From the narrator's point of view, the ring is a present from Alex, a token of their mutual love. The men of the town, who do not believe his story and "were all bored" (239), as it had been "a long, dull year" (239), turn to mob violence, get the narrator very drunk on corn liquor and force him to tell them the truth. When their victim rushes to the plantation house the next morning the men of the town follow him, intending to lynch the witch woman. The narrator is held prisoner as the "dirty, insensitive men" (240) drag the witch woman out, but she is defended by her pet camel who breaks one man's leg with a kick while the others run away in terror. The witch woman leaves the town flying on the camel's back as the narrator, unmolested now, waves good-bye.

In one way the plantation house in the story represents what such properties were always meant to be, "an ideal oasis of civilisation in a corrupt world" (Seidel 89). However, the antebellum stereotypes are both confirmed and transformed. Alex, the imaginary/ghostly descendant of the Londermaines, is the perfect lady, elegant, gracious, generous and loving. On the other hand, the radical witch woman, with both her beauty and all her leadership qualities, is described as the "lord and master" (240) of her household, a deliberate choice of masculine vocabulary to accentuate her strength and independence. Moreover, she is not only a witch by professional choice, and therefore highly suspect in the small Southern town, she also seems to have been (perhaps in another life?) involved in a lover-like relationship with Colonel Londermaine, making her potentially an adulteress too. The brutish men of the town, including the protagonist's own father, are seen to be following an archaic, practically pagan, honor code, which in the American South, as Bertram Wyatt-Brown has pointed out, "required the rejection of the lowly, the alien and the shamed" (4), like the poor, sick boy, suspected of stealing, who has no chance of defending himself against a violent mob, or the supposedly helpless witch woman. And yet, it is the untypical, vulnerable, young hero, who faints, vomits and accepts help from women, who is finally victorious, standing alone, dancing and waving to his mentor, as the cowardly men scatter around him.

After "Poor Little Saturday," L'Engle did not write about the South again for over a decade and, before attempting to do so, decided "to do a good bit of research" (*Summer* 193). While writing *Ilsa* and her short stories, she had relied on her own memories and the stories told by her mother who, in her own words, was "born in 1881 [...] just after the end of the Civil War, with the memory of it still fresh, [...] with the memory bitter indeed" (157). Now, L'Engle read extensively about the history of the region and delved deeply into her family history. She came away with a much more balanced view of her ancestors' world: "as with all worlds, it was good and it was evil. It had vision, and it was blind. It was rich, and incredibly poor" (197). Although, on both sides of the family, she found "examples of meanness and selfishness and greed" (191), she also found ancestors she could be proud of: for example, Justice William Johnson, "Jefferson's first appointee to the Supreme Court, the youngest justice to sit on the bench, and the first dissenting justice" (193), a man who "stood up for the rights of the black man, both slave and free" (193). There was also one of her mother's cousins who was responsible for founding "the first hospital in the Deep South with beds for blacks" (191) and her great-great-grandfather Francis Fatio who made sure that "every child in the household should be taught to read and write at an early age, and the children of the servants learned their letters side by side with the children of the family" (190, also S. L'Engle 51). Another interesting figure was Madeleine's great-grandfather William L'Engle, who appears to have been a most generous and humane doctor. Among the women, Madeleine's great-grandmother,

Mado, and her great-great-grandmother, Susan Philippa Fatio, also provided examples of intelligent women with a strong sense of both justice and mercy. All these gave the twentieth century author "a tradition of compassion and generosity to live up to" (191). Between 1956 and the publication of her second novel of the Deep South, *The Other Side of the Sun* (1971), Madeleine L'Engle had not only researched the South; she had also gone through a difficult period in which she struggled with her "cloud of unknowing to return to the Church and to Christ" (*Walking* 55). One result of this was that the author realized that the message of hope and love which she put in her other writings also had its place in stories about the South.

Madeleine L'Engle herself referred to *The Other Side of the Sun* as "a theological Gothic novel set in the deep South" (qtd. in Hobbs 14), but the theology does not make the South any less difficult than in her previous Southern writings. The novel is full of political plots, racial hatred, lynchings, vigilante killings and voodoo. It is set in 1910 when, as Donald Hettinga explains, "the wounds of the Civil War were still festering" ("Great Cloud" 173) and the characters are living in a situation of growing tensions, where something seems certain to explode sooner or later. The Renier family are based in a dilapidated old mansion on the North Florida coast, not far from Jacksonville (called Jefferson in the novel) and one of the work's greatest strengths is the stifling, ominous atmosphere. As John Conner puts it: "oppressive heat, gusting winds, threatening storms, and shadowy swamps form an uneasy emotional background for the internal strife" (1154).

What is new here is that, for the first time, L'Engle takes the racial tensions and the problems of segregation in the South seriously and she presents some genuinely good, attractive Southern people. There are as many African American protagonists as white ones and, in both groups, there are good people, bad people and those in-between, who cause chaos with the best of intentions. Readers, and particularly those who have never lived in the region, gradually discover the South with its past glories and the legacy of the Civil War and the slave trade at the same time as Stella Renier, the naïve British narrator, who has come to live there with her husband's extended family when he is sent on a diplomatic mission. Loosely based on her great-great-grandmother Susan Philippa Fatio's friendship with an African princess forcibly married to a slavetrader, "in a day when such a friendship was unheard of" (*Summer* 188), *The Other Side of the Sun* presents a community of frail but compassionate people, black and white, "who dared think independently of the social and political mores which controlled the thoughts of their neighbors" (Conner 1155), and as a result risk their own lives. The question of identity is also raised as British-educated, but black, Dr. Ron James struggles to fit back into his native area after several years' absence because, as a doctor, there is no place for him in either black or white society. The enchanting heroine, African princess Honoria, her husband and her support group of elderly aristocrats, their former servants, two middle-aged holy fools (or idiots, depending on who is talking) and her grandson, Ron, slowly communicate their history and values to ignorant Stella until she "cannot pretend that the voodoo and the racist riders do not exist" (Hettinga, "Great Cloud" 175), and has to choose her own side in the ideological battle between good and evil.

The ugliest events take place against a background of glorious sandy beaches, donax soup, long, flowing dresses, fans, a beautifully proportioned house with coquina columns and all the multi-colored flora and fauna of the South. Cousin James Renier is a true Southern, Christian gentleman, in the tradition of Confederate general Robert E. Lee, showing at the same time humility, leadership and respect for his dependents and inferiors. Yet, Clive, Honoria's black husband, shares these qualities. Equally, the seemingly fragile and feminine Aunt Olivia reveals unexpected strength, both in her past as a spy during the Civil War and in her decision to shoot to kill in order to prevent a lynching. Throughout the story it is clear that the South's past must be faced, but it must also be forgiven, and that more violence will not solve any of the region's problems.

Although L'Engle wrote no more works set entirely the South after 1971, several of Stella Renier's Southern descendants appear in later novels which include episodes set in the South. In each case they reveal problematic aspects of the Southern heritage, while affirming that it is possible for both men and women to live a good, honorable life within the Southern tradition. The first to appear is the orphaned thirteen-year-old Simon Renier in *Dragons in the Waters* (1976), who may be assumed to be one of Stella's great-grandsons. Although he is, chronologically, a teenager of the 1970s, Simon has an old-fashioned worldview as he has been raised, since his parents' death five years earlier, by his elderly Aunt Leonis Phair, an impoverished Southern gentlewoman from near Charleston, who was born in the 1880s. L'Engle named this admirable old lady after her ancestor William L'Engle's Aunt Leonis L'Engle Johnson, to whom he wrote regularly when he was a young man (*Summer* 168). Leonis's family is presented as one of many casualties of the Civil War and the old woman herself went "from riches to rags" (*Dragons* 64) because of it. Her family's huge property, Pharoah, was taken over by Yankee officers as their headquarters, but when they left they "burnt the fields and salted them" (50), making the land infertile for several generations. At the time of the action, Simon and Leonis live in a "small cottage on an acre and a half which was all that was left of the once great plantation" (28–29). In spite of their poverty they are content with their lot and completely without bitterness about the disasters their family has encountered.

L'Engle uses this situation to illustrate how the legacy of the Civil War was still relevant in her day and how perceptions of the South were still vastly different depending on one's family origins. Although he is a pleasant and open-minded teenager, Simon has been brought up to believe that the South at the end of the Civil War was "an occupied country like Israel at the time of Christ, or Norway with the Nazis" (60) and that Southerners who did business with the carpetbaggers after the war were collaborators and, by definition, dishonest. His new friends, Poly and Charles O'Keefe, who have only recently moved to the South and belong to a Northern family, are shocked by this point of view. Poly exclaims: "But the carpetbaggers weren't Nazis. They were us…" (61) and then realizes not only how perceptions of history depend on a person's origins and education, but also that everyone has burdens of guilt from their past that they must face up to. Simon has also been brought up to be a Southern gentleman, in spite of his poverty. He considers himself lucky because he is "rich in education and rich in tradition" (63) and identifies with his more glamorous ancestors. He calls adults, even relations, "Sir" or "Ma'am" and is proud that his deceased journalist father "cared about honor" (165). For Poly and Charles, Simon lives in another world, "not in our century" (46), but they find him pleasant and quickly adopt him as a friend.

Although she presents quite an attractive picture of Southern gentle folk in *Dragons in the Waters*, Madeleine L'Engle also shows what was often wrong with their lifestyle. Simon's hero is his ancestor, Quentin Phair, based on Madeleine's own kinsman Miller Hallowes. Like Hallowes, Phair, at the age of nineteen, "left his native England and [went] to South America to offer his services to [Simon] Bolivar" (*Summer* 169). Again like Hallowes, "at Bolivar's death he was given the last portrait ever painted of the great hero" (*Summer* 169) and then came to North Florida "intending to visit for only a short time, but quickly fell in love" (Parker), married a Southern belle, and stayed there for the rest of his life. The trauma for Simon comes when he finds out that Quentin was not, in fact, the perfect gentleman he has always thought him, but that before coming to Florida, he abandoned his first wife and son in Venezuela and did not keep his promise to return to them and their community. As Aunt Leonis points out, "few people in the pioneer South of those days would have thought twice about the rights of some South American Indian girl" (*Dragons* 125), even if they had known about her. However, for Simon, Leonis and presumably Madeleine L'Engle, "fidelity built on broken promises has a shaky foundation" (125) and Quentin's betrayal has left a legacy of bitterness among the people he let down. The reader is given to understand that part of Quentin's problem was that he thought "religion […] was women's work" (223) and that his worldview was not rooted in the Christian faith. Simon has to come to terms with his hero's failure and decides that, although he is very young, as a gentleman and Quentin's descendant, honor requires him to make his home in Venezuela among Quentin's wife's people and fulfil, to the best of his ability, the promises his ancestor once made.

Polly (now with two ls) O'Keefe's adventures continue, two years after the action in *Dragons in the Waters*, with *A House Like a Lotus* (1984). The O'Keefe family are living in a converted motel at one end of Benne Seed Island, South Carolina, and get to know Maximiliana (Max) Horne, a wealthy artist, staying in her beautiful family property at the other end of the island. Polly, now 17, like Madeleine at the same age, has a resident outsider's view of the South and its traditions. She loves Max's mansion by the beach, which has all the charm of the South, "soft pink brick and surrounded by three-story white verandahs" (*Lotus* 23), "Greek revival columns" (25), "soft silvery-grey" (25) woodwork, a delightful couple of devoted elderly retainers to do the housework, lots of art work and especially portraits. Polly notes that "Southerners do seem to have a great many portraits" (25). The grounds contain "great, jungly trees, full of Spanish moss and mocking birds" (25) and the whole island is alive with Cape Jessamine, wisteria, azaleas, Spanish Bayonettes and sea breezes. Like the author again, although fifty years after her time, teenage Polly is happy with her natural surroundings but uncomfortable with the Southern girls, as they "all wore large quantities of make-up and talked about boys" (9), rather than sharing her interests and desiring to go to a good college. She is also considered "snobby" (9) as she does not have a Southern accent. There is beauty in the landscape, the architecture and the culture of the South, but it is much harder to feel at home with the people.

Once again, a descendant of Stella Renier is instrumental in highlighting L'Engle's questions about Southern traditions and codes of behavior. Queron Renier (Renny) is a cousin of Simon's and "a perfect Southern-gentleman type" (68). He is a compassionate doctor, specializing in research into a rare South-American disease. He is proud of his family's status and standards, declaring that "the Reniers believe that there is right and wrong, and a world without restraints is going down the drain" (290). In spite of these standards, Renny gives into temptation and has sex with teenage Polly, which he afterwards regrets. However, Renny is presented as a basically good man who tries to live up to the gentlemanly ideal, respect women and serve the community, even if he does not always manage it. He both shares the positive heritage of the Reniers presented in *The Other Side of the Sun* and provides a contrast to Max Horne's late father, who was perceived by society as a great Southern gentleman, but who was in reality "completely unprincipled" and "a lecherous old roué" (125).

Mr. Horne is a prime example of Robert F. Pace's observation that "Southern men had to exhibit behavior that held them to be dutiful to their responsibilities, respectful of their peers, and [...] honest in their public declarations. This ethic, however, did not say that one actually had to be dutiful, respectful or honest; one simply had to appear" (Pace 5). In fact, Mr. Horne, in addition to being a domestic tyrant, tried to rape his daughter Minerva and caused her death, but he was honored in society as a social benefactor because he built a hospital in Minerva's memory.

L'Engle uses Mr. Horne and his father-in-law to show how, in the patriarchal society of the old South, religion could be misused in order to oppress women. Max's outwardly pious maternal grandfather christened his three daughters Submit, Patience and Hope to show what he expected of them. In a similar way, Mr. Horne had "a God complex" (122) and encouraged his female relations to think of him as having the divine right to impose his will on them and all his dependents. Even years later, the only way Max "can get rid of the false image of Papa as God" (122) is to meditate on the wonders of the creation or concentrate on God as "a benevolent physician" (122). She keeps her father's portrait "to remind [her] that God is *not* like him" (122)—a belief her creator clearly shares.

The final Southern setting to appear in L'Engle's fiction is in *A Live Coal in the Sea* (1996). Mac, the heroine Camilla's late husband, is a Southerner. Mac's mother, Olivia, is a Renier, named after Aunt Olivia from *The Other Side of the Sun* (*Live Coal* 91). His father is from a poor white family "from the wrong side of the tracks" (129) in Jacksonville and becomes the Bishop of North Florida. Mac, an Episcopalian priest, has been brought up as a Southern gentleman and is both rooted in the Christian faith and open and considerate to all classes of society. He is a good priest, husband and father, showing his attachment to the Renier heritage by passing on his mother's family rings to his bride. When Mac and Camilla are called to minister in Corinth, Georgia, the usual problems of Southern tradition are raised. Mac refers to Corinth as "still living in the dark ages [...] segregated but quiet" (219). He copes patiently with teenagers whose fathers say "that Negroes have a lower IQ than we do" (121) and cares for those who have been hurt by their parents' failings in honesty or fidelity. He is also happy to support his wife as she gets her PhD and prepares for a career as a university professor—in spite of opposition from the population of Corinth who expect her to give up her own work to support her husband and family. Although he is not perfect, Mac is portrayed as a man with standards which he attempts to live up to, the Southern gentleman at his best.

Although several of the Renier family provide hope and show the possibility of a good life in the American South, L'Engle is careful to show that they are not perfect and that, even in the mid to late twentieth century, there were many problems in the region. Jewish Mimi Oppenheimer in *A Severed Wasp*, a grand-daughter of Stella's, points out that "there was plenty [of anti-Semitism] in South Carolina" and that some of her "Renier cousins could be pretty insular" (*Wasp* 52). And yet, as with Selina in Madeleine's first Southern story, it is clear throughout her Southern writings that the author has deep roots in the South and that she is criticizing her own people.

Madeleine L'Engle: An American Abroad[2]

Although Madeleine L'Engle was born in New York, spent most of her early childhood in that city and spent several childhood vacations in Florida, she also had links to France and Switzerland from her birth. On her mother's side of the family, as Madeleine would later write, she had "forebears who settled in South Carolina well before the American Revolution." These pioneers were "a conglomeration of French Huguenots fleeing religious persecution, and Frenchmen who had come to Ireland at the time of the Norman conquest [...] and later had to flee Ireland" (*Summer* 191) at the time of Henry VIII. Other ancestors came from Switzerland. For example, Francis Philip Fatio, "born in Vevey [...] in 1724," left his home town to settle in Florida (Willis 174). Her more immediate family also had connections with France. After having four children with Madeleine's grandmother, Carolina Hallowes L'Engle, her grandfather, the Florida banker Bion Hall Barnett, "had run off with a woman to the South of France, leaving behind a note on the mantel" (Zarin 62) and remained there, except for occasional visits, with his new love, until Carolina died. Two of his sons, Madeleine's Uncle William and Uncle Bion, had married Frenchwomen and provided Madeleine with four bilingual and bicultural cousins, including Charles, five years older than Madeleine and the inspiration for her character Charlot. Although William returned to the USA with his family in 1928, Bion, who was an artist married to the well-known concert pianist Yvonne Charvot,[3] remained in France until the German occupation in 1940 and the couple knew many of the artistic community in Paris. Madeleine's father, the journalist and novelist Charles Wadsworth Camp, had also spent quite a lot of time in Europe, particularly during the First World War, and had many close friends in France, including the artist Gilbert White. Madeleine writes of White's portrait of her father hanging over the mantelpiece in her family home, "a charming impressionist piece done long before [she] was born, in an apple orchard in Brittany" (*Summer* 107).

In this context, it is scarcely surprising that Madeleine was "learning French from at least the age of 8," possibly before (*Circle* 143), and started to visit France for holidays in her early childhood. She would remember decades later "when [she] was a little girl in France [...] putting out [her] shoes on the Eve of Epiphany" (*Irrational Season* 39) for the Three Wise Men to fill. The summer when Madeleine was eight or nine, she recalls in the second volume of her published journals that her mother "had cause to drag [...]

her around France" (*Summer* 89). This was her first introduction both to the South of France, which she would claim years later that she "knew with her senses" (*Circle* 94), and also to Brittany where she was "sent on picnics [...] with three small boys," members of her godfather's family, to get them "out of the grown-ups' hair" (*Summer* 89). Her mother remembered Madeleine as "a skinny, awkward, sulky little girl who saw nothing as she was dragged through châteaux and museums" (89), but would later be amazed when her daughter accurately "described places and people of that summer in [her] first serious stories" (90). A photo of Madeleine in Pornic, Brittany,[4] perhaps a year and a half after that summer of discovery, shows that skating and fancy dress were also part of her early French experiences and that the family returned to France at least once during the late 1920s.

However, until the summer she was eleven years old, Europe had only been a holiday destination for Madeleine. This changed in 1930 when, as Leonard Marcus relates: "the Camps left New York for France and took up residence in a picture-postcard alpine château as guests of family friends" (5). The official reason for the move was that Charles Camp's "lungs were so damaged by mustard gas" ("Madeleine L'Engle") from the First World War he needed the cleaner, purer air of the Alps. Although Francis Mason, one of Madeleine's cousins, has cast doubt on this (Zarin 63), another cousin, Mary L'Engle Avent, considers the author's account of the family history in *The Summer of the Great-Grandmother*, which contains several mentions of her father's fragile lungs, to be "an accurate description" (Marcus 34), and it seems entirely possible that a man who was fifteen years old at Charles Camp's death may not have known as much of the story as Camp's wife and child. In any case, Madeleine agreed that the family also moved abroad because "the Depression had hit the United States, and the standard of living in France was lower than in New York" ("Nourishment" 117), making it easier for her parents to survive on their limited income.

The picturesque château where Madeleine spent her twelfth summer and which would later appear, transported to Switzerland, in both *The Small Rain* and *And Both Were Young*, was in Publier, a small village near Evian-les-Bains in the Haute-Savoie region of France. It was almost certainly the Château de Blonay. Although the young Madeleine had the impression that "nothing much had been done to it since the eleventh century" (*From This Day* 6), the neo-Renaissance style building she lived in, built on the site of the former castle, was actually less than a century old and had been occupied for many years by the oblates of St. Francis de Sales until they abandoned it in 1928. Madeleine "spent the summer dreaming and wandering through the dusty rooms of the château" (*From This Day* 7) and imagined herself as "the daughter of the château [...] in the twelfth century, the fifteenth and the eighteenth" (*Summer* 96). While she wandered she "wrote stories and poems and

[...] lived an interior life which protected [her] from [...] the world of the grown-ups" (96). This dream world ended abruptly in the autumn when Madeleine's parents "delivered their daughter without warning to a Swiss boarding school, introduced her to the matron in charge, said their goodbyes and drove away" (Marcus 5). Madeleine would stay there for three years and, in her opinion, "it was, at first, sheer hell" (*Summer* 98).

The boarding school was called Châtelard. Founded by an English woman, Dorothy Braginton, in 1927, it was organized according to the British system of education. As Madeleine herself explained, "The Depression had closed down most of the great resort hotels. There were no "beautiful people" and the world was a war away from the jet set. Most of the available *pensions* around the emptied resort hotels had no indoor plumbing and no running water" (*From This Day* 5–6).

The school had moved into one of these abandoned hotels, the Hôtel des Narcisses in Chamby, just outside Montreux. According to Charles Micklewright, whose mother and aunt, Ella and Molly Marriott, were at Châtelard at the same time as Madeleine, "it was cheaper to send girls to school in Switzerland than to a similar school in England at that time. Switzerland was still a relatively poor country." Unlike Madeleine, Ella and Molly loved it. Madeleine, however, learned to adapt. That same year her parents spent the winter in Chamonix in a rented villa "as inconvenient as the château" (*Summer* 106), but which enchanted Madeleine. Although her parents visited her from time to time, most of the long holidays she spent "in Provence with her grandfather" (Zarin 63), where she recollected spending the long afternoons reading his collection of *Punch* magazines. The situation changed in 1933 when Madeleine's grandmother fell ill and her parents returned from Europe to be with the invalid in Florida. Madeleine would not visit the Alps again until she was an established author.

However, many memories from Madeleine L'Engle's French and Swiss years would find their way into her writing. Her published journals and other autobiographical works contain several passages describing her expatriate life. Equally, much of Madeleine's early fiction takes place in Europe and clear traces of the author's boarding school and holiday experiences may be found in the novels *The Small Rain* (1945), *And Both Were Young* (1949) and *A Winter's Love* (1957) as well as in two short stories, "The Mountains Shall Stand for Ever" (1941) and "Night at the Fair" (1941), published when she was still a student. Among her later works, only *A Severed Wasp* (1982) contains a very few flashback scenes in France. As in her relationship with the American South, the author sometimes seems to be much closer to the natural environment than to the people in Europe, although some of these are sympathetically portrayed. It is also worth noting that her protagonists are all Americans, living mainly as expatriates, surrounded by other foreigners as well as by the local population. To start with at least, all her protagonists experience the feeling of exile, even if some will come to feel at home in their new location. And yet, in all cases, the Americans are enriched by and learn from their foreign experiences. Madeleine L'Engle's attitude parallels that of her father's friend, Gilbert White: "to be a good American, you have to live abroad to get the perspective" ("T. Gilbert White").

Both the early short stories set in Europe would later be rewritten and included in L'Engle's first novel, *The Small Rain*, but they remain interesting as evidence of how soon some of her best-known themes and characters were already part of her imaginative world. Both stories also clearly contain personal memories. For example, in "Night at the Fair" (1941), the protagonist, Paula, who resembles the young Madeleine in many ways, is asked: "Have you ever been to a fair before?" She replies: "Once, in Brittany, with mother, when I was very small" (22). As neither the place nor her mother are important to the story, this is probably one of the author's own memories. Although no indication is given of the setting of the story, internal allusions lead the reader to assume the action takes place in France: Colin drives a Citroën car (4), the protagonists have only met once before, in Paris (22–23), and Paula's aunt appears to have a servant called Gustave (25). The fair in the story is situated "at the edge of the lake" (4). Seeing as an almost identical visit to a fair in *The Small Rain* takes place in Thonon, on the French side of Lake Geneva, it is reasonable to assume a similar setting for the short story. The story's greatest weakness is that all the characters are unattractive, except perhaps Paula who is more neutral. However, Colin has some clear connections with L'Engle's later characters Charlot and Zachary Grey. The story also contains the first written traces of young Madeleine's love for the lakes and mountains, while the haunting music of the carousel and Paula's attempts to reproduce it on the piano both provide a frame to the narrative and will lead to Tom Forrester's *First Kermesse Suite* in *A Severed Wasp*.

"The Mountains Shall Stand Forever" is a sad story with mainly unpleasant characters and is based on Madeleine's feelings of deep depression during her first few weeks at boarding school in Switzerland. The scene appears later not only in *The Small Rain*, but also in *And Both Were Young*. The song the girls are listening to, "Goodnight Sweetheart," fixes the action in 1931, as it was in the charts for several months that year. Although the school could be anywhere and its inhabitants are English-speaking, the story starts and finishes with a view out of the window. At the beginning of the story, the mountains and lake are invisible because of the fog, a frequent occurrence around Lake Geneva, leading Ellen, the protagonist, to imagine that they have vanished and been replaced by a black hole. By the end of the story the fog has cleared, but Ellen wants the black space to come back, so that she can throw herself into it. Yet, the title of story shows that she knows this is an impossible dream, as the mountains provide a fixed point, perhaps the only stability in her world.

On the second to last page of *The Small Rain* Katherine Forrester prepares to return to France from New York and tells herself: "I'm coming home!" (370). Nearly three hundred pages earlier, when Katherine first arrives in Europe, neither she nor the reader would have predicted this. As an American in an English boarding school in Switzerland, Katherine's primary emotion is "a bewildered misery" (92), which, as for Ellen in "The Mountains Shall Stand Forever," is reflected in the weather and the landscape. However, once Katherine meets her piano teacher, Parisian Justin Vigneras, and realizes that she is going to learn and make progress, she is able to see the incredible beauty that is around her:

> The mountain sloped in terraces down to the lights of Montreux and the lake; and across the lake the mountains of France stood, shadowy in spite of the clear outline the snow gave them against the sky. Two lake steamers were moving slowly on the water in opposite directions, two small bands of gold lights approaching each other and crossing. In a straight line down the mountain ran the funicular, and, winding around, ran the small train. They were the only lights on the mountainside, and they seemed like something magic. Leaning there with her nose pressed against the windowpane, Katherine suddenly felt a sense of peace and strength. "I will lift up mine eyes unto the hills, from whence cometh my help," she whispered [110–111].

This sudden connection with her surroundings motivates Katherine to explore and she discovers a ruined castle in the vicinity, which strongly resembles the one Madeleine stayed in at Publier, and which connects her to the country and its past. Now that Katherine's eyes have been opened she, and the reader, can enjoy Thonon and Evian, Territet and Paris. Through Justin, Katherine meets pleasant French people, providing a contrast with the unpleasant English ones she knows at the school and she also becomes more and more at home in the French language, even to the extent of reading Proust's *Albertine Disparue*, a serious exploit for any teenager! French elegance is also celebrated in Pauline Marat, Charlot's fiancée, "a slender young Parisienne, on the tall side, beautifully dressed, with softly waved hair under a small black hat" (253). Pauline also has "the deep black line under the lashes that looks like heavy mascara but is natural, and that is almost unique with French women" (253), which, whether it really exists or not, is L'Engle's tribute to the beautiful French women she knew.

Katherine's initial experience of profound suffering at school, like Philippa Hunter's in *And Both Were Young*, comes from the fact that she "wasn't homesick for a place, but for a person" (*Both Were Young* 26), in Katherine's case both her dead mother and her absent father and step-mother. For Madeleine herself, being left alone for the first time without her parents and with little warning had been equally traumatic. For Katherine, her friendship with Sarah Courmont and her passionate crush on Justin reconcile her to the school and its location. The author herself, although she "had some good friends" in her second year at the school, never had a close friend "with whom [she] was able to talk as Katherine was able to talk to Sarah" (*Small Rain* x). Equally, her piano teacher, Mlle Dunaud, whom she would later describe as "a gentle Frenchwoman who encouraged me" (*Small Rain* x), was hardly the object of any youthful passion, although she certainly did encourage Madeleine by describing her in her school report as "a very gifted pupil and very musical."[5] On the other hand, Madeleine admitted she "had crushes on some of [her] teachers" (*Penguins* 37) and Cindi Bowles, another former Châtelard pupil who talked to Madeleine in the mid–1970s, was surprised by her "starry-eyed memory of the tennis instructor," Roger Parisod, whom Madeleine described as "a young, blond Adonis" and who taught both tennis and skiing. Parisod would have been only 21 years old when Madeleine left the school, an obvious object of admiration for a community of teenage girls! It is highly likely that Madeleine was able to transform her own or her friends' crush on Parisod into Katherine's schoolgirl passion for Justin.

And Both Were Young (1949) was L'Engle first novel to be published for the young adult market, although she had originally intended it for adults. As a result, although the heroine's boarding school experiences are basically similar to those in *The Small Rain*, certain changes had to be made before publication to make the book suitable for children. For example, while Katherine Forrester gets into trouble for her close friendship with Sarah Courmont, L'Engle was obliged "to change the object of Flip's [Philippa's] affections from a girl to a boy" as "in those days even the slightest hint of homosexuality would have killed the book's chances in the children's book market" (Marcus 62). However, the principal change is in the attitude to the Swiss school, because teenage girls usually like the idea of going to a boarding school in Switzerland and an unattractive portrayal of such an establishment, like the one in her earlier novel, would not have been popular. One way L'Engle makes the place more interesting is by changing it from a British school to an international one, in a setting in some ways similar to that of Elinor M. Brent-Dyer's popular Chalet School stories.[6] In L'Engle's fictional school, like the Chalet School, there were girls from several countries and both French and German were frequently spoken, sometimes interspersed with other languages. One girl in *And Both Were Young* even exclaims: "Ach […] I left *mein ceinture dans le* shower *ce morgen. Quelle* dope *ich bin*" (32). This change comes from the post–World War II context of the novel, where Madeleine seeks to draw her readers' attention to the need for international reconciliation and has the most attractive teacher, a former member of the Resistance, point out to Philippa that "the girls who are in the difficult and defensive position are the German girls. They've had a hard time of it here" (95–96).

Erna, one of the Germans, is portrayed very positively and has a best friend with a Jewish surname, Jacqui Bernstein—probably named after Madeleine's former neighbor in New York, the composer Leonard Bernstein—providing an example of how former barriers could be broken down.

In addition to the more attractive school, as Donald Hettinga has pointed out, "L'Engle makes it clear that while some aspects of Philippa's situation are objectively repressive, others are subjective—a kind of imprisonment that Philippa makes for herself" (*Presenting* 138). She decides to "pretend the school is the château of Chillon and [she's] the prisoner" (7) before she has even seen the school. In spite of her sufferings and initial isolation, however, Philippa is able to appreciate her surroundings from the very start. Even on the very first horrible day, she looks down the mountainside to the lake and begins "to feel the wonderful sense of elation that always came to her when beauty took hold of her" (25). The sky, the valley, the lake, the flickering lights at night, the stars and, later, the snow all entrance her. Like Katherine Forrester, she finds an old castle and loves to explore it. Philippa is an artist, so it is predictably the art mistress who becomes her inspiration and mentor. The name of the teacher, Madame Perceval, conjures up the image of a knight in shining armor coming to the rescue of the damsel in distress. Her first name, Colette, may be a tribute to the famous author whom L'Engle appreciated. In *A Circle of Quiet* she quotes, in French, Colette's words to a young poet who complained that he was unhappy: "Mais personne ne t'a demandé d'être heureux. Travaille!" (But no one asked you to be happy. Work!—*Circle* 53), which is good advice for Philippa in her Swiss school. The names of Philippa's other rescuers also had personal significance for L'Engle: the character Georges Laurens and his adopted son Paul are probably named after the artistic Laurens family[7] who taught both L'Engle's Uncle Bion and the artist Gilbert White at the Académie Julian in Paris.

Some critics have mentioned that L'Engle's stories based in Europe, and in particular *And Both Were Young*, "avoid her usual focus on religion and science" (Ness, "Development"). In the case of *The Small Rain*, while there is very little science, there is quite a lot of religion. Katherine quotes Psalm 121 (111 and 206) in English and Romans chapter 5 in French (212). She is also quite happy to talk about God with Charlot, coming to the conclusion: "I do believe in God.... I do believe in God. The mountains and the lake and the possibility of people like Mother and Justin being born, that's really enough" (206).

However, *And Both Were Young* and *A Winter's Love* were written before the author's full return to the Christian faith and were also based on a period in her life when she knew little about science and found religion difficult.

> In boarding school in Switzerland [...] I felt so alienated that I nearly lost Jesus completely [...] I knew that Jesus calls us all by name, but I could not hear the call in this

cold school, English and Anglican [...] Nobody mentioned Jesus. An Anglican clergyman came to the school and talked about the world of Jesus' day, but not about Jesus [*Bright Evening Star* 27].

This is almost certainly an exaggeration. Madeleine mentions elsewhere that it was "an Anglican school, with mandatory Morning and Evening prayer" ("Nourishment" 117), which includes Gospel readings together with psalms and other Bible stories. She also explains that, at school, she "got into the habit of slipping away from the common room and going to the chapel to pray" (117). To her great surprise, one of the mistresses found her there one day and dragged her out by the ear "as though going to be alone with God was something obscene and perverse" (117). This incident appears in fictional form in *And Both Were Young*, however there is no mention of prayer. For Philippa, the chapel is, as Mari Ness points out, "genuinely just used as a hiding place" and has no real religious significance. On the other hand, Philippa appreciates the evening chapel service at the school when her favorite teacher takes it and finds herself listening "for the first time to the beauty of the words" (*Both Were Young* 34) of the liturgy. As she recites Psalm 98, she can feel "the mountains reaching gladly to the sky, and the sound of the wind on the white peaks must be their song of praise" (34). As with Katherine, the mountains enable Philippa to relate to the Creator.

In 1957, the publication of *A Winter's Love* brought to an end Madeleine L'Engle's barren years when none of her novels were accepted for publication. Like several of her early works, it is, as Mari Ness has noted, "a bit depressing" ("Love in the Mountains"). Surprisingly, although this is L'Engle's only European novel with no major non–American characters, it is also the one which is the most explicitly French in its atmosphere and setting. The action takes place in Chamonix, even if the town's name is never mentioned, and the descriptions of the landscapes, the alpine slopes, the sea of ice, the run-down hotels, the sanatoria overlooking the town and the inconvenient rented villa with its gaudy furniture come from Madeleine's Christmas vacation in that town in the winter of 1930/1931, although the novel is set several years after the end of the Second World War. Courtney reads *L'Aurore* and *Le Figaro* (21) and various locals sing or play well-known French songs, even if it is unlikely that Fred Gouin's 1931 hit, *Coucou*, would really have been played all the time at the skating rink in the 1950s. The main characters catch snippets of untranslated French conversation as they walk about the town: "la belle petite poupée, qu'elle est mignonne!" or "dis, dis le beau chemin de fer" (21), or even, rather less politely, "espèce de putain!" (107).[8] A more literary allusion may be found in the name of Gertrude's deceased French husband, Henri de Croisenois, named after an attractive young nobleman in Emile Gaboriau's *Les Esclaves de Paris* (1867).

One of the minor themes of the book is the perceived differences in French people's and Americans' attitude to love and marriage. Half-French Mimi advises her American friend Virginia Bowen to "just marry money" (103) if she wants to have the financial freedom to be a poet and novelist. This is referred to as "the practical French way of looking at it" (103). The highly skilled French doctor, Michel Clément, also shows an un–American attitude to marital fidelity. His "beautiful and expensive" (190) wife, who is "far too beautiful for her own good" (197), has made it clear to her husband that she "would not stay with [him] for a minute were [he] not reasonably successful" (197). He therefore feels free to have discreet affairs with other women and also refuses the idea that a married woman who falls in love with another man is in any way sinful or depraved (199). The vocabulary of puritanism is "distasteful" (199) to him, although he understands the issues at stake. Madeleine also clearly shows, through the characters, her own "European attitude" that "the very young can be charming and delightful and pretty, but only a mature woman can be beautiful and only a mature man can be truly tender" (*Circle* 11).

Although the protagonist, Emily's, dilemma: leave her husband for her new love or stay with him and move to small town Indiana (presented as the middle of nowhere), is presented as a specifically American problem, the novel's setting does influence the action. The plot moves forward slowly and deliberately, "restrained partly by its majestic setting in the French Alps" (Ness, "Love in the Mountains"). Everything that happens is influenced by the snow, the freezing cold, the poor visibility and the need to put on several layers of clothing and strap on your skis before emerging from any building and by the fact that the American characters are only there temporarily and know they must one day move on. Aspects of Madeleine herself at different ages can be seen in many of the characters: she too was tall and clumsy like Mimi, she was always writing from a young age like Virginia, in 1957 she was in a professional impasse like Courtney and, like Emily, she was 38 and short of money and living in a small town away from New York. However, Emily, Courtney and Gertrude all share characteristics with Madeleine's parents and their experience during "that winter of outer and inner cold in Chamonix" (*Summer* 183). Courtney and Gertrude, like Charles Camp, are tempted to drink too much and refuse the obvious solution to their problems. Emily, like Madeleine's mother, felt that "the mountains closed in on her" (*Summer* 106, *Winter's Love* 12) and yet was able, in spite of the "pain and confusion" (*Summer* 111) she was experiencing, to transform the ugly rented villa into a home.

Although L'Engle did not write in detail about France or Switzerland again after her return to faith and the Anglican Church, her understanding of what it means to be an American abroad and, in particular, an expatriate, may be seen in the experiences of the O'Keefe family in Gaia, an island off the coast of Portugal, and of all the Americans in Lisbon portrayed in *The Arm of the Starfish* (1966), remembering in particular that, in these circumstances, if you did anything wrong "it was an international incident" (*Circle* 161). The author continued to enjoy reading in French, including the French Bible (*Irrational* 57), rejoiced in her Huguenot heritage, and even "occasionally [...] used to dream in French" (*Sold* 145), a sign, in her opinion, of being "completely fluent" in a language. Despite this, she may have realized that her childhood and adolescent memories and her understanding of what she saw in Europe were insufficient for adult fiction or stories set in a more recent period. Perhaps unsurprisingly, of all her European writings, her young adult story with the happy ending, *And Both Were Young*, has survived the best. One reviewer in 2010 says she turns to it when she wants "to be reminded that the world and the people in it can be beautiful despite the darkness" (Angie).

New York, the American South and the Alps were all, at various times in her life, places Madeleine L'Engle knew well and, in different ways, loved. As a result, the places, the people, the atmosphere and various remembered incidents all turn up, transformed in her published fiction. Madeleine's granddaughters have written, perhaps paradoxically, that "all of Madeleine's writing, fiction and non-fiction, was an example of how all narrative is fiction, and all fiction can be true" (*Unicorns* 1), seeing the way that her memoirs, novels and short stories are all carefully constructed works of literature, rooted in their grandmother's sometimes unreliable but always vivid memory, and also in her understanding of genuine values and keen observation of real people and places. While L'Engle is most famous for her imaginary, fantastic worlds, it is unfair to neglect her real ones or omit to analyse how new aspects of these familiar settings come alive and take on new meaning in her works.

Notes

1. L'Engle's thinly disguised fictional portrait of the real Community of the Holy Spirit.

2. Some of this section was originally published in "Transforming Memories: Madeleine L'Engle's Recreation of Her Childhood Experiences in France and Switzerland," in Marcel Arbeit and Roman Trušník, eds., *A View from Elsewhere* (Olomouc: Palacký University, 2014), 135–154.

3. Yvonne was also the daughter of the famous artist Eugène Louis Charvot (1847–1924).

4. The photo may be seen in the Madeleine L'Engle archive, Wheaton College, Illinois.

5. Châtelard School report, Summer 1932 : "Élève très douée et très musicienne."

6. See Elinor M. Brent-Dyer, *The School at the Chalet* (London: W & R Chambers, 1925) and the following novels in the series.

7. The father Jean-Pierre Laurens and his two sons Paul Laurens and Jean-Pierre Laurens all taught at the Académie Julian. The sons, who both died in the 1930s, were certainly known to Madeleine's parents and uncles. She may have met them during

her childhood, but we have no proof. However, the name Paul Laurens, which is given to the object of Philippa's affections, could not have been chosen without evoking the artist.

8. "What a pretty doll!" or "Look at the beautiful railway" or "Silly whore!"

WORKS CITED

Adams, Nancy. "Madeleine L'Engle's The Young Unicorns." *Saints and Trees*, 14 November 2013. Web.
Angie. "Retro Friday Review: *And Both Were Young* by Madeleine L'Engle." *Angieville*, 30 April 2010. Web.
Auster, Paul. *New York Trilogy*. London: Faber and Faber, 1987. Print.
Baldassarro, R. Wolf. "Banned Books Awareness: *A Wrinkle in Time*." 5 December 2011. Web.
Baptiste, Tracey. *Madeleine L'Engle*. New York: Chelsea House Publications, 2013. Print.
Bowles, Cindi. Personal email. 27 January 2014.
"A Cheerful Tragedy: Madeleine L'Engle's *Ilsa*." *The Sydney Morning Herald*, 28 November 1946. Print.
Fitzgerald, Katie. "Old Sunday School Review: *The Young Unicorns* by Madeleine L'Engle." *Storytimes Secrets*, 9 September 2012. Web.
Gonzales, Doreen. *Madeleine L'Engle: Author of* A Wrinkle in Time. New York: Dillon Press, 1991. Print.
Hettinga, Donald R. "A Great Cloud of Witnesses." *The Swiftly Tilting Worlds of Madeleine L'Engle*. Ed. Luci Shaw. Wheaton, IL: Harold Shaw Publishers, 1998. 165–178. Print.
_____. *Presenting Madeleine L'Engle*. New York: Twayne Publishers, 1993. Print.
Hobbs, Helen D. "Memorable Portrait: 'The Other Side of the Sun' by Madeleine L'Engle." *The Living Church* 187. 30 October 1983. Print.
Holsaert, Eunice. "Hollow Lives." *The New York Times Book Review*, 28 April 1946. Print.
Kirkpatrick, Katherine, ed. *A Circle of Friends*. New York: Circle of Friends Publication, 2009. Print.
L'Engle, Madeleine. "The Birthday." *The Smith College Monthly*, April 1941. 2–4, 28, 31–32. Print.
_____. *And Both Were Young* (1949). New York: Dell Publishing, 1983. Print.
_____. *Camilla* (1951). New York: Bantam Doubleday, 1982. Print.
_____. *Certain Women* (1992). San Francisco: HarperCollins, 1993. Print.
_____. *A Circle of Quiet*. New York: Farrar, Straus & Giroux, 1972. Print.
_____. *Dragons in the Waters* (1976). London: Hodder & Stoughton, 1991. Print.
_____. *18 Washington Square South*. New York: Walter H. Baker, 1944. Print.
_____. "Evening of a Governess." *The Tanager*, February 1945. 16–19. Print.
_____. *From This Day Forward*. Oxford: Lion, 1988. Print.
_____. "George MacDonald: Nourishment for a Private World," in Ed. Philip Yancey, *Reality and the Vision*. Dallas: Word Publishing, 1990. 111–121. Print.
_____. *A House Like a Lotus* (1984). New York: Bantam Doubleday, 1985. Print.
_____. *Ilsa*. New York: Vanguard Press, 1946. Print.
_____. *The Irrational Season*. San Francisco: Harper, 1977. Print.
_____. *A Live Coal in the Sea* (1996). San Francisco: HarperCollins, 1997. Print.
_____. "The Mountains Shall Stand for Ever." *The Matrix*, 1941. 3–6. Print.
_____. "Night at the Fair." *Opinion: Smith College Monthly*, 1941. 4, 21–25. Print.

———. *The Other Side of the Sun* (1971). Greenwich, CT: Fawcett Crest, 1972. Print.
———. *Penguins and Golden Calves*. Wheaton, IL: Harold Shaw Publishers, 1996. Print.
———. "Please Wear Your Rubbers." *Mademoiselle*, November 1944. 128–29, 190–91. Print.
———. "Poor Little Saturday" (1956). *Witches: Wicked, Wild and Wonderful*. Ed. Paula Guran. Germantown, MD: Prime Books, 2012. 227–41. Print.
———. *The Rock That Is Higher*. Wheaton, IL: Harold Shaw Publishers, 1993. Print.
———. *A Severed Wasp* (1982). New York: Farrar, Straus & Giroux, 1990. Print.
———. *The Small Rain* (1945). New York: Noonday Press, 1996. Print.
———. *Sold into Egypt*. Wheaton, IL: Harold Shaw Publishers, 1989. Print.
———. *The Summer of the Great-Grandmother*. New York: Farrar, Straus & Giroux, 1974. Print.
———. "Transfiguration" (1992). *Miracle on Tenth Street and Other Christmas Writings*. Wheaton, IL: Harold Shaw Publishers, 1998. 25–32. Print.
———. *Walking on Water* (1980). Tring: Lion Publishing, 1982. Print.
———. "White in the Moon the Long Road Lies." *Opinion: The Literary Section of the Smith College Weekly*, June 1939. 1–4. Print.
———. *A Winter's Love* (1957). New York: Ballantine Books, 1984. Print.
———. *The Young Unicorns*. New York: Square Fish, Macmillan, 2008. Print.
L'Engle, Susan. *Notes on My Family and Recollections of My Early Days*. New York: The Knickerbocker Press, 1888. Print.
"Madeleine L'Engle." *Gale Encyclopedia of World Biography*, 2004. Web.
"Madeleine L'Engle Library: A Literary Landmark." n.d. Web.
Marcus, Leonard S. *Listening for Madeleine: A Portrait of Madeleine L'Engle in Many Voices*. New York: Farrar, Straus & Giroux, 2012. Print.
Micklewright, Charles. Personal email, 17 January 2014.
Ness, Mari. "The Development of a Heroine: *And Both Were Young*." *Tor*. 28 November 2011. Web.
———. Intrigue and Lasers in Manhattan: *The Young Unicorns*." *Tor*. 12 January 2012. Web.
———. "Love in the Mountains: *A Winter's Love*." *Tor*. 29 March 2012. Web.
Pace, Robert F. *Halls of Honor: College Men in the Old South*. Baton Rouge: Louisiana State University Press, 2004. Print.
Parker, Susan. "The Nation's Oldest City: The Story of Colonel Miller Hallowes and the Cove Named for Him." *The St. Augustine Record*, 1 September 2002. Web.
Patell, Cyrus R.K., and Bryan Waterman, eds. *The Cambridge Companion to the Literature of New York*. Cambridge: Cambridge University Press, 2010. Print.
Pick, Robert. "Three Families, One Town." *The Saturday Review*, 6 July 1946. Print.
Roberts, Diane. "Ladies and Gentlemen." Ed. Charles Reagan Wilson. *Myth, Manners and Memory: The New Encyclopedia of Southern Culture*, vol. 4. Chapel Hill: University of North Carolina Press, 2006. 86. Print.
Rosenberg, Aaron. *Madeleine L'Engle*. New York: Rosen, 2006. Print.
Seidel, Kathryn L. "The Southern Belle as an Antebellum Ideal." *The Past Is Not Dead: Essays from the* Southern Quarterly. Jackson: University Press of Mississippi, 2012. Print.
Silber, Nina. *The Romance of Reunion: Northerners and the South, 1865–1900*. Chapel Hill: University of North Carolina Press, 1998. Print.
Smith, Harrison. "Camilla Dickinson." *The Saturday Review of Literature*, 1 September 1951. Print.
Staino, Rocco. "Author Madeleine L'Engle Remembered as the Cathedral of Saint John

the Divine Is Named a Literary Landmark." *School Library Journal*, 3 December 2012. Web.
"T. Gilbert White—St. Mark's Square Venice, Painting." *Live Auctioneers*, 5 March 2006. Web.
Weeks, Edward. "Atlantic Bookshelf." *The Atlantic Monthly*, June 1945. 123–126. Print.
Wilkerson, David. *The Cross and the Switchblade*. New York: Bernard Geis Associates, 1963. Print.
Willey, Margaret. "Girls in Towers." *The Horn Book Magazine*, 5 November 2014. Web.
Willis, William Scott. "A Swiss Settler in East Florida: A Letter of Francis Philip Fatio." *The Florida Historical Quarterly*, October 1985. Web.
Wyatt-Brown, Bertram. *Honour and Violence in the Old South*. New York: Oxford University Press, 1986. Print.
Zarin, Cynthia. "The Storyteller: Fact, Fiction, and the Books of Madeleine L'Engle." *The New Yorker*, April 12, 2004. 60–67. Print.

A Scientific Girl and Two Intuitive Boys
The Unconventional Protagonists of A Wrinkle in Time

Anne-Frédérique Mochel-Caballero

Although *A Wrinkle in Time* (1962) now belongs to the classics of American children's literature, the early days were not easy as Madeleine L'Engle allegedly approached twenty-six publishers before John Farrar eventually agreed to take on the job. This is because, in her own words, the novel was "too different" (*Go Fish* 236), "[dealing] overtly with the problem of evil [...] really difficult for children" (*A Circle of Quiet* 5–6, 21, 66, 217–8). What made it even more original was that it featured "a female protagonist in a science fiction book" ("A Special Message"). This was a rarity at the time and is not so common even in the twenty-first century. As Pierre Bruno wrote in 2012: "Even today, there are more males than females among heroes in children's literature"(28), and according to a 2010 American study mentioned by Pamela Paul in the *New York Times*, science fiction is still mainly read by men: "Half of 18- to 24-year-old men say that science fiction is their favorite type of book, compared with only one-fourth of young women [...] And while a sizable portion of men continue to read science fiction throughout their lives, women don't."

Yet in spite of these unusual characteristics, a year after it was published, the novel had become a best-seller and has since then been awarded several prizes, among which the prestigious Newbery medal. It is often studied in schools and has helped a lot of American teenagers in the construction of their gender identities as was made clear by the numerous testimonies posted on the Internet when *A Wrinkle in Time* celebrated its fiftieth anniversary in 2012. One example is that of Meghan Miller, a writer for the *Forever Young*

Adult site, who referred to her younger self as "a dress-hating, tangle-haired, Lisa-Frank-shunning, chatterbox tomboy who occasionally got into fistfights with boys" and who described how *A Wrinkle in Time* became "one of [her] favorite books of all time," defining it as her "go-to comfort book, the one that reminds [her] to be [herself], to not give up." To quote another example of the novel's influence, the astronaut Janice Voss claimed in a 2007 interview on National Public Radio that she made her choice of career after discovering *A Wrinkle in Time* when she was ten:

> I happened to pick up the year before my sixth grade, which is in 1966 (sic), a copy of Madeleine L'Engle's *A Wrinkle in Time*. I was just fascinated. So it was the most interesting thing I had ever read. I went back and checked out the entire science fiction section when I got back and had been reading science fiction ever since (sic). And that's what got me an interest in space and my path to be an astronaut.

On the one hand, a number of clichés based on the outside/inside and strength/weakness duets can be found in this novel: they concern family structures, gender-based roles and behaviors. However, subversive representations reversing traditional patterns are also present and even dominant. Thus, the pairs rationality/intuition, activity/passivity, and exact sciences/humanities are respectively associated with feminine and masculine characters. Considering the novel as a whole, I will endeavor to show that Madeleine L'Engle was ahead of her time in that she perceived the notion of gender as being socially constructed long before this was popularized, thus preparing a generation of young Americans for the emergence of feminist ideology at the end of the sixties, as Catherine Hand has stated: "The engine that drives [*A Wrinkle in Time*] is Meg's inner life, and it's astonishing, because here is a girl who at that moment is stronger than her father. For some of us, it planted the seeds of the women's movement" (qtd. in Elizabeth Bird).

Dolls and Trains

There are three protagonists in *A Wrinkle in Time*: a girl, Meg Murry, aged around thirteen, her five-year-old brother, Charles Wallace, and her fourteen-year-old school friend Calvin O'Keefe.[1] However, although it is a third-person narrative, Meg is given a special place as the focalization is internal: the reader sees everything through her eyes and experiences the whole range of her feelings, starting with her fear and discouragement in the first chapter and ending with a love and joy "so tangible that Meg felt that if she only knew where to reach she could touch it with her bare hands" (226).

In a certain number of respects, Meg is an ordinary girl, raised in a rather conventional nuclear family at the beginning of the sixties. Her father is missing at the start of the story, but even before disappearing, he was frequently absent from home, travelling for professional reasons. As for her mother, she stays at home, is a good cook and her children occasionally confide in her or ask for her advice. At the Murrys,' toys are shared out along traditional lines: dolls for Meg, a rocking-horse for baby Charles Wallace and trains for their brothers Sandy and Dennys (5). When it comes to housework, Mrs. Murry and Meg wash the dishes whereas the twins lay the table (474) and raise vegetables (50), gardening usually being seen as one of the more masculine chores (Héritier, *Masculin/Féminin II* 377). When Calvin is invited for dinner, he is given the nobler task of reading Charles Wallace a bedtime story while Meg and her mother stay in the kitchen and the twins watch television (46). Of course, he is perhaps simply being honored as a guest, and at least he is making himself useful, albeit in a pleasant way: after all, let us remember that the novel was published in 1963, at a time when children's books still routinely presented apron-clad mothers busying themselves in the kitchen while fathers were smoking pipes and reading newspapers on the sofa.[2]

Meg often behaves in a way which is traditionally considered typically feminine: she cries a lot (2, 55, 78, 134, 209, 224), throws tantrums (24, 51, 209), shrieks in terror (35, 58) and generally lacks self-confidence. She hates her looks (4), reproaches herself for her aggressiveness (2), for not being popular at school and for being oversensitive (2, 54). Her friend Calvin—whom she will marry between Books 2 and 3 of the Trilogy—reassures (36, 72), protects (38, 50, 61), calms (51) and comforts her (55). He is almost systematically the one who initiates physical contact (36, 38, 51, 72–78, 84, 85, etc.). When he does, the wording suggests a strong guiding masculine presence, coming to the rescue of a more fragile female, as in the following example: "Meg stumbled as the land sloped suddenly downhill, but Calvin's strong hand steadied her." (50) Some readers have complained about Meg's conventional personality or about her excess of tears (R.L. Stine qtd. by Jen Doll) but she can also be seen as a typical teenager as described by the research of Carol Gilligan and the Harvard Project on the Psychology of Women and the Development of Girls, as well as that of the American Association of University Women, which has shown that

> at about age eleven or twelve girls are in danger of "losing their voices" and "hitting the wall" (Gilligan et al. 25, 19), falling from the positions of strength, freedom, and self-confidence they had in childhood into "traditional patterns of low self-image, self-doubt, and self-censorship of their creative and intellectual potential" [Orenstein xvi qtd. in Clark, Higonnet 197].

Actually, part of the reason for the great success of the novel could be that generations of female readers[3] have identified with this awkward girl, wearing big glasses and braces (4). Although in the film versions this aspect is played down, with the part of the heroine played by actresses who are systematically beautiful, *A Wrinkle in Time* is not the only youth novel where the protagonist is an ugly duckling: in *Twilight*, Bella is so clumsy that sport at school is like torture (23, 32, 44, 61, 64, etc.) and Katniss Everdeen[4] sees herself as lacking charm (15) in the first chapter of *The Hunger Games* trilogy. Madeleine L'Engle herself had a difficult time as a teenager as she was clumsy (Hettinga 4), did not do well at school, spent a lot of time on her own (Chase 88) and she confessed in an interview with Scholastic students that "Meg couldn't keep her hair nice and she was not a beauty. She was a difficult child. She is a lot like me!"

While her attempt to be true to life led the author to set her story in a rather conservative frame, she also chose to reverse a certain number of common patterns.

"The Privilege of Accepting This Danger" (215)

Right at the beginning of the novel, Meg behaves in a "masculine," aggressive manner, fighting boys at school to defend her little brother Charles Wallace. The ten-year-old twins unconsciously react in a conformist way, being "disgusted" (2) with their sister's attitude and wanting to fulfill their "masculine" role: "Let *us* do the fighting when it's necessary" (emphasis in the text) (2). In the 2003 television adaptation, this scene is presented in a more stereotyped fashion since, as soon as Meg starts fighting, Calvin comes to her rescue, which proves, if needs be, that forty years later, the public still preferred more customary gendered behaviors, or at least so the director thought. Although no date has been given for the release of the movie, *Frozen* director Jennifer Lee is said to be currently working on a Disney adaptation of *A Wrinkle in Time* (Ben Child). It will be interesting to see how she handles the issue of gender. Judging from the *Frozen* scenario, we can guess her approach will be very different from that of John H. Kent, who directed the television adaptation.

In the novel, a certain number of representations of masculinity and femininity are subversive: for instance, Meg is very good at math (44) whereas Calvin's strong subjects are Literature and History, thus reversing the tendency for boys to be better at science than girls, which is still a reality in classes today. Admittedly, Mrs. Murry's laboratory is next to the house, allowing her to work without leaving home, but she is a brilliant scientist—a doctor in biology and in bacteriology (27)—like her husband (52), or even better, since she is the one who will win the Nobel Prize in the third volume of the trilogy, *A Swiftly Tilting Planet* (474). The two boys, Calvin (33–4) and Charles

Wallace (7), are both uncannily intuitive, which is usually viewed as a feminine attribute. They remain rather passive in comparison to Meg, who saves both her little brother and her father from the enemy's clutches. When she finally meets Mr. Murry, Meg is angry with him for not being the patriarchal figure she was expecting. The beginning of the novel deals with her search for her father, whom she expects to solve all their problems by his mere presence: "Her father had been found but he had not made everything all right. Instead everything was worse than ever, and her adored father was bearded and thin and white and not omnipotent after all" (168). However, she is expected to change her attitude. Indeed, the magical glasses needed to enter Mr. Murry's prison were given to Meg, and she is the one who has to go back to the planet Camazotz to save Charles Wallace. Her father and Calvin suggest going in her stead, but the chances of success are greater if she goes since she knows her little brother much more intimately than they do. They must therefore allow her "the privilege of accepting this danger," as Mrs. Whatsit tells Mr. Murry (215). Meg wins the fight against evil with totally unexpected weapons. Her little brother's "masculine" pride leads him to overestimate his strength (108) and though Meg first attempts to fight by resisting her enemy (171–2, 175), she nearly loses her life in the process (190–1). She eventually manages to escape from IT, the giant brain trying to take possession of her soul. She wins the battle because of the love which flows in her when she thinks of her little brother (223), in a passage which may have inspired J. K. Rowling with a similar scene in which Harry Potter drives Voldemort out of his own body thanks to the same feeling.[5] For "God has chosen the weak things of the world to confound the things which are mighty" (216), as Mrs. Who tells Meg just before leaving, quoting the first letter to the Corinthians.[6] Although the enemy is of infinitely superior strength in every other way, the weapon he lacks is precisely love (217). Hence the traditional contrast between strength and weakness is here reversed.

Meg, Charles Wallace and Calvin are not on their own in this adventure. Admittedly, their parents remain discreet, as is often the case in children's literature, but the protagonists get help from three mysterious characters, Mrs. Whatsit, Mrs. Who and Mrs. Which. Their identities seem to fluctuate in the course of the novel. They are first seen as eccentric old ladies with supernatural powers, capable of reading people's minds (18), of flying (20) and of appearing or disappearing at will (56–7). These charming witch-like figures choose to live in a supposedly haunted house in order to drive nosy people away (37) and they "get a lot of fun out of using all the typical props" (36). However, it is later made clear that they only decided on this form so as not to frighten human children (66). In reality, they are former stars[7] having given up their status in their fight against evil (97), and they are capable of changing shape. When the children need to travel from one planet to another, Mrs. Whatsit becomes a sort of majestic winged centaur, with the beauty (67) and the song[8] of an angel (71). Calvin falls to his knees, ready to worship it, but just like Saint John in the book of Revelation (Rev. 19, 10), he is asked to abstain (67). Later, on the planet Ixchel, he refers to the three creatures as "guardian angels" and "messengers of God" (204).

The glorious being Mrs. Whatsit has become has nothing feminine about it and the children accordingly lose their bearings when she transforms: they don't know what to call her anymore (68), or whether they should use "she," "he" or "it" when referring to the creature who is smiling at them (68). Nevertheless, she and her two companions remain associated with the feminine throughout the novel, because they first choose to reveal themselves in this form. Since Madeleine L'Engle rejected the idea of a purely masculine God,[9] it is interesting that these mighty tutelary feminine figures fighting evil should be the closest manifestations of the divine the reader comes across in this story.

With its mixture of conformism and subversion, the novel has a double function, as Hans-Robert Jauss put it: "the function of a work of art is not only to *represent* reality but also to *create* it" (emphasis in the text 36).

"The Happy Medium" (96)

The protagonists in *A Wrinkle in Time* cannot be classified in a simplistic binary manner. For instance, just after fighting like a lion, Meg mistrusts herself and cries: the juxtaposition of the two scenes presents the reader with a personality which is complex and therefore true to life. Faced with the grief caused by the disappearance of a loved one, two female characters, Meg and her mother, react in different ways, the former by expressing her pain, the latter by keeping it locked inside (3). At school, Calvin adapts to his surroundings and manages to be popular (46, 102), whereas Meg and Charles Wallace are considered to be "subnormal children" (7), like monsters inspiring fear and rejection because of their differences, consequently placing themselves on the side of what has long been believed to be "feminine," as French anthropologist Françoise Héritier put it: "[…] for Aristotle, the first stage of abnormality, of monstrosity is when a female is born rather than a male" (*Masculin/Féminin I* 195).

Moreover, the characters are not static in that they learn through their mistakes: this is true of Charles Wallace and Mr. Murry (179), but even more so of Meg, who, during her initiatory journey, learns, among other things, to accept herself as she is: "And Mrs. Who said—I don't understand what she said but I think it was meant to make me not hate being only me, and me being the way I am" (220). Even if Meg lacks self-confidence at the beginning of the novel, her quest transforms her, as suggested by Donald R. Hettinga:

> When Meg discovers that love can break the bonds of evil, her quest is complete, for the love that she has discovered is a love that can set her free just as it released Charles Wallace from the power of IT. ... Equipped with such a love, a love that gives her the assurance that she need not conform in order to be "good," Meg is ready to reenter reality. No chronological time has passed on earth, but she is a changed person, confident enough of who she is to face social difficulties she might meet. Her quest is over [31].

Madeleine L'Engle is not an essentialist: all her characters, whether male or female, have their own unique non gender-based personalities, and it gives them—and the reader—a sense of freedom. As Dorothy L. Sayers stated in an address delivered to a Women's Society in 1938, "what is repugnant to every human being is to be reckoned always as a member of a class and not as an individual person" (24).

The combination of clichés and more original representations seems to be deliberate on the part of the author. Indeed, Madeleine L'Engle interestingly created a character who was similar to herself, with one exception: "I made Meg good at math and bad at English, and I was good at English and bad at math. Otherwise, we were very much alike!" (Interview, Scholastic). Charles Wallace and Calvin's sense of intuition is probably not fortuitous either, as Madeleine L'Engle rued the restrictive fashion in which boys were raised: "the world of intuition has, for many years, been more available to women than to men, who are taught from early childhood on to live in a restricted, rational world. If they delve into the realms of the intuition it must be apologized for, or explained" ("Foreword," *Companion* xiii).

Nevertheless, she was not a militant; she herself claimed she "did not know that one was not supposed to have a female protagonist in a science fiction book, so perhaps it was [her] first *unconscious* affirmation of feminism" (Emphasis mine. Foreword to *Suncatcher* 14). While wanting to fight inequalities, Madeleine L'Engle did not fall into extremes as authors sometimes do. In a French study on sexism in children's literature, a book called *Inès la piratesse* was quoted as displaying a lack of balance in this area. Indeed, Inès and her female accomplices turn Pablo, a man they have caught, into a slave: "Instead of suggesting a new balanced relationship between men and women, the reversal of roles makes one think it is impossible to escape the domination of one sex over the other and it perpetuates the clichés" (Mazzone, Barthe-Gay 46). American children's literature expert Charlotte Huck warned against the same snare in her introduction to *Beauty, Brains and Brawn, The Construction of Gender in Children's Literature*: "We need stories of adventurous girls, but they should reveal some of the caring, responsible aspects that made them a girl in the first place. We do not want to substitute one stereotype for another" (ix).

On the contrary, Madeleine L'Engle created genuine characters who avoid excesses, according to Carol F. Chase: "She does not seek to right the gender imbalance of the centuries by belittling or downgrading males. Just as strong, accomplished women populate her books, so do strong, gentle men" (142).

Madeleine L'Engle chose to pun on the expression "the happy medium" by creating a character who is a literally a jolly seer and whom the children get to meet in Orion's belt (88). But she must have realized that this expression could be applied to the personalities her characters developed throughout the novel because she also uses it in this context for example in the first chapter, when Mrs. Murry's remarks to her daughter: "A happy medium is something I wonder if you'll ever learn" (11). Indeed, Meg does learn, though not in the way Mrs. Murry had in mind (Scheebaum 31). As Thomas A. Barron comments, L'Engle's heroines are accomplished beings:

> Madeleine L'Engle [...] ha[s] deepened and strengthened the concept of the female hero in a mythic context. [She has] shown convincingly the traumas and triumphs by which women and girls can be great leaders, gifted healers and also fierce warriors. And such characters need not simply mimic the male hero's journey. They may reject the established patterns, cast aside the old rules, and prevail on their own terms [31].

In imagining characters who are simultaneously "masculine" and "feminine," Madeleine L'Engle also avoids the trap of transforming the masculine into a "neutral," as Sylvie Cromer put it, "pretending to be universal, while the feminine is erased and marginalized" (45). In Madeleine l'Engle's imaginary world, both the masculine and the feminine are allowed room, consequently conveying an impression of authenticity.

In fact, she does not reject the idea of instructing through her writing, but she intends to do it with characters who are genuine, as did C. S. Lewis, in her view: "I believe that if a writer is writing out of his own truth, then the reader is going to learn from that truth; it need not and should not be didactic, but it is nevertheless teaching, and I am grateful for it" (Foreword to *Companion* xv).

Conclusion

A Wrinkle in Time conveys an impression of balance as far as the personalities of the male and female characters are concerned. This impression may also be due to the specific genre of the novel, *science-fantasy*. Indeed, science fiction and fantasy may be considered as respectively "masculine" and "feminine," or at least that is how they were viewed by the American public in the eighties, according to Professor Charlotte Spivack:

> Fantasy fiction in America has suffered from a persistent critical ambivalence [...] Even while science fiction and detective novels have become academically acceptable as worthy of intellectual analysis, fantasy is often rejected as frivolous (what one science-fiction writer called "cute stories about unicorns") or categorically relegated to the juvenile shelves [...] Ursula K. Le Guin, posing the question of why Americans are afraid of dragons, [...] attributes the fear in part to Puritanism, the work ethic, and profit-mindedness. She further suggests that our sexual mores are also partly to blame, for Americans tend to regard reading (and writing) fantasy fiction as effeminate [ix–x].

It also seems that setting a story in an imaginary world facilitates the transmission of novel values (Barron 31), for the gap between reality and fiction allows the reader to question his/her routine, as Isabelle Smadja remarked in her study on *Harry Potter*. To her mind, the fact of dealing with wizards gives the books an exotic aura, thus allowing the author to convey a moral message without the children realizing it is intended for them (23). Even so, *A Wrinkle in Time* is a surprising work, if one compares it to twenty-first century books, which are often less daring as far as representations of the masculine and the feminine are concerned, whether in children's literature or in school books (Mazzone, Barthe-Gay). Let us, for instance, put side by side the three protagonists of both *A Wrinkle in Time* and *Harry Potter*: the former are far less conventional than the latter. Admittedly, both groups are composed of two boys and one girl, however the main protagonist is not Hermione in J. K. Rowling's novels and her characters are more stereotyped than L'Engle's. Nevertheless, let us rejoice that the girl Meg and the boy Harry win the fight with the same weapon, love, which eventually transcends gender.

Notes

1. Meg's exact age is not given: we know she is younger than Calvin (31) who is fourteen and in eleventh grade. His remark "I'm bright" suggests he might have skipped a class or two (33). She says he is a couple of grades above her (32) so she must be twelve or thirteen. Charles Wallace's age is given in my edition (9) but seems to be missing from earlier editions. However we know he is in his first year at school so he will be either five or six.

2. In a more recent novel for teenage girls, *Twilight*, Bella gets the food ready *and* does the dishes while her father watches television (27, 30, 32). This seems to be a general trend in children's literature, according to a 2012 study: "In the twenty-first century, a lot of sexist stereotypes can still be found in children's literature [...] There are still more girls working at home, occasionally helping their mothers with nurturing or domestic tasks. On the other hand, little boys are active outside with their friends in public places where they do mischief or play a game of sport" (Mazzone, Barthe-Gay 67–68).

3. Men have also identified with Meg Murry, as playwright John Glore stated in an interview he gave after adapting *A Wrinkle in Time* for the theater: "I'd say I relate to Meg's sense of alienation, of feeling like she's the weirdest person in her family and perhaps in the world. I think most of us feel that way as kids, as we're trying to figure out how we fit in."

4. Katniss Everdeen and Meg Murry have a lot in common and *The Hunger Games*' author, Suzanne Collins, said that she had loved *A Wrinkle in Time* as a child (qtd. in Jen Doll).

5. "That power also saved you from possession by Voldemort, because he could not bear to reside in a body so full of the force he detests. In the end, it mattered not that you could not close your mind. It was your heart that saved you" (*Harry Potter and the Order of the Phoenix* 743).

6. "The foolishness of God is wiser than men; and the weakness of God is stronger than men. For ye see your calling, brethren, how that not many wise men after the flesh, not many mighty, not many noble, *are called*: But God hath chosen the foolish things of the world to confound the wise; and God hath chosen the weak things of the world to confound the things which are mighty. And base things of the world, and things which are despised, hath God chosen, *yea*, and things which are not, to bring to nought things that are" (*King James Version* 1 Cor. 1. 25–28).

7. Narnia's Ramandu and Coriakin spring to mind here. Madeleine L'Engle knew and admired C.S. Lewis, referring to him in terms of "reading friendship" and "kinship" ("Foreword" to *Companion* xiv).

8. They sing a "new song" to the Lord, taken from Isaiah 42.10. In Revelation, the angels also sing a new song to the Lamb (Rev. 5. 9–14).

9. "Noting the patriarchal nature of the Bible, she views the scriptural presentation of God as incomplete, partly because it is seen only through male eyes. She expresses this in *The Rock That Is Higher*" (Chase 144).

Works Cited

Barron, Thomas A. "The Unquenchable Source: Finding a Heroic Girl Inside a Man?" *Beauty, Brains and Brawn: The Construction of Gender in Children's Literature.* Ed. Susan Lehr. Portsmouth: Heinemann, 2001: 30–35. Print.

Bird, Elizabeth. "Top 100 Children's Novels #2: *A Wrinkle in Time* by Madeleine L'Engle." *The School Library Journal.* 28 June 2012. Web. 5 August 2015.

Bruno, Pierre. "Le sexisme dans la littérature pour la jeunesse : une évaluation et une explication complexes." *Le sexisme dans le livre jeunesse, actes de la journée d'études du 16 janvier 2012.* Eds. Fanny Mazzone and Clarisse Barthe-Gay. Toulouse: Presses de l'Université Toulouse I capitole, 2012. Print.

Chase, Carole F. *Suncatcher: A Study of Madeleine L'Engle and Her Writings.* 1995. Philadelphia: Innisfree, 1998. Print.

Child, Ben. "Frozen Director Jennifer Lee to Adapt *A Wrinkle in Time*." *The Guardian.* 5 August 2014. Web. 5 August 2015.

Clark, Beverly Lyon, and Margaret R. Higonnet, eds. *Girls, Boys, Books, Toys: Gender in Children's Literature and Culture.* Baltimore: Johns Hopkins University Press, 1999. Print.

Collins, Suzanne. *The Hunger Games.* New York: Scholastic Press, 2008. Print.

Cromer, Sylvie. "Genre et littérature jeunesse en France : éléments pour une synthèse." *Filles intrépides et garçons tendres, genre et culture enfantine.* Ed. A.J. Ireman. *Nordiques* No. 21. Paris: Choiseul, Winter 2009–10. Print.

Doll, Jen. "*A Wrinkle in Time* Turns 50: Meg Murry Made Katniss Everdeen Possible." *The Wire*. 7 February 2012. Web. 5 August 2015.

Glore, John. "An Interview with *A Wrinkle in Time* Playwright John Glore: Part Two—The Play and Beyond." Interview by Jacqueline Lawton. Round House Theater. 24 November 2010. Web. 5 August 2015.

Héritier, Françoise. *Masculin/Féminin I, La pensée de la différence*. Paris: Odile Jacob, 2012. Print.

_____. *Masculin/Féminin II, Dissoudre la hiérarchie*. Paris: Odile Jacob, 2012. Print.

Hettinga, Donald R. *Presenting Madeleine L'Engle*. New York: Twayne, 1993. Print.

Huck, Charlotte. "Introduction." *Beauty, Brains and Brawn: The Construction of Gender in Children's Literature*. Ed. Susan Lehr. Portsmouth: Heinemann, 2001. Print.

Jauss, Hans-Robert. *Pour une esthétique de la reception*. Trans. Claude Maillard. Paris: Gallimard, 1978. Print.

Lehr, Susan, ed. *Beauty, Brains and Brawn: The Construction of Gender in Children's Literature*. Portsmouth: Heinemann, 2001. Print.

L'Engle, Madeleine. *A Circle of Quiet*. New York: Farrar, Straus & Giroux, 1972. Print.

_____. Foreword. *Companion to Narnia*. 1980. Paul Ford. New York: HarperCollins, 1994. Print.

_____. Foreword. *Suncatcher: A Study of Madeleine L'Engle and Her Writings*. 1995. Carole F. Chase. Philadelphia: Innisfree, 1998. Print.

_____. "Go Fish: Questions for the Author," *A Wrinkle in Time*. New York: Square Fish, 2007. Print.

_____. Interview by Scholastic Students. Scholastic. Web. 5 August 2015.

_____. "A Special Message from Madeleine L'Engle." Penguin Random House. Web. 5 August 2015.

_____. *A Wrinkle in Time Trilogy*. 1962, 1973, 1978. New York: Farrar, Straus & Giroux, 2012. Print.

Mazzone, Fanny, and Clarisse Barthe-Gay, eds. *Le sexisme dans le livre jeunesse, actes de la journée d'études du 16 janvier 2012*. Toulouse: Presses de l'Université Toulouse I capitol, 2012. Print.

Meyer, Stephenie. *Twilight*. 2005. London: Atom, 2007. Print.

Miller, Meghan. "Alike and Equal Are Not the Same Thing at All (Or: Remembering *A Wrinkle in Time*)." *Forever Young Adult*. 18 January 2012. Web. 5 August 2015.

Paul, Pamela. "*A Wrinkle in Time* and Its Sci-Fi Heroine." *New York Times*. 27 January 2012. Web. 5 August 2015.

Rowling, J. K. *Harry Potter and the Order of the Phoenix*. London: Bloomsbury, 2003. Print.

Sayers, Dorothy L. *Are Women Human?* 1947. Grand Rapids: Eerdmans, 2005. Print.

Schneebaum, Katherine. "Finding a Happy Medium: The Design for Womanhood in *A Wrinkle in Time*." *The Lion and the Unicorn*, vol. 14. Baltimore: Johns Hopkins University Press, 1990: 30–36. Print.

Smadja, Isabelle. *Harry Potter, les raisons d'un succès*. Vendôme: Presses Universitaires de France, 2002. Print.

Spivack, Charlotte. Preface. *Merlin's Daughters: Contemporary Women Writers of Fantasy*. New York: Greenwood, 1987. Print.

Voss, Janice. Interview by Jacki Lyden. National Public Radio. 8 September 2007. Web. 5 August 2015.

A Wrinkle in Time. Writ. Susan Shilliday (teleplay), Madeleine L'Engle (novel). Dir. John Harrison Kent. Disney. 16 November 2004. DVD.

Thinking, Doing and Delaying Insemination in L'Engle's *Many Waters*

Chantel Lavoie

> If [Sandy] and Dennys were not interested in mythical beasts, neither were they interested in girls. They went to the regional school dances, but usually stuck with the other members of the hockey and basketball teams. There was going to be plenty of time for girls later.—*Many Waters* 169.

> "We've never been exposed to heat like this before."—*Many Waters* 26.

Madeleine L'Engle's novel *Many Waters* (1986) revisits much that is familiar in the other books that make up her Time Quintet (or Quartet, if one excludes *An Acceptable Time* [1989], in which case *Many Waters* is the last in the shorter series). Here again we meet with members of the Murry family, and quantum leaps drive the plot. This time the protagonists are the twin boys, Sandy and Dennys, middle children between the troubled genius older sister, Meg, and their empathic younger brother Charles Wallace, both of whom have been central characters in previous books. Whereas the twins also have higher than average intelligence (Sandy will grow up to be an environmental lawyer, Dennys a doctor), compared to their siblings, astrophysicist father, and Nobel prize-winning microbiologist mother, the boys are "the ordinary, run-of-the-mill ones in the family" (6). In *Many Waters,* while playing with one of their father's computer experiments, Sandy and Dennys are thrust back to a time before the Common/Christian Era—to the oasis tenthold of Noah in the months prior to the flood. Like all heroes, Sandy and Dennys are tested, and theirs is a test of faith. Natural disasters and historical context come up against myth ("Isn't there some kind of flood story in all cultures?" 201), thereby entangling, as L'Engle so fruitfully does, faith and reason, theologies and sciences, with an emphasis on the challenging quotation she includes from Ralph Hodgson, "Some things have to be believed to be seen" (290). Less inclined than other members of their family to believe in what they cannot see, Sandy and Dennys now encounter mythical creatures which inhabit L'Engle's rewriting of the Old Testament story—the Seraphim and Nephilim of the Old Testament are here[1]; so too are miniature mammoths, manticores, and virtual unicorns (virtual in that they exist only when they are believed in). Dennys says of himself and his twin: "We've never had very willing suspensions of disbelief. We're the pragmatists of the family" (24). Yet they come to believe that they are now part of the story of the flood, or in a different version of it. It is both impossible and true.

Their time travel gives them a reprieve from the ordinary; normal falls away, and they start to wonder what such words as *ordinary* and *normal* even meant, and how they apply to themselves. At the same time, the dread of knowing that annihilating waters are coming to flood the world mirrors the anxiety in their own lives about nuclear war. Both inevitabilities challenge their faith, their sense of purpose, and lead them to question the value of human endeavor. If destruction is assured, why does it matter what anyone does or refrains from doing? In light of these two end-of-the-world scenarios, *Many Waters* takes a stand on three seducers of teenagers: aggression, lust and despair. This paper argues that L'Engle's book about boys exposed to the heat of a desert and to temptations at the cooling oasis where they are saved, as well as to their own mid–1980s adolescence—offers a strategy to the average adolescent male for approaching sex, and love, in a dangerous time.

Leaving Normal

The adjectives mentioned above—*ordinary*, *normal*—pepper the lexicon with which Sandy and Dennys Murry talk about themselves. In the first book, *A Wrinkle in Time* (1962), we see little of them, but know that the twins defend their sister and brother from bullies when they have to, that they get consistently good (not bad and not great) marks, and that they get along fine with other children. The reader sees that this can take its toll: "'I wish our parents did ordinary things,' Sandy complained. 'If Dad were a plumber or an electrician and Mother were somebody's secretary, it would be a lot easier for us […] And we wouldn't have to be such great athletes and good guys at school…'" (*Wrinkle* 16). The telling phrases "have to be" along with "good guys" indicate much about how the twins believe they perform their identities.

In *Many Waters*, no longer children but fifteen-year-olds, they continue to define themselves as united in their differences from the rest of their family. Sandy reminds his brother, "We're the ones who *do* things, remember?" (*Many Waters* 11). However, as the novel progresses, normal and ordinary are increasingly problematized, as in a conversation with a Seraphic being named Alarid, whom they encounter in the ancient world: "'Sandy and I are the squares of our family. Our older sister and our little brother are the special ones. We're just the ordinary...' Alarid interrupted him. 'Because that is how you are, or because that is how you choose to be?'" (113). Alarid will not allow them to dismiss themselves—nor to excuse themselves—arguing "there must be some reason for [them] to be here" (113). At this point he is telling the twins that they have a special gift. This matters, as the Seraph knows about the future, identifying them as being from "A time of many wars" in which "the heart of the atom has been revealed" (115). Of the twentieth century too, Alarid notes, "You have soiled your waters and your air" (115).

The boys' acceptance of the new, seemingly unreal reality they encounter in the ancient world is enriched by the fact that *they* are mythical creatures in the land they come to visit. Noah and his family, and the less welcoming people at the oasis, are confused by twins, which they have never seen before. The patriarch remarks: "They told me you look like one boy in two bodies. Now I believe them" (156). Being much larger than the Old Testament people they encounter, they are also— relatively—giants, and referred to as those other mythical beasts. "'I'm not a giant,' Sandy said, 'really. I'm just a boy. Dennys and I are still growing, but we're not giants, we're just ordinary tall'" (26). Here again, in a different context, that word *ordinary* signals something apart from itself, because in their new environment of the distant past they are far from ordinary. It is hard for those they encounter in this past to understand that the boys are only fifteen, for these forebears are—in accordance with biblical lore—well over a hundred years old.

Peace, Enlightenment, Disaster: Caution Against Aggression

Being brothers transported to times of Genesis connects the Murry twins, albeit obliquely, to another biblical tale, that of Cain and Abel. Unlike in that story, though, both of these brothers are peacekeepers. Sandy and Dennys manage to reconcile Noah and his father, Lamech. This is something no member of the patriarchs' family has managed to do. They achieve this despite concerns voiced by the Seraph about the twins altering the past—a common trope in time travel narratives. Moreover, when they are helping to build the ark, and a hostile crowd of onlookers gathers to jeer, "A stone was thrown." The boys, towering over the small people, "walked with deliberate steps toward the mob of little people. Dennys did not put down the plank he was sanding. Sandy still held the stone he used for a hammer. Neither boy threatened in any way; nevertheless, the people drew back slightly. Sandy spoke in a commanding voice. 'No stone throwing'" (327). It is impossible not to recall Christ at this moment, as L'Engle hints at a typology that shifts from Old Testament to the promise of the New, along with the argument for human progress.

The boys must grow close to the people they encounter in order to survive the harsh environmental conditions, but they also choose to do so; they become like members of Noah's family and weep when Grandfather Lamech dies. Like Christ himself, they are invested in a story that has taken on flesh, and the disaster will be real.

Further, in worrying about the seemingly pointless flood to come, the twins are especially concerned about the women they have met who are not mentioned among the few saved in the Bible. Dennys says to the Seraph Alarid, "Listen, it's a stupid story. Only the males have names. It's a chauvinist story. I mean, Matred [Noah's wife] has a name. She's a mother. And Elisheba and Anah and Oholibamah. They're real people, with names" (317). The Murry twins are therefore enlightened males—resistant to violence, respectful of women—who land in an unenlightened, patriarchal desert. As such, the Murry twins are aware of their own feelings, cooperate with nature, and do all that's in their power to include the feminine.[2] Threatened as they seem to be at this moment along with everyone else, the attitudes Sandy and Dennys bring with them from the twentieth century are signs of hope for futurity; they are part of the rainbow.

Playing with the Bible

Katherine Paterson has written that L'Engle's emphasis on freedom "teaches us [...] the ability to see the Bible as an icon rather than an idol—a window to God rather than an object of worship" (1998: 86). Whereas *Many Waters* is set later in Genesis, the novel also reimagines the transgression of Adam and Eve, conflating the story of that fall with the story of two brothers, as noted above, like and profoundly unlike Cain and Abel in that Sandy and Dennys heal the breach in a family, love one another, and humbly tend the land together. In this way L'Engle pulls away from the story of the apocalyptic flood to consider other tales in which individual human decisions—like loving one's brother as oneself—can make all the difference. Further, Sandy and Dennys are associated with gardens—in two previous books the twins' vegetable garden has been made much of. They are hard-working natural gardeners, earning money as children while contributing to the well-being of the family, and most importantly, enjoying the work. In *A Wind in the Door* (1973), they also help save their younger brother, Charles Wallace, whose life is threatened when Echthroi (microcosmic and macrocosmic forces of nihilism) attack the boy's mitochondria (organelles found in all cellular life). Because everything in the universe is connected, the twins merely doing what they know how to do in favor of life ultimately helps their brother: "They went on with their preparation of the garden for the winter cold and snow" (188).

In *Many Waters*, again, they toil in the garden—now pulling prehistoric weeds larger than they are, protecting and honoring the gentle life of the ancestors of our tomatoes and onions. Cheerfully, they take up Adam's fate to bring forth life with the sweat of their brow. Sandy and Dennys's labor shifts in the final quarter of the book to helping build the ark that Noah has been told by El (Noah's family's name for God) to build. All of this revisits an earlier punishment for transgression: as Grandfather Lamech, father of Noah, explains "When our forebears had to leave the Garden they were told Accursed shall be the ground on your account. It will grow thorns and thistles for you. You shall gain your bread by the sweat of your brow" (98).

It is neither a simple nor a condemnatory story that L'Engle weaves through her testament to the Old Testament tale. In her work, the Bible becomes among other things a tale of mystery and intrigue. When Dennys learns that he is really in the presence of Noah, he recalls his mother reading to her children when they were little: "What did she read? Stories. Greek and Roman myths. Indian tales, Chinese tales, African tales. Fairy Tales. Bible stories" (106). The list might suggest a levelling of fictions; the effect, however, is an identifying of deep truths—the myths across the globe and time being like many deep waters, inseparable. Sandy and Dennys are as surprised as anyone that they share a remarkable gift: "You come from a far time, and yet you speak the Old Language?" asks a Seraph, "the language of creation, of the time when the stars were made and the heavens and the waters and all creatures. It was the language which was spoken in the Garden […] The Garden of Eden, before the story was bent" (113). The statement is radical. Since the story was already "bent" with the expulsion from the garden, L'Engle implies, we are free—and perhaps on some level obliged—to play with how we retell it; biblical authority is inspired by God, but written by fallible humans. As Donald Hettinga argues, "story itself is part of her story" (1).

Where God the Father stands in L'Engle's reimagining of the flood is compellingly unclear. Sandy and Dennys achieve (or are pulled into) the quantum leap that takes them on this adventure because they entered their mother's laboratory and played around on their father's computer. Having typed into the latter a request to go "SOMEPLACE WARM AND SPARSELY POPULATED," adding "LOW HUMIDITY," it is then they are transported to Noah's desert oasis. "'Hey.' Sandy pointed. 'We didn't see this.' There was a small note taped to the door. EXPERIMENT IN PROGRESS. PLEASE KEEP OUT" (9). Theirs is a transgression, therefore, but an honest mistake rather than a sin. Indeed, the too-small note troubles the story of God's injunction against eating of the tree of the knowledge of good and evil. Interestingly, that the twins' mild mischief leading to the sonic boom and a quantum leap takes place in their mother's laboratory and while using their father's computer could also be read as an insemination and fertilization. The request for a place 'sparsely populated' might speak therefore to a subconscious awareness of the results of women and men coming together—they become mothers and fathers. Enormous consequences can result from small mistakes.

Donald Hettinga, again, refers to L'Engle's vision in *Many Waters* as "a gradual fall." Not only is the fall gradual, it is nuanced. Dennys teaches Noah himself about filial love and duty when he says, "Sandy and I get mad at our father. He pays more attention to our sister and our little brother than he does to us, because they're the geniuses and we're only—but even when we get mad at him, he's still our father" (153). "We're only" what? Ordinary again? Arguably this lacuna might stand too for 'only human,' as were Adam and Eve. Clearly the father is in the wrong here, as he is in having placed the too-small sign on the lab door. But his children owe him respect because he is what he is, even though this father, Mr. Murry, is only human too. Dennys's attempt at an explanation about their father being unequal in his attention is suggestive, moreover, of the extent to which some form of sibling jealousy is at work in the story of so many falls, a message reinforced throughout the text.[3] For example, at one point the Seraph Alarid attempts to convince the dark and fallen Nephilim, "You are still our brothers," only to be rebuffed with: "No. We have renounced you and all you stand for. This planet is ours. Its people are ours" (142). There are so many forms of seduction. Jealousy and possession are among them.

The Readiness Is All: Caution Against Lust

The Murry twins' adventure is more question than quest. More remains unanswered than otherwise here, and no one gets the girl. They both want the girl, however, and this carefully managed sibling rivalry when it comes to Yalith, Noah's youngest daughter, is intriguing, since another seductive—and potentially destructive—emotion much associated with young males is lust. And still *Many Waters* is a decidedly 1980s text. Kimberley Reynolds argues that, in contrast to the largely asexual, protective texts written for twentieth-century postwar children, "the epoch of sexual liberation that occurred in the years after the contraceptive pill and before AIDS coincided with the rise of Young Adult Fiction, and it was not long before pubescent and adolescent readers could find books about people of their own age, with feelings they recognised doing things with their bodies that they wanted to do—or indeed were succeeding in doing" (*Radical Children's Literature* 115). *Many Waters* participates in this sea change, though by 1986 AIDS had been identified along with its causes of transmission—and the novel does not abandon those efforts that Reynolds identifies with literature for young adults earlier in the century, "efforts to protect and prolong childhood including attempting to shield the young from sexual knowledge and discouraging interest by associating sex with transgression and punishment" (115). A balancing approach to the life-giving and life-threatening sides of sex explains the connection between sex and water itself in L'Engle's book.

The title *Many Waters* refers to what will happen after the novel closes—the flood, of which we see only the first drops by the end as the ark is finished and the Murry twins each travel by unicorn back to their own time. In Noah's desert there is so little water that none is wasted on drinking (the twins are given fig juice; water is reserved for the garden). Often, parched and sunburned, one or another of the boys longs for cold fresh water to drink, or a refreshing shower. Instead, bodily odors in the world they have come to inhabit are partly rubbed away, partly covered up with scent that can itself be cloying. This means that they cannot disregard the bodies around them, just as sunburn and other hardships along with being far larger than the hundred-plus-year-old humans of that world keep reminding them of their own *em*bodied existence. The normal world they left in the first few pages of the novel highlighted those bodies growing from boyhood to manhood: there they were playing hockey with other guys on a pond, then returned to their house and ate ravenously, remarking on how tall they were growing. Now, in the desert and the oasis where they find succor, they are made increasingly aware of the maleness of their bodies.

Noah's youngest daughter is attractive to and loved by both boys, and she, Yalith, returns those feelings although she is confused by their doubled bodies. She is a hundred years old yet "barely out of childhood and into womanhood" (72). Sandy, the first to meet her, "could see that the girl, covered only in a loincloth [...] was gently curved, with small rosy breasts. Her skin was the color of a ripe apricot" (39). Meeting Yalith, "For the first time in his life, Sandy had a flash of gratitude that Dennys was not with him" (41). This is amusing, understandable, and also sad. Each twin is a blocking agent to the potential romance of the other; each feels "washed over with a sick wave of jealousy" because of her interest in his brother (169). Again this is unsurprising, given that "Yalith smiled on both of them with equal loveliness" (229). The imagery of the "sick wave" is obviously important, as that wave about to wash over humanity results from succumbing to those temptations which have pulled people away from God.

At fifteen, Sandy and Dennys are past puberty, yet not adults. Before they take their quantum leap and throughout the book, their age is described as significant also in relation to their not having, but being in the position soon to acquire, their drivers' licenses. This fact is mentioned at least thrice after they leave the twentieth century, first when they are asked by Japheth whether they are virgins, because upon this depends their ability to touch a unicorn without it disappearing:

> "Oh!" Japheth exclaimed, "it's a good thing you're both so young. For the moment, I'd forgotten that unicorns will not let themselves be touched by anyone who is not a virgin."
> The twins glanced at each other. "Well, we don't even have our driver's license yet," Dennys said [28].

By drawing on unicorn lore, L'Engle makes a point about the advantages of remaining in childhood's kingdom rather than rushing to grow up—to do, or undo—what cannot be altered. This point is less, I think, about the loss of virginity itself, than about the varied entanglements that come from altering that state of being.

Sex is a very real drive in the novel, and threatening. Yalith, for example, "feared the manticores [who are man-eaters] less than she feared some of the young men in the town, and she kept a dart in her hand in case she needed it" (48). A genuine temptation for her comes in the form of the Nephil, Eblis, seeking to seduce the girl: "You were a child, and now you are not a child any longer [...] There are many pleasures ahead for you to taste, and I would help you to enjoy them all" (50). Here we have an Eve who does not succumb to the forked-tongue temptation, largely due to the fact that her twin Adams are now in her world; yet in their brotherhood and youth, as reminders of Eve's *sons* they become reminders of the life that sex engenders.

As noted above, the "giant" Murry twins exist outside of the usual categories in their new (prehistoric) surroundings. When first discussing where to care for the sunburnt and battered Dennys, for instance, the women of Noah's tenthold argue his liminality as a male:

> "He's just a child [...] What about the women's tent?"
> In Yalith's eyes, Sandy/ Dennys was not a child.
> Elisheba asked, "How near to the time of the moon is it for any of us?" [83].

Those eyes, Yalith's, are "beautiful eyes. Pure." By contrast, the red-haired seductress, Tiglah, described as "gorgeous" and "spectacularly beautiful" is not pure. She cannot touch a unicorn, though she is constantly touching the twins as much as they will allow, and attempting to get Sandy to go for a walk with her. When she first bends close to him, he is "half-fascinated, half-repelled by the strong odor of perspiration mingled with heavy perfume. She had rubbed something red onto her lips and over her cheekbones" (173).

Later he tells his twin, "Hey, I don't like the way Tiglah keeps coming around. I don't think I'm ready for Tiglah.' 'Tiglah,' Dennys said, 'is what the kids at school would call an easy lay'" (212). Not the Murry twins themselves, of course, "the kids at school." The indirection of the judgment here protects the character who voices it.

Sandy does go on a walk with Tiglah. When Tiglah kisses him, he draws away: "He knew what she wanted, and he wanted it, too; he was ready, but not, despite her gorgeousness, with Tiglah. Tiglah was not worth losing his ability to touch a unicorn" (228). When he pulls away she protests, asking if he does not like their kissing. "Yes, I like it." His voice was hoarse. "I like it too much" (229). Genuinely tempted, he is heroic in resisting. This decision is justified later when Tiglah betrays him and her father and brother accost and kidnap him for the Nephilim. He wakes bound in a tent, his life in danger, gagging at the smell of "goat, urine, sweat" (256). No perfume can sweeten Tiglah's little hand.

The text offers positive sexuality to counteract instances of (negative) lust: When Dennys sees Noah's son Japheth kiss his wife on the lips, the boy "thought that it was a nice kiss. It was the kind of kiss he had seen his father give his mother. A real kiss. If he lived through this, he would like to kiss someone like that" (90). There is therefore a reward for those who are patient, an implicit recommendation to wait for intimacy that mirrors the patience the twins must exercise even while knowing that the apparently senseless flood is to come.

Being identical, Dennys and Sandy are who they are because a single egg was fertilized by two sperm to form one zygote, which then divided into two separate embryos. The desirable Yalith, however, cannot (or must not) be like that egg. Indeed, the jealousy that the brothers feel—and keep under control—echoes, as I have indicated, the Cain/Abel/God triangle far more than the Adam/Eve/Serpent ménage. But the Murry brothers stand united, and the dual solution to the problem that Yalith causes the twins, and that they cause her, is that she is taken up directly to El (God, perhaps heaven) before the flood, after which the twins ride unicorns back to their own time and place. When Yalith says goodbye, she declares her love for both of them, and they to her:

> "If we had been older," Sandy started.
> Dennys laughed. "If we had been older, it would have been very complicated, wouldn't it?'
> Yalith, too, laughed, "Oh. I love you both! I love you both!"

She kisses each boy—"Full, long kisses" (337). Not being older is therefore an asset to the boys, for now. Yalith then ascends in a shimmer of light, accompanied by an angel. She is not Eve, not Mary, without sin, although she shares characteristics of both. Myth thereby competes with myth in L'Engle's novel; past and present, BC(E) and AD, before the flood and thereafter—opposites are entwined, and twinned.

After the Flood: Caution Against Despair

Whereas lust and sibling rivalry are more nature-based temptations—and sins—despair is a theological one. The first two are also, perhaps, more closely associated with males than with females (rightly or wrongly) whereas the last transcends gender. As a book aimed at teenagers in 1986, *Many Waters* speaks forcefully to the anxiety felt at that time about the arms race and the likelihood of nuclear war (there is also on the second page mention of "the population explosion") causing damage to the modern world. Their sojourn with Noah and his kin occurs *at* and is itself a metaphorical oasis, but the desert is all around them, and it damages them too. The sun burns their tender skins, some of the people they encounter are harsh and violent, and inevitable destruction looms. Dennys's appreciation of the kiss that Japheth gives his wife accompanies the bleak thought that he will only reach manhood "if he lived through this," echoing (and chronologically foreshadowing) Cold War nuclear despair. In *Postapocalyptic Fiction and the Social Contract*, Claire Curtis recalls in the mid–1980s, wondering whether bombs would be coming soon: "And if so was there anything to be done? The TV film *The Day After* [1983] premiered my freshman year in college and as quaint as it seems now I remember warnings not to watch the film alone, televisions set up in common rooms for communal watching and counselors made available for consultation with students who might be traumatized" (1). *The Day After* was seen by over 100 million people during its first broadcast.

Given the state of the world for two teenagers transported from 1986 back to the weeks before the flood, it is unsurprising that, at one point, "Sandy said in a flat voice, 'Maybe we'll get drowned, too. Maybe it would be better than being nuked […] If we get nuked, it will be because of people. Power and greed and corruption. It wouldn't be a natural disaster. But a flood is a natural disaster'" (202).[4] Dennys responds, "Nothing that hasn't happened yet has to happen" (202). But when Sandy is kidnapped later in the story, the boy thinks, "Terrorism was not just a twentieth-century phenomenon. It was evidently part of human nature, and it didn't get wiped out by the flood. There seemed less and less point to the flood" (258). It is a mystery, yet it connects the world and suggests a curious kind of hope: human life recovered and carried on after the flood; it might do so again.

Hopefully, however, now that the choice is with humanity (the arms race) rather than mass destruction as an act of God (flood), history is teaching us something. When Sandy is tempted to succumb both to meaningless sex and to violence in response to Old Testament terrorism, he thinks of the seductress trying to tempt him to escape by physical force: "Tiglah had never heard of the great heroes of lance and spear, of longbow and sword. But this was what she was tempting him to be. What he could be if he wanted to be" (239).[5] However, "violence was not going to work. Violence was what these little men turned to, and he did not want to be like them" (265). In pretending to be big, such men lessen themselves. The twin "giants," although so much younger, are wiser and more mature—invested with a length of cultural memory and human progress—than most of the literally and figuratively small men of the oasis.

However when the flood threatens or the missiles proliferate, hope is not easy to find. *Carpe diem* then can make more sense. Moreover, given the biblical theme taken from Song of Solomon 8.7—"Many waters cannot quench love, neither can the floods drown it"—would sex with the willing and "easy lay" Tiglah necessarily diminish what either twin feels for Yalith? There is also, for example, the biblical verse "Hope deferred makes the heart sick, / but a longing fulfilled is a tree of life" (Proverbs 13.12). In 1986, with a mad arms race informing world politics and a doomsday clock counting down, why should teenagers concern themselves with the consequences of their actions? The only answer can be—again—hope, human reason, and restraint.

At the very end of L'Engle's text, when Sandy and Dennys have returned to their farmhouse, their family, and their boyish winter pallor in 1986, the penultimate line is uttered by Sandy, "As soon as we have our birthdays, we can get our driver's licenses." His brother answers, "And about time [...] Now let's makes that cocoa" (352). It was searching for this cocoa after the hockey game that had drawn them into their mother's lab in the first place, before they erroneously became involved in one of their father's computer experiments. Here with the cocoa we encounter a return to childish things as far as they are willing to do so.

The transgression with the computer in the lab led to knowledge, and to wisdom, for the boys, and is never referred to in terms of sin rather than innocent (somewhat careless) error, and so the lab is not the Garden of Eden, the cocoa is not the forbidden fruit. Rather, when the family enters the kitchen from the lab, "there was the familiar odor of fresh bread, apples baking in the oven, and warmth, and rightness, and all the reassurance of home" (352). This is a far cry from the "goat, urine, sweat," the animal skins and even the pungent, highly sexualized aroma of the easy Tiglah. We might nevertheless read the combination of bread and apples both baking in the oven as a final nod toward metaphorically taking a bite of fruit that is knowledge, and fruit that is death, too, and the new life (bun in the oven) that often arises from that.

Among those many, many waters in the novel are the punishing raindrops from menacing clouds at the end, the coming flood which cannot drown love, the right amount of water to nurture a garden, the steaming mugs of cocoa, and Sandy's and Dennys' semen, still stored, still in wait, for timely fruition. When the flood waters receded, Genesis says, Noah and his sons and all their wives left the ark, "Then God blessing Noah and his sons, said to them, Be Fruitful and increase in number and fill the earth" (Genesis 9.1). Sex is ultimately a good thing in this novel too, and a symbol of hope in futurity. It is not condemned, but something for which to wait and prepare. Its promise in the Murry boys' lives is reassuring, warm. That is how families like theirs come to be.

Evidently every action does have a consequence, and we can choose to think about it or not. L'Engle makes a connection between the Earth in the weeks before the flood and the mutually *assured* destruction of an arms race that seemed to many to *ensure* destruction. A terrifying depiction of childbirth undergone by Yalith's sister Mahlah, who gives birth to a half-Nephil infant, is a near-death experience for the girl: "The baby was so large that Yalith could hear Mahlah's flesh rip as the child came out" (234). Combined with complaints about the "population explosion" in the modern world, the passage reads like a contraceptive cautionary tale. Love cannot be drowned by many waters, but sex (and the "sick wave of jealousy" that laps at different characters throughout the book) *might* lead to death. Despair will surely do so.

On a cruder level, the American association between a license to drive a car and dating might suggest that semen will be spent on the back seat. In our current political climate, too, the violence enacted around the global demand for oil to fuel the motorized heart of the American dream must color our reading of drivers' licenses to come. Nevertheless, with that association L'Engle yokes freedom and responsibility in her possible allowance for sex at the age of sixteen.[6] Sex becomes something earned, a privilege rather than a right, and power is twinned with taking care of others and oneself. The novel, then, is about resisting certain kinds of adventures that "normal," "ordinary" adolescent males are supposed to want. The twins—the ones in their family who "*do* things"—must think long and hard about thinking and doing, thinking *before* doing, and sometimes do nothing at all.

Conclusion

The story of the flood is a troubling one. It is a massacre, caused with intent, by a not merely seeming wrathful God but a peevish one, who "regretted" he had made men whose hearts had turned wicked (Genesis 6.6). It is also a story we like to retell, a favorite in children's literature, children's songs: consider the animals two by two, the rainbow, and the dove. The author of *Many Waters* muddies them all. Despite the frequent refrain—seen elsewhere in L'Engle's work—that sometimes we are not meant to *do* anything, but merely to await God's will, when things are looking bleak and Dennys complains "I don't like this story.... I don't like it at all" we know that the author is in sympathy with her character. Later, when Sandy predicts, "Noah's surely going to have to shovel out a lot of manure" (319), the text does not merely refer to the ark, but to the legacy of this story, the patriarchal oppression it nurtures, the narratives of exclusion and purging it engenders. This manure takes us back to the "old manure, rotting" that first brought the unfortunate Dennys to consciousness early in his sojourn, along with "a smell that made the urinals in the lavatories at school seem sweet. And over it all, but not covering it, a cloying smell of perfume and sweat, body sweat which had never seen a shower" (57). The vulture, rat, and other animal forms taken on by the Nephilim "eat flesh" and boast that this is how they "help keep the world clean" (133). No one can engage in life's pleasures without paying a price. L'Engle reminds us of this with rot and stench and sour bodily fluids, with the biblical flood and nuclear war. As hopeful as the twins' return to boyhood is at the end of *Many Waters*, this is a story about life and death, and everybody will soon see a shower.

NOTES

1. Genesis 6.4: "The Nephilim were on the earth in those days, and also afterward, when the sons of God came in to the daughters of man and they bore children to them. These were mighty men who were of old, the men of renown."

2. As such, they also stand for a resistance against the kind of "masculine mystique" that Yoshida Junko identifies as having influenced Ursula K. Le Guin in her early books. This myth, "based on a narrow image of white middle class heterosexual males," privileges descriptions of the dark side of masculinity, with "features of being power-hungry, always 'in harness' (suppressing human feelings), disturbing the balance of nature (exploiting nature), and excluding the feminine from his gender construct (using and exploiting femininity)" (187–88).

3. Obviously the bond between siblings is powerful, which is why it is so devastating when sundered completely. Prior to the events of the novel Sandy and Dennys had never gone to sleep in separate places; in the opening pages Sandy remarks of an upcoming trip to the dentist (in their own world) "*we've* never had a cavity" (3, italics mine). They are united, profoundly kindred. Yet they are also differentiated one from the other with such pieces of information as: "Dennys was the thinker, Sandy was the doer" (165). Whereas they have evidently been distinguishing themselves from the extraordinary members of their family for most of their lives, the function of the story they live in this book is to differentiate from one another—a special part of growing up for twins: "Sandy said, 'I've been thinking.' After all, not only Dennys could think" (166). It is important, and newly challenging, that they are separated in new ways here while remaining united in purpose.

4. When a more familial disaster is occurring in *A Swiftly Tilting Planet* (1978),

the now older brothers "suggest that the destruction of the planet could set off a chain reaction with unforeseeable consequences to the galaxy" (16): "Obviously, the beleaguered planet in L'Engle's title is swiftly tilting out of control (ethically, politically, and spiritually) is our own" (Pepetone 16).

   5. I have written elsewhere about L'Engle's *Wrinkle in Time* and Suzanne Collins's *Gregor the Overlander* (forthcoming in *Jeunesse: Young People, Texts, Cultures*). With Sandy's refusal to be like medieval knights, I see a precursor to Gregor's final rejection of that model, and of the sword, at the end of Collins's series.

   When Dennys is cruelly treated by people at the oasis and thrown out on a garbage pit, the stench overwhelms him so that he tears off his clothing and scrapes his already burnt skin raw with sand: "sobbing like a child.... He sat there, naked as Adam, on the white desert, his back to the oasis" (62).

   6. In *An Acceptable Time* (1989) the now grown twins' seventeen-year-old niece, Polly, is courted by the unworthy Zachary, whose lack of caution and excess speed while driving indicate other forms of selfishness and dangerous behavior.

WORKS CITED

Collins, Suzanne. *Gregor the Overlander.* New York: Scholastic, 2003. Print.
Curtis, Claire P. *Postapocalyptic Fiction and the Social Contract: "We'll Not Go Home Again."* Lanham, MD: Lexington, 2010. Print.
Hettinga, Donald R. *Presenting Madeleine L'Engle.* New York: Twayne, 1993. Print.
Junko, Yoshida. "The 'Masculine Mystique' Revisioned in *The Earthsea Quartet.*" *The Presence of the Past in Children's Literature.* Ed. Ann Lawson Lucas. Westport, CT: Praeger, 2003. 187–93. Print.
L'Engle, Madeleine. *An Acceptable Time.* New York: Farrar, Straus and Giroux, 1989. Print.
_____. *Many Waters.* New York: Farrar, Straus and Giroux, 1986. Print.
_____. *A Swiftly Tilting Planet.* New York: Farrar, Straus and Giroux, 1978. Print.
_____. *A Wind in the Door.* New York: Farrar, Straus and Giroux, 1973. Print.
_____. *A Wrinkle in Time.* New York: Farrar, Straus and Giroux, 1962. Print.
Paterson, Katherine. "Taking the Bible Seriously." *The Swiftly Tilting Worlds of Madeleine L'Engle.* Ed. Luci Shaw. Wheaton, IL: Harold Shaw, 1998. 85–102. Print.
Pepetone, Gregory G. *Hogwarts and All: Gothic Perspectives on Children's Literature.* New York: Peter Lang, 2012. Print.
Reynolds, Kimberley. *Radical Children's Literature: Future Visions and Aesthetic Transformations in Juvenile Fiction.* New York: Palgrave Macmillan, 2007. Print.

Narration of the Poet as a Young Woman
Intertextuality, Genre and World-Building in L'Engle's Austin Family Novels

CAROL S. FRANKO

Artists populate Madeleine L'Engle's fiction. Musicians, painters, writers, and actors appear as protagonists, mentors, and the occasional villain. With *Meet the Austins*, her sixth novel and first juvenile fiction, L'Engle expands the field to include, along with artists, also doctors, homemakers, research scientists, and clergy. This prominence given to meaningful work that pulls characters to its pursuit exemplifies L'Engle's theme of serving one's vocation in *Meet the Austins* (1960) and the four subsequent Austin novels: *The Moon by Night* (1963); *The Young Unicorns* (1968); *A Ring of Endless Light* (1980); and *Troubling a Star* (1994). Except for *The Young Unicorns*,[1] each is narrated by Vicky, the second of the four Austin children (John, Vicky, Suzy, and Rob). Focusing on three of the Austin novels, this article explores L'Engle's use of intertextuality and genre to portray Vicky Austin's development from active receiver of family and literary traditions in *Meet the Austins*, to apprentice poet and powerful but vulnerable "poe[t] mind" (*Ring* 179) in *A Ring of Endless Light*, and finally to committed, practising poet in *Troubling a Star*. The novels depict a fictional world that features the artist's role in two related projects: a fruitful coexistence of modern science with "ancient" religious belief, and loving family communities that foster intensely individual vocations. Vicky's mother is a special case within this second project. A former professional singer, Mrs. Austin is portrayed as choosing to leave the performing arts to become a homemaker (*Meet the Austins* 98–99). Mrs. Austin's choice, as she consistently terms it (*Ring* 90–91; *Troubling* 38) allows the formation of the Austin family world since Mrs. Austin brings music and literature, as well as nurturing to the family.

L'Engle portrays Vicky's developing sexuality, engaging the traditional role of women as nurturers, and L'Engle's own preoccupation with the artist's responsibility to transform pain into affirmation. Vicky matures largely through her relationships with people and with texts, rather than by separation and autonomy. Feminist critics identify this relational model of subjectivity as characteristic of female *bildungsromans* and artist-novels (Abel, Hirsch, and Langland 9–11). Another characteristic of women's artist novels is the conflict between a necessary selfishness of the artist and the selfless ideal traditionally accorded to women (Huf 5–6). Vicky navigates this conflict in *A Ring of Endless Light* and *Troubling a Star* in such a way that her identity and work as a poet is affirmed and she is not forced "to choose between her sexuality and her profession" (Huf 5). L'Engle's treatment of gender roles has been explored by Katherine Schneebaum in "Finding a Happy Medium: The Design for Womanhood in *A Wrinkle in Time*" and Tanya Avakian in "The Wildness of Christianity: the Legacy of Madeleine L'Engle." Schneebaum finds limiting the feminine roles foisted on Meg in *A Wrinkle in Time*, despite how the novel's "portrayal of women was truly progressive for its era" in the early 1960s (30). Avakian critically observes L'Engle's historically situated commitment to "all-aroundness" as she terms it, finding it both a strength and weakness in L'Engle's oeuvre (8). She argues that societal expectations of both women and gifted people during the 1940s and 1950s—women to be nurturing homemakers and gifted people to "sublimate their individuality to the demands of society"—shape L'Engle's determination to be an all-around writer, housewife, and theologian. They likewise shape her fictional depictions of families and her nonfictional theological writings (8). Avakian's commentary on Vicky's trials in *A Ring of Endless Light* differs from my interpretation of them, as I will explain in that section. Schneebaum and Avakian offer important contexts for studying L'Engle, which I will return to after an analysis of what Vicky is offered by, or more accurately, of how Vicky's character is constructed through, L'Engle's manipulation of genre and intertextuality.

The "world" that Vicky narrates and which nurtures her is given depth and meaning through L'Engle's manipulation of intertextuality—especially allusions, references, and quotations from a variety of texts—and through her experiments with three genres that she blends with the developmental novel: the family story (in *Meet the Austins*); a realism harboring mythopoeic science fiction (in *A Ring of Endless Light*); and the suspense thriller (in *Troubling a Star*). The Austins' world is built as much on Vicky's and her siblings' responses to texts and traditions, emphasizing the arts, sciences, and theology, as it is on settings like Seven Bay Island, a fictional island off the New England coast and home to Vicky's maternal grandfather, the retired Reverend Eaton. In *Meet the Austins*, L'Engle uses intertextual references to insert herself into writing for children and teens. In this first volume, twelve-year-old Vicky is primarily an appreciative chronicler of her siblings' and also of her Grandfather's engagement with taking new meanings from known texts. In *A Ring of Endless Light*, fifteen-year-old Vicky responds to the terminal illness of her beloved Grandfather Eaton, the forefather figure of the Austin family culture, through rewriting poems from his library. A year later, sixteen year old Vicky (in *Troubling a Star*) explores her place in a new extended "family" and a new set of texts that she assembles or writes herself. She brings these texts with her on a trip to Antarctica during which she composes more poetry. Vicky's own poems begin to be quoted, helping to shape the fictional worlds evoked in *A Ring of Endless Light* and *Troubling a Star*.[2]

Regarding L'Engle's use of genre, in *A Ring of Endless Light*, the science fiction component unsettles an otherwise realist narrative, complementing Vicky's world being broken by her grandfather's illness. The blend of realist and fantastical elements allows Vicky to fail fortunately to meet all of the demands placed on her and to defer strategically some of the potential experiences offered to her. In *Troubling a Star* L'Engle's combination of thriller and developmental novel allows Vicky to explore new locales, as well her own limitations and potential, as she investigates, misreads, endures, and creates.

Lacking telepathic communication or international intrigue, the genre of *Meet the Austins* is easier to overlook, but the craft of L'Engle's first novel for children becomes visible when it is viewed as a "family story," as defined by Brian Attebery. Attebery identifies five characteristics in this genre of children's literature: "domestic comedy"; "a bundle of parallel bildungsromans"; the "family as a whole" as protagonist; "an ethnography of a specific and distinctive tribal culture"; and a hybridity that "combines a fantastic structure with a realistic surface" (Attebery 125). "Fantastic structure" here refers to plots reminiscent of traditional forms like the "magical folktale"—story structures openly patterned, leading through tests to a happy ending (Attebery 129–30). The Austin folk culture and domestic comedy plays out in the children learning responsibility even while they creatively own the cultural and literary texts in their environment. Although not formal *bildungsromans*, each of the children has a developmental arc, while four adults temporarily subvert their normal roles. Who is the protagonist in this array—Vicky or the family? The answer is both. On the one hand, Vicky's preoccupation with her responses and potential (a preoccupation affirmed as reasonable by her mentor, Uncle Douglas), as well as her vivid depiction of her bike accident, tips her into a protagonist position. On the other hand, the patterned and "fantastic" plot shows the Austins as collective protagonist, being tested and graced by Maggy joining their family for an unspecified period because of the deaths of two pilots, her father and "Uncle" Hal, a dear friend of the Austins. Maggy is an assertive, alienated ten-year-old who has spent little time with her now dead parents or with her wealthy invalid grandfather. Disruption escalates; mistakes yield spectacular and edifying consequences. The final chapter, "A Visit to the Stable," features an adventure that riles Vicky on account of her own and Maggy's failure to monitor Rob, the youngest child's, movements on the seashore. But the deeper fantastic structure of Rob's disappearance and return is a hopeful bookend to the deaths of chapter one. The Austin family protagonist expresses their gratitude for this fortunate reunion as grandfather says grace before supper (214).

Few critics treat the Austin novels, and the only sustained analysis of them as a group is Donald Hettinga's "The Assurance of Things Hoped For," in his *Presenting Madeleine L'Engle* (1993), published a year before *Troubling a Star*, the fifth and final volume in the Austin chronicles. In his analysis of the first four novels Hettinga praises L'Engle for treating subjects like death that publishers of children's literature were then reluctant to accept. He argues that the novels offer age appropriate depictions of such subjects, even while L'Engle admirably persists in presenting "unanswerable questions" (Hettinga 49). He shows how *Meet the Austins* tackles selfishness, as Vicky learns to stop blaming her own mistakes on Maggy. He stresses how the beauty of nature and the faith of Vicky's grandfather aid Vicky's developing faith in a God that cares for creation despite death and suffering. Although Hettinga does not focus on intertextuality per se, he explains how, in *The Moon by Night*, Vicky's viewing of a play based on *The Diary of Anne Frank* moves her to an interrogation of Psalm 121 (59–62). Hettinga is also insightful on how L'Engle manages Vicky's romantic relationships in *The Moon by Night* and *A Ring of Endless Light*, so that her growth is not determined by her shifting from her family's worldview to the views of a boyfriend, but instead by her testing all views (Hettinga 56, 70).

That Hettinga did not have access to *Troubling a Star* when he valuably assessed the Austin novels shapes our different approaches. My focus on L'Engle's intertextual world building and Vicky's vocation leads me to consider L'Engle's theme of artistic and scientific vocations and the related theme of the potential compatibility of religious and scientific orientations. In the Austin novels, the arts and sciences stand in part for a fulfillment of a person's deepest self, and this position is in dialogue with the novels' rejection of selfishness and their interest in making room for God through a self-emptying. "Science" also reminds us repeatedly in the Austin chronicles that in Nature all creatures live at the expense of other creatures. Hettinga does not consider these issues, nor does he treat Vicky's vocation for writing.

L'Engle did not write a single development-of-the-artist novel for Vicky; instead, in novels whose publications span thirty-four years she came close to completing such a *künstlerroman*.[3] Novels that portray an artist's growth typically suggest ties to their authors' lives, and studying the Austin novels necessitates acknowledging biographical contexts although this study is not exploring those connections.[4] The home appearing in similar guises in her books about the Austins, the Murrys, and the O'Keefes is based on the old farmhouse in Connecticut that L'Engle and her husband Hugh Franklin bought and lived in during the 1950s with their three children. They named the home Crosswicks; Franklin, an actor taking a hiatus from the stage, ran the village store; L'Engle wrote at night after the children were in bed, sometimes falling asleep at the typewriter but other times very irritable if she didn't keep writing (Hettinga 8). In their 2008 introduction that now prefaces each Austin novel, L'Engle's granddaughters Charlotte Jones Voiklis and Léna Roy share that "people would joke that *Meet the Austins* could have been called *Meet the Franklins*" (2), but they grew up learning that such a "simple translation" did not exist (2), even though they were intrigued by how "family lore" (1) contained events and locations similar to but different from those in the first three Austin novels. *Listening for Madeleine* (2012), Leonard Marcus' collection of interviews with family, friends, and colleagues of L'Engle, is an invaluable resource and very thought-provoking on the relations between fact and fiction. Although L'Engle spoke of her connection to her characters (Hettinga 14–15), I avoid treating Vicky as an author-surrogate. My exploration of these novels treats instead their fictionality—their craft and the values they promote. I focus first on L'Engle's creating a fictional world for her growing poet and maturing girl out of materials both ancient and modern, and secondly on how the fifteen- and sixteen-year-old Vicky balances, or doesn't, several facets of her experience: her understanding of her responsibilities; her struggle to develop an affirmative faith and to support the people she loves; her entry into sexual and romantic desire; and her increasing activity and self-identification as a poet and more generally, as a writer. Finally, I will consider Schneebaum's and Avakian's concerns about gender roles in relation to what intertextuality and genre have provided for Vicky's character and will offer suggestions for how the Austin novels connect to L'Engle's broader authorial identity as a mythopoeic fantasist.

The Space Suit and the Stable: L'Engle's Modern and Ancient Placement of the Austins

In *Meet the Austins* (1960), L'Engle first builds a world in a children's book in which intertextuality serves several purposes. Before Mrs. Who of *A Wrinkle in Time* (1962) manifests L'Engle's own "quotitis"[5] and thereby helps substantiate and focus the science-fantasy realm of *Wrinkle*, Vicky Austin narrates how she and her family listen to and debate stories and sing poems as well as read poetry painted on walls. In part, L'Engle uses allusions and references in *Meet the Austins* to develop her career as a children's writer. I suggest two examples, one explicit and the other implied. First, while Vicky often alludes to Kipling's *The Jungle Book*, as well as mentioning numerous other books, the contemporary E.B. White's *Charlotte's Web* (1952), and the Austin children's response to it, are prominent. L'Engle pays homage to this beloved work and asserts her own fictional realm, one where characters are also, as in *Charlotte's Web*, dealing with death. Subtler is L'Engle's probable allusion to Robert Heinlein's 1958 *Have Space Suit Will Travel*, the popular and critically acclaimed final volume in Heinlein's science fiction series for teens. Heinlein's story hinges on the protagonist winning a functional space suit in an advertising contest. Vicky's older brother John is fine-tuning his own space suit when *Meet the Austins* begins. L'Engle was apparently reading science fiction in the 1950s[6]; moreover, *Meet the Austins* emphasizes a synthesis of scientific with artistic and religious orientations. John's spacesuit implies that L'Engle is inserting her voice into thoughtful, modern, and adventurous fiction for children.

A second way that intertextuality functions is by complementing L'Engle's first indications of Vicky's vocation. Vicky is in one sense already a writer, since she narrates "a specific and distinctive tribal culture" (Attebery 125), introducing readers to her family's culture from her role as participant in it. But the child Vicky does not identify herself as a writer. Instead, she confides her need to find her own pursuit within her characterization of her family as people who celebrate, apparently equally, commitment to loving, family community with individual dedication to demanding vocations. Chapter One details how the telephone call announcing Uncle Hal's death disrupts the "happy and noisy and comfortable" hour before supper (6). In the first two pages, Vicky refers to four vocations: her father's (doctor who is out delivering a baby), her Uncle Douglas's (artist; a painter we learn later), her older brother John's (scientific researcher, out in the barn with his spacesuit) and her younger sister Suzy's (doctor of people or animals, using a carrot scraper both on carrots and, as a scalpel, on dolls). "Aunt" Elena, Hal's wife and Mrs. Austin's lifelong friend, is a concert pianist (9), while Hal himself was a test-pilot, "one of the first … to go through the sound barrier" (10). This focus on vocations extends to Uncle Douglas outlining for Vicky the scientific and artistic temperaments. When she asks him why she remains tongue-tied while her brother John is able to express his sympathy to Aunt Elena, Douglas says that those like John with scientific temperaments can feel strongly but more objectively about the sorrows of others, while those, like Vicky, with artistic temperaments, must learn to deal with their tendency to be empathic: "you get right inside her suffering, and it becomes your suffering, too" (30). When Vicky protests that she has no artistic talent, Douglas promises her that the talent, and the ability to manage empathy, will come (30).

The first chapter thus raises and defers Vicky's vocation, before detailing the Austins being tested by the deaths of Uncle Hal and Maggy's father and by Maggy's coming to live with them. Maggy bites one of Dr. Austin's patients and accidentally disables the music box in Rob's favorite toy; Suzy and Maggy trespass on Dr. Austin's home office, notably his sterilized tools; Suzy steals candy and then lies about it; Vicky floods the upstairs when trying to bleed the radiators and then rides her bike at night, crashes and is hospitalized for a broken arm and wounded jaw. Even the fifteen-year-old John loses his temper and quarrels rather viciously with Vicky.

But beyond their learning from mistakes, the novel's manipulation of intertextuality showcases another way the children grow: by contributing to their family's customs and lore. Three examples show the novel making a theme of intertextual work, by which I mean characters responding to texts and creating their own theories and stories. In the first two the children are involved in retelling a story about where people go after they die and in debating whether *Charlotte's Web* is usefully considered as a text to inspire vegetarianism. John, he of the scientific temperament, is an instigator for both. In a final instance of characters using texts to debate issues, Grandfather counters John in a move that unites Christian mystical poetry and scientific pursuits.

The children's participation in intertextuality stems from their environment. The Austin children are positioned to enjoy the benefits of country and city, with ready access to mountains from which to view the Milky Way and parents who bring their professions into the home: Dr. Austin's home doctor's office and Mrs. Austin, a former singer, often playing her guitar or the piano and singing. In chapter four, the family uses her old costumes to trick a snobbish visitor. While the family's situation is idealized, the novel also shows how hard both parents work and how the children each have duties to help keep the farmhouse warm and livable. The Austin world is also both old and new. In addition to growing up with reading aloud, regular chores, and family prayer times—the "God bless" rituals—the children are immersed in modern scientific pursuits, including Suzy's and John's developing vocations for medicine and astrophysics.

Their positioning in an environment that synthesizes nature and civilization peaks in the final chapter, "The Visit to the Stable," a title that evokes Christmas (although it's a summer visit) and hence the nondenominational Christianity of the Austins. The stable belongs to Grandfather Eaton, Mrs. Austin's father and a retired minister. Grandfather lives on Seven Bay Island (L'Engle's invention) a three-hour boat ride from the mainland (181). Grandfather's stable is on a hill on the ocean side of the island; a steep path winds down to a cove. Grandfather thus lives far out and into nature. At the same time, Grandfather is a "bibliomaniac"; Vicky invites readers to consider that word and shares that she too is one, so that her family has called her "bookworm" so often that they have shortened it to "worm" (167). Grandfather's renovated stable is packed with books on every conceivable subject. The stable walls are also lettered: in the one actual bedroom the wall is painted with "one of Grandfather's favorite things [...] by Hildevert of Lavardin, who wrote it sometime around 1125": "God is over all things, under all things; outside all; within, but not enclosed; without, but not excluded; above, but not raised up; below, but not depressed; wholly above, presiding; wholly without, embracing; wholly within, filling" (183).[7] Hildevert's twelfth-century hymn acts as "ancient" textual verification of recent transcendent moments in nature. At the end of chapter one Vicky and John go to Hawk Mountain with their mother to view the stars and ask questions about death and change. In that episode Vicky feels the love joining her to her mother and to John as she prays silently for her family (35). In chapter four, the family witnesses the crystalline aftermath of an ice storm; here Vicky's joy sweeps away her worries about whether Maggy's distant relatives will take her from the Austins (132–33). Hildevert's affirmation of God's presence in nature implies a basis for Vicky to negotiate her and her family's encounters with death and change. Vicky quotes two other texts that "live" in Grandfather's stable: the poem "Indwelling," by Thomas E. Brown, painted on the walls of the loft where the children sleep, and autobiographical writings of Albert Einstein that Grandfather quotes at supper.[8] Before considering that scene, we'll consider the children's intertextual work.

Rob, who is about five years old, is the first to incorporate Uncle Hal's death into a family ritual. At bedtime Mrs. Austin reads aloud to the children followed by prayers including each person's God Bless. Rob's are distinctive for how he puts in whatever is on his mind and tonight Vicky is fervently hoping he will speak of Uncle Hal (15). After stopping and starting again when he reaches Hal's name, Rob proceeds: "and especially Uncle Hal, God, and make his plane have taken him to another planet to live so he's all right because you can do that, God, John says you can, and we all want him to be all right, because we love him" (15). This story reappears in chapter two, after Dr. Austin's patient, a condescending teacher from school, is screaming because Maggy has bitten her. As Maggy tells Dr. Austin, "She said my father's plane couldn't have gone to another star. I was telling the kids about it at recess, and she was listening and said it couldn't be true and I hate her" (58–59). As Maggy cries, Dr. Austin hugs her, each saying "I love you" (59). John tells his father: "You know what I told you last year—how I'd figured out that after we died we maybe went to different stars to kind of go on learning? [... Maggy] wanted to know, if her father's plane had exploded in the middle of the sky, what had happened to him and where he had gone, and I said maybe he'd gone on to another star. And I guess she thought the plane had gone on to another star" (59). John's theory becomes Rob's prayer for Uncle Hal and

Maggy's belief about her father. In the final chapter when Rob asks Grandfather what is beyond the end of space and Grandfather says even Einstein couldn't answer that, Maggy interjects that her father knows because "he's living on another star now and he knows everything. John explained it all to me" (190). Grandfather replies "John knows that God has taken care of your father." (190). Vicky reports these instances with no editorial comments on the scientific or religious propriety of imagining that people go to other stars after death to keep on learning, thus leaving the impression that she is in between believing the story and considering the story as one creative way that people might cope with what her mother spoke of on Hawk Mountain as "things we would never understand" (37), such as "why Uncle Hal and Maggy's father had to die" (36).

Charlotte's Web, which Mrs. Austin has been reading aloud to the children, frames the "The Terrible Week" (chapter three's title, 61) when Suzy, Vicky and John misbehave in ways Vicky is troubled by, but she cannot explain. The debate over eating pork provides comic relief but raises its own disturbing issues. Nine-year-old Suzy has two passionate responses to White's novel: grief at Charlotte the spider's death and anger at the threat to Wilbur the pig's life (62–63). Suzy decides that she won't eat pork anymore, and John seeks out Vicky to discuss how he understands Suzy's outrage, but can't agree to dietary changes as a solution. He also values the family activity of eating (63). The clash between Suzy and John recurs at the family dinner table, and John shocks everyone by claiming that cutting up and eating apples is as much an attack against life as eating meat and sums up the situation: "it's just a place where we have to disapprove of nature and that's that" (70). When asked by Suzy and Dr. Austin to explain this point, John tells how he has been learning in science class about how "every species lives by preying on another" (70). While his father chides him for getting Suzy upset, John's work with texts and ideas is not discouraged. Likewise, Suzy maintains her own response to *Charlotte's Web* as Vicky reports at the end of the chapter: "And Suzy still doesn't like to eat pig" (93).

During the final chapter Rob goes missing and is fortunately found; likewise, the threat that Maggy will be taken from the Austins is averted. These happy endings coincide with the family's visit to Grandfather Eaton, their beloved patriarch. "He's always thinking about what will make other people happy," notes Vicky (187). Grandfather, the "bibliomaniac" (167), is passionate about the intersections of faith and science. Vicky notes that the poem that Grandfather painted on the wall of the loft probably has a "good influence" on her and her siblings (187):

> If thou could'st empty all thyself of self,
> Like to a shell dishabited,
> Then might He find thee on the ocean shelf,

> And say, "This is not dead,"
> And fill thee with Himself instead.
> But thou art all replete with very thou
> And hast such shrewd activity,
> That when He comes He says, "This is enow
> Unto itself—'twere better let it be,
> It is so small and full, there is no room for Me'" [186–187].

Thomas E. Brown's poem becomes a touchstone for Vicky, generating consideration of the right and wrong ways to be one's self. Here Brown's poem provides subtle, "ancient" commentary on the children's earlier, extravagant misbehavior; it also underscores Grandfather's celebration of the intersection of science and religion. When Maggy states that her father now knows everything, Suzy shares that she would "'like to know everything in the world,'" and Grandfather notes that the "'search for knowledge and truth can be the most exciting thing there is as long as it takes you toward God'" (190–91). When John replies that "Einstein didn't believe in God" (191), Grandfather finds a book in his stalls and reads to them Einstein's description of "the scientist's religious feeling" that "takes the form of a rapturous amazement at the harmony of natural law" and "reveals an intelligence of such superiority" that all human endeavor and thinking is revealed as "utterly insignificant" (191).[9] Akin to Browne's poem, Einstein explains that the scientist's religious feeling "is the guiding principle of his life and work, in so far as he succeeds in keeping himself from the shackles of selfish desire" (191). John cheerfully concedes his mistake about Einstein; while back home Vicky reports that he is in the barn with his spacesuit. Vicky has not yet found her own vocation, but the domestic comedy and tribal lore of L'Engle's family story nurtures her own bibliomania and affirms that despite death and the "shackles of selfish desire," life is rich with natural and cultural resources and overseen by a loving deity.

To the Ocean, to the Ice: Vicky the Poet Seeks Her Place

Shifting to *A Ring of Endless Light* and *Troubling a Star*, the fifteen and sixteen-year-old Vicky is now a poet and full-fledged protagonist narrating developmental novels that blend with science fiction (*Ring*) and the thriller (*Troubling*). Vicky's way of writing changes the feel of the narration, lending a sense that the novels are overlapping with the writing that Vicky reports doing in her journal.[10] *A Ring of Endless Light* chronicles the summer following the Austins' nine-month sojourn in New York City. The family is now caring for Grandfather Eaton on Seven Bay Island as he dies of leukemia and several other tragedies punctuate the narrative, including a late scene in a hospital when a very sick little girl dies while Vicky is holding her. Also key to the plot are the internships of John (Vicky's older brother) and his friend Adam Eddington at a marine research center on the island.[11] Vicky works with Adam on his project involving dolphins. *Troubling a Star* begins the following autumn at the Austin family home, but soon sees Vicky traveling to Antarctica where she and Adam separately become endangered by criminals exploiting the continent's resources. L'Engle's blended genres render Vicky's adolescence both adventurous and protected, allowing her to balance strong claims: her writing vocation; sexual desire and love; and her desire to nurture others. Intertextuality also develops these themes. In *A Ring of Endless Light* Vicky's relationship to Brown's poem painted on Grandfather's wall shifts fundamentally as she succeeds as a poet and partially fails as a nurturer. In the foreground is Vicky's poem, a rondel, in which she weaves lines from poems by the seventeenth century Welsh poet Henry Vaughan, while in the background L'Engle apparently alludes to turning points and extraordinary communication in Charlotte Brontë's *Jane Eyre*. Intertextual references work differently in *Troubling a Star*. Vicky's imagination no longer rests within Grandfather's library and she begins to assemble and to write her own touchstone texts, a process that coincides with making new friends and mentoring relationships; investigating a murder from the past; and living through what she believes to be the loss of love.[12]

Any analysis of *Ring* must acknowledge Vicky finding a way through multiple tragedies including her own deeply felt despair at a death, to her grandfather's naming of her as a "light-bearer" (325),[13] and on to a final joyful vision of creation connected by love, within nonlinear time—the ring of "pure and endless light" that Vicky experiences in the ocean at the novel's end through her empathic connections with dolphins and her friend Adam (331). I argue that the novel's final affirmation crowns three achievements in Vicky's development as a poet and young woman. First, as Vicky communes with Grandfather this final summer, she exchanges feelings and ideas, shows him her poems, and thus furthers their ability to offer comfort and wisdom to each other, even while she also achieves a new independence within the holistic faith that he has long offered his family. Emblematic of this deeper relationship and Vicky's more independent perspective on the Austin "world" is the rondel that she composes in chapter two after a long talk with Grandfather in which he quotes from Henry Vaughan's poems "The World" and "The Night." For the rest of the novel, Vicky brings into her narration the two lines that initiate and then form refrains in her rondel: "A great ring of pure & endless light / Dazzles the darkness in my heart" (72). Her woven references to "dazzling darkness" and less frequently to "endless light" bring lyrical order to the increasing suffering, including Grandfather's two hospitalizations caused by internal bleeding and Vicky's sudden, tragic encounter with Binnie, the little girl who dies in the hospital waiting room.

Vicky's second and third developmental steps sound negative baldly stated—she avoids having sex and she fails to be a super nurturer. Young men are paying attention to Vicky this summer, and her relationship with the rich, cynical and charming Zachary Gray (first met in *A Moon by Night*) includes a mutual attraction that could easily lead to sex, but Vicky declines. She is put off when she finds herself imagining Adam when she's kissing Zachary (193) and also, as she tells Zachary, she's not ready (194). She doesn't have sex with Adam either; instead, the literally oceanic experiences with Adam and the dolphins act partly as an extraordinary alternative to sexual experience. As Smedman points out, L'Engle depicts Adam as Vicky's "soul-mate" (Smedman 186); likewise, Adam affirms and is attracted to Vicky's being a poet. In addition to their conversations, Vicky and Adam's best times include joy and physical pleasure as they swim and play with Basil, Norberta and the other dolphins. When Vicky's telepathic communion first with the dolphins and eventually also with Adam are added in, the results are peak experiences made possible by science fiction, since no definitive experiments have established how dolphins communicate or if humans can be included therein.

Vicky fortunately fails to be a super-nurturer—this is shorthand for a confluence of motifs and allusions in *Ring* involving selfhood, vocation, and relationships. Vicky experiences her limitations as a consoler; Vicky makes a poet's contribution to Adam's dolphin research; she reflects on the choices made by her multi-talented mother and by Mrs. Rodney, a recent widow and professional nurse (90; 134). At the same time, she reevaluates Brown's poem that for many years has taught her that if she could "empty all [herself] of self" she could make room for God to fill her (24).

Awaking late the first night on the island, Jane Eyre–like by the light of a full moon, Vicky reads Brown's poem on the wall, commenting that it makes her "think of Grandfather, empty of all the horrid things, and filled with gentleness and strength." Vicky laments: "I felt replete with very me, full of confusions and questions for which there were no answers" (25).[14] Vicky's parents have asked her to give up a paid job so that she can help take care of grandfather, and Vicky is glad to do this, although she also finds times to work on her writing and with Adam and the dolphins. Vicky knows she can't protect her mother or her grandfather from his failing health but she longs to "hold them both against the dark" (18). She is also tempted to believe that Zachary with his multiple problems "needs" her, as Zachary himself insists (16; 60–63). She and Grandfather disagree over the extent that she should take responsibility for Zachary, with Grandfather urging: "There's a kind of vanity in thinking you can nurse the world. There's a kind of vanity in goodness" (67).[15] Grandfather adds a reference to John Donne's insight "*Other men's crosses are not my crosses*" (66). Sadly, Grandfather thus gives Vicky a perspective for later when, his alertness deteriorating, he tells Vicky that he's afraid he won't know when to let go of life, and that she will have to be the one to decide (279). Vicky realizes she can't accept this responsibility and that Grandfather's earlier advice and Donne's words are pertinent (281). Still, as people around her suffer, Vicky keeps trying to comfort them until she and the novel crash in the penultimate chapter when Binnie dies in Vicky's arms. As Binnie's mother screams, Vicky reports that she too screamed but with "no sound" (315). Her narration in the final chapter alternates between her usual mode and a spare, free-form prose poetry that describes first her despair and then her reclamation.

The Austins have brought Grandfather home from the hospital to die. Her family cannot penetrate Vicky's despair; she can't explain to them how death is stifling any consoling paradoxes in the play of dark and light; Suzy and John scold her for wallowing; even Grandfather cannot reach her. He apologizes for and withdraws his request that she tell him when it is time to die (324). He refers to Brown's poem, urging Vicky "Empty yourself, [...] You're all replete with very thee," but the words don't resonate (325). Vicky remembers him earlier proclaiming faith in the Resurrection while performing a funeral service, but she cannot respond now to his naming her a light-bearer (325). Vicky's inability to respond either to Grandfather quoting Brown's poem or to his light-bearer announcement is critical to how the novel develops her character, a point where I differ from Tanya Avakian's reading. Avakian suggests that Grandfather's insistence that Vicky be a light-bearer is a "scold[ing]" example of "what [Flannery] O'Connor called 'a nasty dose of orthodoxy'" (8), apparently a strong corrective medicine to balance how Vicky and all L'Engle heroines, Avakian claims, are treated and advised specially because of their giftedness (8). Avakian's larger argument is that all of L'Engle's fiction for younger audiences enacts the all-roundness that L'Engle was devoted to through an emphasis on gifted characters who are disciplined through pain. While I have characterized the Austin books as heavily populated with characters drawn to vocations in the arts and sciences, Avakian, grouping the mythopoeic science fiction novels that begin with *A Wrinkle in Time* with the "more realistic" Austin books, characterizes them as all populated by gifted people who become famous, "often intermarry," and "nearly always lear[n] that a harsh destiny lies in wait" (8). She has a point; the whole issue of gifted and famous people in L'Engle's fiction turns up frequently in readers' responses, understandably, but I have avoided the term gifted because I think the values of the Austin novels present more a shared passion for learning and doing, with a commitment to vocation, than they do a highlighting of individually gifted people. In relation to this understanding of the novels, Avakian's observation of conflicting values in the decades when L'Engle was becoming a writer is relevant: "gifted [people] of the 1940s and 1950s were expected to sublimate their individuality to the demands of society at large" (8). But Avakian is right that Vicky's desire to find her "talent" is nurtured. Clearly interested in words and texts of all kinds in *Meet the Austins*, Vicky is eager to find her pursuit with the same confidence that Suzy knows she wants to do some kind of medicine. Vicky wants individual fulfillment and status within her family; in addition, she is given special mentoring by Uncle Douglas in the first two novels and by Grandfather in *A Ring of Endless Light*. To return to Vicky's apathy when Grandfather names her a light-bearer, Avakian apparently thinks this is a moment when Vicky is chastened by strong Christian medicine. But that characterization does not fit what happens as the medicine doesn't work.

Only Adam bringing her to the ocean to commune with the dolphins brings Vicky out of her withdrawal. This reclamation holds a couple of layers of L'Engle's portrayal of Vicky's development as a poet and young woman. First, Adam "hears" Vicky's interior scream when Binnie dies, and comes to the hospital, convinced that Vicky has called him (319, 320, 322). The novel's final scene affirms his inner hearing when Vicky tells him, "I called you" (332). Vicky and Adam's telepathy is akin to the climax in Charlotte Brontë's *Jane Eyre*: Jane, about to give in to St. John Rivers' urging her to accept a loveless marriage with him so that they can be partners in missionary work, hears her name being called soundlessly by Edward Rochester, whom she loves but has been separated from (ch. 35; 357). She later learns that Edward had called out to her on the same night, with its full moon, when Jane was about to give in to St. John Rivers' temptation to a kind of suicide (ch. 37; 381). Like Jane, Vicky experiences a crisis relating to the temptations of selflessness for women. Vicky's is a terribly literal lesson in the impossibility of nursing the world; despite her care of Binnie, the child dies. But the apparent allusion to *Jane Eyre* is not a simple parallel. While Brontë's insertion of telepathy prevents Jane from an excess of selflessness and rewards her and Edward with a loving union, Adam and Vicky's telepathy underscores Vicky's identity as a poet, as well as her deep connection to Adam. Adam "hears" Vicky's scream because she has earlier communicated nonverbally with Basil and other dolphins and then with Adam himself.

Apparently through the intuitive openness of her "poet's mind" (179) as Adam terms it, Vicky earlier has aided Adam in his research, confirming his hunch that dolphins communicate not just through sounds but by "non-verbal communication" as they attempt to classify it (179). This scientific breakthrough also leads to Vicky reimagining selfhood and to a confirmation, through Vicky and Adam sharing the dolphin's mindset, of a joyful, nonlinear perspective on time. Working with Adam leads Vicky to realize that experiences of intense selfhood are not identical to the deadening selfishness described in Brown's poem. She and Adam talk about her fear of death as a fear of annihilation, prompting Adam to ask her, "When are you most completely you?" (167). As Vicky and Adam speculate about what aspect of the self might survive death, Adam's questions push Vicky to consider how her encounters with the dolphin Basil as well as when she is deeply at work on a poem are times when she is most herself but not "replete" with self (167). This positive completeness of self comes, for example, when she names Basil's skin "resilient pewter" (107). "Resilient pewter" is Vicky's most original poem in *Ring* and becomes a motif in her narration: in the conclusion it joins phrases from her rondel in a description of the dolphins: "resilient pewter bodies spraying off dazzles of light, pure and endless light" (331). The science fictional subplot that features Adam Eddington's secret project with dolphins thus validates Vicky's identity as a poet while it also furthers L'Engle's theme in the Austin novels of how arts and sciences cooperate to reveal, or to help construct, a thoughtful faith.

In his study of detective fiction, Marty Roth remarks that "the thriller begins out in the cold, with misanthropy and alienation as its nominal topics" (70). Drawing on genre conventions of the isolation and misanthropy of the sleuth, legacies of unsolved crime impinging on the present, and international settings entwined in conspiracy, L'Engle adapts the thriller in *Troubling a Star* for a further developmental story of Vicky as poet and young woman. L'Engle blends genres to produce an adventure for this bereft, in-between time that requires "patience," as her new mentor Serena Eddington tells Vicky (74). Serena is Adam's gracious and wealthy great-aunt; ninety years old, her active intelligence and wisdom complement Adam, who tells Vicky that Aunt Serena reminds him of Vicky's grandfather (11). Vicky and Serena become friends and Vicky's first fully quoted poem is one that she writes for her (54). Also early in the novel is an important conversation between Vicky and Serena that wanders through different angles on penguins: on the serious side Serena argues that because of the constant threat of predators, the penguins' communal life does not equate with intimacy, which would be too risky, and they discuss comparisons with human communities in different historical periods. On the comic side, Vicky learns from Serena that penguins have feathers, very closely packed. "If it has feathers, it is a bird" (74). This talks overlaps with Serena urging Vicky to have patience with herself in this period where she is seeking her "place" and waiting to go to college (74).

L'Engle manipulates intertextuality to accommodate the thriller plot and Vicky's growth as a poet after her grandfather's death. The novel's frequent references to Shakespeare's writings and Vicky's own poems structure and unify this strategy. Although he is mentioned several times in *Troubling*, Grandfather's book-filled stable, home of his and the Austins' ancient and modern Christianity, is here not the culminating setting as in *Meet the*

Austins, or the daily resource for Vicky's rewriting of this heritage as in *Ring*. In its absence, Vicky explores the books, journals and letters in Serena's attic, an activity that connects her to current and old favorites—to Shakespeare's sonnets and to books her mother used to read aloud like *The Jungle Book* and *Charlotte's Web* (41)—while also leading her to find clues to the death of Serena's son (and Adam's uncle), Adam Eddington II, a marine biologist and advocate for Antarctica, who disappeared a couple or more decades ago during his second expedition there. With a gothic strangeness and a thriller use of coincidence, Adam III, Vicky's friend, looks remarkably like Adam II, as Vicky sees in a portrait and photographs of Serena's son. As Vicky makes her own journey to the icy continent, her backpack holds her journal and her copy of *Hamlet* in which she files the letters and postcards containing puzzles and clues, the latter often Shakespearean hints from Adam III, who is taking a Shakespeare course while Vicky's English class is doing a Shakespeare unit. On the journey Vicky makes new friends, notably Siri Evenson, a biochemist and musician who introduces her to Francis Thompson's poem "The Mistress of Vision" (which includes a line about troubling a star) and a mysterious conservationist who dresses like a bird and references works she knows, like Mozart's *The Magic Flute* and St. John's *Revelation*. Antarctica—its ice-scape and wildlife, especially penguins—yield information that Vicky adds to her growing "library." This array of "texts" continues the tradition of the Austin fictional world where vocations for science or art mingle with a faith that continually seeks knowledge and aesthetic expressions of meaningful patterns. Yet another example of intertextuality in *Troubling a Star* is L'Engle's invented South American country, Vespugia. Fictionally located "in the middle of a sizeable area along what are now the boundaries of Chile and Argentina" (L'Engle, *Walking* 173), Vespugia first appears in L'Engle's mythopoeic science fiction *A Swiftly Tilting Planet* (1978). Vespugia has now reverted to a police state. An officer in its army as well as two drug traffickers, one from Vespugia and the other from Texas, engage in nefarious activities that pull in four young adults: Esteban Manuel, a Vespugian oboist and soldier; Otto Zlatovitcx, prince of a nation recently free of the Soviet Union and in need of resources; Adam Eddington III, Vicky's boyfriend, who has received a grant to study penguins in Antarctica; and Vicky herself, whom Serena sends to Antarctica as an extraordinary sixteenth birthday present in this, Vicky's "winter of discontent" (29).

Troubling a Star is set after the events in *Ring* from late summer through winter. Each chapter begins with brief, italicized flash-forwards of Vicky stranded on an iceberg in the Antarctic Ocean in the deadly cold of Antarctic summer (January). After these openings that place Vicky literally "out in the cold" of the thriller scenario (Roth 70), the chapters proceed chronologically, beginning right before school starts: "I was still fifteen then, feeling lost and alien, though I had yet to learn what being truly alien feels like" (8). Back in her hometown of Thornhill and starting her junior year in high school, Vicky feels displaced and lonely. Adam is returning to Berkeley; Vicky's brother John, himself returning to MIT, is urging Vicky that Adam is too old for her, and that she doesn't want to "get pregnant and married and drop out" of school like some girls are doing (57). Vicky's sister Suzy is offering to get Vicky dates to school dances and calling Vicky a snob for not wanting the dates and for quoting Shakespeare (29, 37). Although Vicky is enjoying her English class and working diligently on her poems and journals, she is disappointed that their school does not offer French or Latin, which she studied the previous year in New York City. Vicky decides not to take Spanish because she doesn't want to be in the same class with Suzy (28). Later Vicky is unable to communicate with Esteban because of their language barrier (131; 230), although her knowing introductory Spanish would not have rescued him from his destructive involvement in Vespugian conspiracies.

Vicky is excited to go, but it might seem she goes to Antarctica for other people rather than for herself. She looks forward to seeing Adam at LeNoir Station (68). Aunt Serena admits that she wants to go to Antarctica again but since she can't, sending Vicky is "the next best thing" (64). Vicky does go because of her relationships, but also because she is a poet. Her family sees it as a balancing kind of learning experience: as Suzy puts it, Vicky is "a politically illiterate literary snob" (29) or as her mother puts it, "Even the dreamiest poets have to know something about the world they're writing about" (48). In the tropes of the thriller, Vicky goes to a remote place because she is alienated; rather like Roth's description of the young male characters from works by Stevenson and Conan Doyle, Vicky's "unwilling witness of an adventure" in a remote locale leads to her increased "social participation" (Roth 70). But while Stevenson's and Conan Doyle's characters perform heroic actions and fall in love (Roth 70), Vicky detects but does not heroically defeat criminal action; moreover, she is already in love but she endures what she thinks is the loss of Adam's love during her adventure.

L'Engle plots *Troubling a Star* to suggest that Vicky goes to Antarctica because she is a poet whose involvement with texts leads her to be a detective even before Serena presents her with the gift of the trip on Thanksgiving, a couple of weeks after Vicky's sixteenth birthday. Vicky is drawn to the familiar and the unfamiliar reading material in Serena's attic. She acknowledges a large book on economics, which apparently belonged to Serena's husband, Adam Eddington I, who disliked his work but made the money that funded past and present trips to Antarctica (34, 41, 84). Serena shares the one remaining journal of her son, Adam II, whose writing strongly attracts Vicky: "He may have been a marine biologist, but he was also a poet" (45). She admires his description of wind and notes that the poems she has recently sent off to a contest include a poem about wind blowing round their hilltop house at Thornhill. The day after Vicky and her mother discuss South American politics, leading Mrs. Austin to remark that poets need to learn something of the world, Vicky finds a clue, a never mailed letter from Adam II to Adam Cook—currently Serena's cook, a former monk, best friend of Adam II, and an important new friend of Vicky's. Vicky is certain that there was foul play in Adam II's death; later it is confirmed that he must have been murdered and the political reasons are understood although the specifics of his death are never discovered (127–128).

Vicky and Adam III become peripherally but dangerously entangled in a conspiracy involving drug trafficking and post-cold-war competition for Antarctic resources and for technology available from former Soviet satellites. While the conspiracy stems from greed and political ambitions, it is fueled also by miscommunication. Adam III's letters to Vicky and to Aunt Serena are opened by the Vespugian military and misread to mean that the current Adam is continuing his uncle's cooperation with the CIA to thwart Vespugia's illegal drilling in Antarctica. Vicky and Esteban, the Vespugian musician and soldier, have friendly mutual feelings but a huge language barrier. Shared knowledge of Shakespeare allows Adam to send Vicky coded warnings, but Vicky misreads as real a letter Adam writes to her as a warning, in which he says they need to "cool it" on their relationship. Vicky's pleasant flirtation with Prince Otto is shadowed by her realizing he is somehow involved with the conspiracy. While the miscommunications further the suspense they ultimately lend the thriller plot a sad aura of revealing the petty and sometimes deadly limitations of all "Adams"—male and female.

Although Vicky continues to detect, and gets some pieces right, her poetic work on the journey takes a ninety degree turn away from thriller conspiracy into serious and comic poems that address human vulnerability, the inhuman beauties of nature, and hints of spiritual transcendence. As Vicky completes her unofficial writing internship in Antarctica, this final volume of the Austin family series presents her as a poet both working alone, throwing out bad starts, revising more promising pieces, and working socially, bringing her poetry to an audience, through cooperation with Siri, whose hobby is playing and composing songs for her Celtic lap harp. "Getting braver" (248) about her poems, Vicky shares some of them with Siri, and finds a new venue for them, as lyrics for songs. The sung poem in this novel becomes a way for art to interact with nature (when Siri plays and sings to seemingly intrigued penguins on an ice floe) and, even more so, a way for humans to bond together inside their ship, temporarily protected from nature. The novel concludes with a scene of reunion for the people who have survived the unraveling of the conspiracy. Vicky has shared two new poems with Siri—one a moving, short lament for Esteban, who has been killed, and the other

her most recent revision of a comic poem that spins off her continual musings on Serena's early proclamation about penguins: "If it has feathers, it is a bird" (74). This final revision is lighthearted and rhythmic and affirms storytelling, accepting the absence of answers, and welcoming the unexpected (315–316).

Notably, the final pages of *Troubling a Star* effectively enact a theme that seems over told in *Ring* and *Troubling*: the theme that Vicky will be a light-bearer (*Ring* 325), that as a poet her job will be to bring news of hope and comfort while acknowledging the darkness and risk in life. Vicky's poems that Siri sings for the group are more accomplished but also recognizably kin to the other poetry Vicky has been working on; they are lyrical and vivid, convincingly a lament and then a whimsical comic song. Thus, the public performance of her work *shows* her being the light-bearing poet and doing so on her own terms. As people ask for Siri to play again the feathers song, Vicky takes a moment to remark on the performance and ends the novel: "I was glad we'd had the lament first, because I knew that something light was needed now. Benjy and Siri sat together. Then Adam put his arm around me and I leaned back and listened" (316).

Vicky is still only sixteen years old in this final volume of the Austin novels. What seems certain about her future is that she will continue to work at poetry. Romantic love is also affirmed but in a qualified way. Siri is divorced; her new union with Benjy is a second chance at love. Vicky and Adam are reunited but for them still remains the puzzle of how to continue their relationship while fulfilling their individual commitments to their educations. Returning to Vicky's story after the 1980 *A Ring of Endless Light*, here in the 1994 *Troubling a Star* L'Engle appears to want to keep imaginative options open for teen and other audiences.

The final episode in *Troubling a Star* is also a striking blend of the new and the homelike for Vicky Austin. Traveling all these thousands of miles, Vicky has become part of a new extended family of friends and they end an evening in the way the Austin family often does, with singing. So what has intertextuality and genre "done" for Vicky and how do these novels relate to Schneebaum's concerns that *A Wrinkle in Time* participates in a problematic supermom ideal and to Avakian's assessment that L'Engle's fiction is energized but limited by L'Engle's fashioning of her career to be an "all-around" writer, house-wife, and theologian? As I address these points, I will bring in one additional thread: how the intertextual and genre strategies of these Austin novels both resemble and differ from L'Engle's fantasy novels.

Avakian's identification of L'Engle's all-aroundness is astute: these three Austin novels do indeed appear to be shaped by L'Engle's self-fashioning as writer, housewife, theologian, and also as "perpetual student" of the arts, sciences and theology (Avakian 8). However, as argued above, Vicky is not disciplined by orthodoxy in the episode when her grandfather names her a light-bearer. L'Engle's crafting of quotation, reference, allusion and genre in *Meet the Austins*, *A Ring of Endless Light* and *Troubling a Star* characterizes Vicky as nurtured by a textual tradition that is also her "world" since she grows up both hearing texts read aloud and sung and reading them in books and on walls. This immersion in texts is an excellent environment for a girl with a vocation for poetry; her family is also crowded with people who are eager and dedicated to pursuing the work they love and who likewise are committed to mutual responsibility and love. Vicky's talented nurturing mother is characterized as choosing her version of homemaking, one that is akin to a mother with a vocation for homeschooling. This multifaceted ideal, this idealized "all-aroundness," to borrow Avakian's term, extends to how the textual components of the Austin world are portrayed as connecting the arts with "modern" science and "ancient" faith. Within this world Vicky becomes an apprentice poet who rewrites certain mystical Christian poems (her rondel in *Ring*) and revises how other such poems shape her identity—specifically the poem on the wall, Brown's "Indwelling." To Brown's two alternatives: the repleteness of self that leaves no room for God and the emptied self that God notes is "not dead" and has room for His entrance, Vicky adds a third category, that of being most truly oneself through meaningful work (poetry in her case) or engagement with creation (like the interesting texture of dolphins' skin). Vicky's third category of selfhood builds on the Austin family's valuing how vocations in the arts and sciences can contribute to faith. L'Engle's mythopoeic portrayal of Adam's dolphin research, for which Vicky's empathic poetic mind aids discovery of dolphins' nonverbal communication, paired with Vicky's failure to be a super-nurse, yields affirmation of Vicky as apprentice poet whose reclamation from despair connects to her poet's identity, rather than to her being "spiked" back into discipline through a strong dose of Grandfather's faith (Avakian 8). This elaborate narrative strategy is furthered by the allusions to *Jane Eyre*, which again underscore that Vicky is a poet developing her own version of all-aroundness as well as a faithful apprentice in the Austins' multi-faceted ideal. *Troubling a Star* uses the thriller genre to place Vicky "out in the cold" (Roth 70) in an exciting environment where she becomes a working poet with an audience. The final scene in *Troubling* harks back to the family community in the earlier novels, while the lyrics that Vicky sings, and then listens to, are her own.

With Schneebaum's concern about women characters in *Wrinkle* portraying either the supermoms of the 1960s or perpetuating the idea that girls truly mature only when they enact maternal love (36), she might be pleased with how *Troubling a Star* ends, with an emphasis on Vicky's satisfying work, even while she also would probably be interested in the way the Austin novels keep circling back to the issue of Mrs. Austin's former career as professional singer and currently chosen role as homemaker. Schneebaum draws attention to how the admirable Dr. Murry, Meg Murry's mom and renowned biologist, was glamorously overworked (33). Concerning *Meet the Austins*, Mrs. Austin's choice to excel at all the work she does in her home is a necessary piece in the working of the Austin world with its dual ideal of ambition and community. Vocation becomes a more flexible ideal in the later *Ring of Endless Light* and *Troubling a Star*, which show an interest in the choices that women characters make over the course of their lives—Mrs. Rodney and Mrs. Austin in *Ring*; Siri in *Troubling*.

Finally, Hettinga found the Austin novels distinctive for their then groundbreaking realistic treatment of hard issues like death in literature for children and teens (48–49), but if we focus on these novels as developments of Vicky as a poet, common ground and significant contrasts emerge between L'Engle's strategies with genre and intertextuality in them and in the body of work she is best known for: mythopoeic fantasy and science fiction. In "The Time Quartet as Madeleine L'Engle's Theology," Marek Oziewicz defines mythopoeic fantasy as "a genre in which the existence of the supernatural is assumed with all seriousness and whose stories provide an imaginative experience of a world in which metaphysical concepts are objective realities" (212), adding that among Christian mythopoeic fantasists L'Engle's work is unique in her "endeavor to recover a more profound vision of Christian spirituality in the context of modern scientific thought" (215). In the Time quintet, L'Engle asserts the objective reality of metaphysical concepts through human characters interacting with stars who may also be angels and traversing cosmologies in outer space or in mitochondria. A quick way to contrast the Austin novels with *Wrinkle* is to say that they have libraries instead of fantastic beings—Grandfather Eaton's library on a cliff over the bay rather than tesseracts enabling galactic travel. The Austins' library-world asserts a "vision of Christian spirituality in the context of modern scientific thought" (Oziewicz 215): its mythopoeic realism, as we might term it, is further defined by L'Engle's use of genres that are partially fantastic—the family story—and by her blending of realism with genres that inhabit the rationalized neighborhoods of the fantastic—science fiction and thriller. Her female poet narrates and grows in an environment that partakes of the worldview of mythopoeic fiction, of Christian belief that is informed by artistic and scientific ambition as well as faith and that imbues her with a value for her vocation while maintaining her relationship to her "home world." Vicky is not forced to choose between art and faith or between her vocation and her sexuality, while the fantastic elements in these novels, especially in *Ring*, make this wholeness possible. But I must correct the generalization that the Austin novels have libraries instead of angels and aliens, since all of L'Engle's fiction is shaped by intertextual "libraries." More specifically, the poetry in the intertextual libraries of the Austin novels and the Time novels manifests differently its contribution "to an imaginative experience of a world in which metaphysical concepts are objective realities" (Oziewicz 212). In *A Swiftly Tilting Planet,* the third novel in the Time books, poetry has supernatural power: beginning in chapter one, the reciting of St. Patrick's "Rune" can become an incantation that effects physical and metaphysical realities. In contrast, the poetry in the Austin novels points to realities and gives Vicky a tradition to inhabit and extend, and poems are recited, sung, painted on walls, and composed rather than adopted as supernatural powers. Granted, when in *A Ring of Endless Light,* Vicky is at her most Romantic, individualist point of affirming her identity as a poet, the ability of her poet's mind to connect metaphysical realities is posited, as she communes with dolphins and experiences their vision of non-linear time. But Vicky hasn't written very much poetry at this point, and her cosmic experiences with the dolphins are shared only with Adam. *Troubling a Star* complements *Ring* in being more mundane—much more toward the "realistic" side of L'Engle's mythopoeic realism in the Austin novels. Balancing the absence of cosmic connection in the ocean, in *Troubling a Star* Vicky's enduring of ice brings her to that ending where her poems are sung and she listens.

Notes

1. *The Young Unicorns* (1968) is a dark suspense thriller set in New York City that alone in the Austin books shifts from first to third person, casting Vicky as one of four young co-protagonists.

2. Stemming from the literary theory of Mikhail Bakhtin and of Julia Kristeva (who coined the term), intertextuality "refers to the presence of a text A in a text B" (Moraru 261). Its scope and meanings have been elaborated by many more theorists whose diverse agendas include emphasizing how textual interdependency can mark either the poststructuralist death of the author (as in Roland Barthes' approach), or conversely, the occasion for an author to enlarge literary history by misreading and rewriting former authors (as in Harold Bloom's criticism) (Wilkie 130–31; Moraru 258–59). Christine Wilkie argues that children's literature is "charged with the awesome responsibility to initiate young readers into the dominant literary codes of the culture" with the consequence that "literature for children has to tread a careful path between a need to be sufficiently overreferential in its intertextual gap filling so as not to lose its readers, and the need to leave enough intertextual space and to be sufficiently stylistically challenging to allow readers free intertextual interplay" (135). As Anne Lundin, library scientist and professor of a children's literature course, explains it: "Stories draw on each other, often unconsciously, as the literature of a culture is interwoven in themes, motifs, and people and natural landscapes. Texts draw upon texts, which themselves are based on yet different texts. The meaning is produced from text to text; new worlds are made out of old texts" (210). My study emphasizes such basic strategies of intertextuality as an author's use of allusion, reference, and quotation to and of a variety of texts, cultural practices, and literary and popular genres. I have not attempted the level of technical language that, for example, Maria Nikolajeva employs in her analysis of intertextuality in Katherine Paterson's *Bridge to Terabithia* (pp. 42–45 in Maria Nikolajeva, *Aesthetic Approaches to Children's Literature: An Introduction* [Lanham, MD: Scarecrow, 2005]).

3. L'Engle published the first three Austin novels in the 1960s. *A Ring of Endless Light* appeared in 1980, twelve years after *The Young Unicorns*, and finally, *Troubling a Star* was published in 1994, fourteen years after *Ring*, after the death of L'Engle's husband Hugh Franklin in 1989, and after L'Engle's 1992 trip to Antarctica with Bion and Laurie Franklin, her son and daughter-in-law.

4. L'Engle's creation of the Austin family has not been enjoyed by her children the way it continues to be enjoyed by her readers. See Cynthia Zarin's essay and Leonard Marcus' book. Zarin's essay states that *Meet the Austins* has been in print continuously since its publication.

5. L'Engle's granddaughter Léna Roy has said: "I always identified with Vicky because she was a writer, and I liked it that Gran said that she was Vicky too. I'm sure she made use of some of my experiences. And I'm sure that being close to both Charlotte and me helped her to write young adult literature ... she read everything.... She would read scientific journals. She had memorized passages from Schopenhauer and Plato and Shakespeare and Chekhov and could quote from these and many other writers. She had 'quotitis,' as she liked to say. My sister, my mother, my grandmother, and I all read the same books together. We had our own little book club" (Marcus 189–190).

6. The collection of magazines that Mrs. Austin brings on the family camping trip in *A Moon by Night* includes "science fiction magazines" (75).

7. This appears to be a modern English paraphrase of a section from Hildebert's "An Address to the Three Persons of the Most Holy Trinity," and grandfather could be thought of as translating it from the Latin when he inscribed it on the wall. See Hildebert, Archbishop of Tours, 1056?–1133. *Hymn of Hildebert and Other Medieval Hymns*. Translations by Erastus C. Benedict. New York: Anson and F. Randolph, 1867.

8. James Eason explains that the poem "Indwelling," first published anonymously and then perhaps misattributed in later printings, is by Thomas E. Brown, or T.E. Brown (1830–1897), not Sir Thomas Browne (1605–1682).

9. The quote appears to be from Albert Einstein, *The World as I See It* (*Mein Weltbild*). Translated by Alan Harris. Philosophical Library, 1949.

10. For example in the opening chapter of *Ring*, Vicky comments that it will be difficult to find privacy this summer "to write in my journal, to write and rewrite, and rewrite again, poems and stories. To try to find out not only who I am but who everybody else is, and what it's all about" (13). L'Engle often commented on how much she enjoyed the *Emily of New Moon* novels by L.M. Montgomery (Hettinga 2). Emily has a vocation for writing and in the second and third volumes Montgomery switches between third person narration and long sections of Emily's journals—a strikingly different style from Vicky's first person narration that begins to include her poems and references to her journal. *Troubling a Star* includes the texts of some letters and postcards from Adam, a journal entry of Vicky's and several of her poems.

11. Adam Eddington appears in an earlier novel by L'Engle, *The Arm of the Starfish* (1965).

12. Vicky has become a poet offstage. In *A Moon by Night*, the second Austin novel, Vicky narrates her family's cross country camping trip, has her first serious boyfriend, and tests her family's faith against her boyfriend's nihilism. The fourteen-year-old Vicky is self-conscious about her moody adolescence and is frustrated that John and Suzy have talents that point toward vocations. Uncle Douglas assures her that she "is an artist of some kind" (*Moon* 182). Then in the third-person narrated *The Young Unicorns*, when the Austins spend a school year in New York City, Vicky is a secondary character and is shown writing poetry both as part of schoolwork and for herself.

13. Smedman and Hettinga each give valuable accounts of this movement.

14. Vicky mistakenly states that Brown wrote his poem "three centuries ago"; this is due to the confusion of T.E. Brown, 19th century, with Sir Thomas Browne, 17th century. See note 7.

15. The novel is dedicated to Sandra Jordan, the editor L'Engle was working with on *Ring*. See Zarin and also Jordan's section in Marcus for Jordan's comments on how she and L'Engle had a key discussion where Jordan criticized Vicky as being too perfect, a discussion which in Jordan's memory led to L'Engle including "the scene with Grandfather, when he tells Vicky that other men's burdens are not your burdens. Madeleine had turned it around and spun straw into gold."

WORKS CITED

Abel, Elizabeth, Marianne Hirsh, and Elizabeth Langland, eds. "Introduction." *The Voyage In: Fictions of Female Development*. Hanover, NH: University Press of New England for Dartmouth College, 1983. 3–22. Print.

Attebery, Brian. "Elizabeth Enright and the Family Story as Genre." *Children's Literature* 37 (2009): 114–136. Print.

Avakian, Tanya. "The Wildness of Christianity: The Legacy of Madeleine L'Engle." *Commonweal* 26 (Oct. 2007): 8–11. Print.

Brontë, Charlotte. *Jane Eyre*. Norton Critical Ed. 3rd ed. Ed. Richard J. Dunn. New York: Norton, 2001. Print.

Eason, James. "A Different Brown: A Poem not by Sir Thomas." Web. 13 Jan 2016.

Huf, Linda. *A Portrait of the Artist as a Young Woman: The Writer as Heroine in American Literature*. New York: Frederick Ungar, 1983. Print.

"Künstlerroman." *Twentieth-Century Literary Criticism*. Ed. Linda Pavlovski. Vol. 150. Detroit: Gale, 2004. *Artemis Literary Sources*. Web.

L'Engle, Madeleine. *Meet the Austins*. New York: Farrar, Straus and Giroux, 1960. Print.

___. *The Moon by Night*. New York: Farrar, Straus and Giroux, 1963. Print.

___. *A Ring of Endless Light*. New York: Farrar, Straus and Giroux, 1980. Print.

___. *Troubling a Star*. New York: Farrar, Straus and Giroux, 1994. Print.

___. *Walking on Water: Reflections on Faith and Art*. New York: North Point Press of Farrar, Straus and Giroux, 1995. Print.

___. *The Young Unicorns*. New York: Farrar, Straus and Giroux, 1968. Print.

Lundin, Anne. "Intertextuality in Children's Literature." *Journal of Education for Library and Information Science* 39.3 (Summer 1998): 210–213. Print.

Marcus, Leonard S. *Listening for Madeleine: A Portrait of Madeleine L'Engle in Many Voices*. New York: Farrar, Straus and Giroux, 2012. Print.

Moraru, Christian. "Intertextuality." *Routledge Encyclopedia of Narrative Theory*. Ed. David Herman. New York: Routledge, 2005. 256–261. Print.

Oziewicz, Marek. "The Time Quartet as Madeleine L'Engle's Theology." *Journal of the Fantastic in the Arts* 17.3 (2006): 211–220. Print.

Roth, Marty. *Foul & Fair Play: Reading Genre in Classic Detective Fiction*. Athens: University of Georgia Press, 1995. Print.

Schneebaum, Katherine. "Finding a Happy Medium: The Design for Womanhood in *A Wrinkle in Time*." *The Lion and the Unicorn: A Critical Journal of Children's Literature* 14.2 (1990): 30–6. Print.

Smedman, M. Sarah. "Out of the Depths to Joy: Spirit/Soul in Juvenile Novels." *Triumphs of the Spirit in Children's Literature*. Eds. Rancelia Butler and Richard Rotert. Hamden, CO: Library Professional Publications, 1986. 181–197. Print.

Wilkie, Christine. "Relating Texts: Intertextuality." *Understanding Children's Literature: Key Essays from the International Companion Encyclopedia of Children's Literature.* Ed. Peter Hunt. London: Routledge, 1999. 130–137. Print.

Zarin, Cynthia. "The Storyteller: Fact, Fiction, and the Books of Madeleine L'Engle." *New Yorker* 80.8. 12 April 2004. 60–67. Web.

What Madeleine Inherited from Her "Grandfather George"
The Influence of George MacDonald on Madeleine L'Engle in Her Children's Fantasy Books

Sophie Dillinger

Madeleine L'Engle once said: "heroes are essential for our own development, because they are models for us, giving us hope that we, too, can do amazing things, beyond ordinary capacity. I still need heroic people to look up to in order to live my own life creatively" ("The Heroic" 121). Interestingly, George MacDonald (1824–1905) was one of her "heroes" (Rosenberg 79). During the Victorian Age, the Scot had to resign as minister of Trinity Congregational Church in Arundel on account of his "distasteful" "universalist beliefs" (H. Ellison). However, as "a Born Preacher," he could not "abandon his calling," so he decided to preach through the characters in the stories he had started to write (H. Ellison). Thanks to his fiction, he became, as L'Engle later admitted, "probably the most important influence in deepening my mythic understanding [of the universe]" ("Nourishment" 113). However, to come to a better understanding of the universe, L'Engle also relied on science.

Her interest in this field and her Christian faith are visible in all her work from the 1960s onward, especially in the well-known Time Quintet: *A Wrinkle in Time* (1962), *A Wind in the Door* (1973), *A Swiftly Tilting Planet* (1978), *Many Waters* (1986) and *An Acceptable Time* (1989). In those five books, her characters travel back and forth through time and space. While doing so, they take part in the struggle between good and evil, a struggle that was already at the heart of MacDonald's work: especially in his two fantasy novels for adults—*Phantastes* (1858) and *Lilith* (1895)—three of his fairy tales[1] and the *Princess* books that L'Engle loved (*Circle* 158). Indeed, *The Princess and The Goblin* (1872) tells how Curdie, a young miner, saves the Kingdom and Princess Irene from the wicked schemes of the Goblins. In the sequel, *The Princess and Curdie* (1883), Curdie thwarts an awful plot against the King. In both books, he succeeds with the help of Irene's mysterious great-great-grandmother who personifies the powers of good.

This acknowledged literary influence[2] invites us to study, through the books mentioned, what L'Engle inherited from the one she called "Grandfather George" (*Circle* 158), while developing her own particular way of writing. First, the way both MacDonald and L'Engle invite their readers to follow their characters in and out of another world will be discussed. Then, the link between story, history and legend will be examined. This progression will, finally, help us to realize that, in most areas, the two authors convey much the same message.

Madeleine L'Engle seems to have adopted a similar narrative method to George MacDonald's. Their readers follow the characters in and out of their imaginary worlds. The physical journey they undertake reflects an inner journey, a spiritual one. In *Phantastes*, Anodos finds the way into Fairy Land in his bedroom at the beginning of the book. His journey lasts twenty-one days but he learns so much through it that, when he is back home at the end of the book, he feels that it has lasted twenty-one years (204). The relationship between what happens within and without is even more obvious in chapter eight of L'Engle's *A Wind in the Door*, entitled "Journey into the Interior," when Meg, Calvin, Progo and Mr. Jenkins travel inside Charles Wallace, "in one of his mitochondria" (170), in order to save his life. To do so, they have to fight against the evil Echthroi and restore harmony within Charles Wallace's body.

Thus, through this kind of pilgrimage, the characters are in fact taking part in the battle against Evil. Indeed, *echthros* means "enemy" in Greek and the Echthroi are said to be "fallen angels" (*Wind* 111), "evil forces at work in the world" (161). These forces contribute to spreading darkness. In L'Engle's work, The Shadow stands for "the Dark Thing," "Evil" and "the Powers of Darkness" (*Wrinkle* 106). The Earth is "shadowed" (109); on account of wars, starvation, misunderstanding and hate, among other ills (110–111). This imagery is entirely biblical: "*And the light shineth in darkness; and the darkness comprehended it not*" (John 1.5, quoted by Mrs. Who and recognized as a biblical quotation by Charles Wallace in *Wrinkle* 108). It was also used by MacDonald: in *Lilith*, The Great Shadow epitomizes Evil here too and in *Phantastes*, Anodos's evil side is embodied in the shadow that follows him everywhere after his fall.

In both corpora, symbolically, light always defeats darkness. However, evil people are not destroyed: they are called upon to change. Violence is excluded because it cannot be redemptive (Rosenberg 81). L'Engle agrees with the following words of MacDonald: "It may be infinitely less evil to murder a man than to refuse to forgive him. The former may be a moment of passion: the latter is the heart's choice. It is spiritual murder" (*Circle* 157). In some cases, like with L'Engle's Zachary Grey, a physical heart problem mirrors a symbolic or spiritual problem. "There is no harmony" in his heart (*Acceptable Time* 236). As a distortion of good, evil has altered the original harmony. Zachary has become proud and self-centered. For MacDonald and L'Engle, shadowed characters have to see themselves as they really are, become aware of the evil in their own hearts, in order to change. The Wise Woman, for example, helps Rosamond and Agnes to do so in MacDonald's eponymous tale. In *An Acceptable Time,* Polly is not allowed to walk near the gate between circles of time because it could be dangerous for her, and yet Zachary insists on going there and forces her to cross the time gate so as not to leave him alone (205–209). Once in this prehistoric era, three thousand years before his own time, Zachary is ready to have Polly sacrificed to pagan gods so as not to miss the chance of having his heart healed. He realizes a bit "late" (341) how selfish he has been. Despite his self-centeredness, Zachary can be forgiven and is "not beyond redemption" (353). For L'Engle, as for MacDonald: "Change is always possible" (360). "Zachary hit bottom [...] But in the pit he saw himself" (360). Zachary can therefore become good again: "From this moment on, your behavior must be such that when you go to bed at night you will be happy with what you have done during the day" (362).

Two pages later, L'Engle's characters are back in their own time. In a few lines, in *Lilith*, Mr. Vane can also go from the chamber of the dead in the other world to his own library. The characters' ability to move through time and space makes everybody wonder: is their adventure a dream or is it real? Mr. Vane wonders: "Which was the real–what I now saw, or what I had just ceased to see? Could both be real ..." (*Lilith* 35)?

"What is real?" is an anaphoric question in L'Engle's work, first asked by Blajeny, the teacher in *A Wind in the Door* (62; 74), and then echoed by his pupil, Meg (83; 141) and by the unicorn and time traveler, Gaudior (*Swiftly Tilting* 49; 247). At the beginning of the second volume of the Time Quintet, Meg has difficulties believing in her six-year-old brother's story: "In a strange way she did believe him. Not, perhaps, that he had seen actual dragons—but Charles Wallace had never before tended to mix fact and fancy" (*Wind* 9). "Fact" is a word that had already been opposed to the word "Fancy" in MacDonald's work (*Goblin* 26–28). This was common at his time, and especially stressed in Charles Dickens's novel, *Hard Times*. Its first sentence announces the "One thing needful" according to Mr. Gradgrind: "Now, what I want is,

Facts" (Dickens 7). However, the clown's fanciful daughter, Sissy, is the one who is happy and with a family at the end. So, everything appears to depend on perspective and equilibrium. L'Engle seems to find the right balance between fact and fancy, advocated by Dickens, in her characters' lives.

Indeed, L'Engle's imaginary worlds, sometimes inhabited by dreamlike creatures, are based on theories of physics, especially Einstein's theories of time and space. Meg's parents are research scientists who work on these theories and explain them. Their job is to acquire more knowledge. In *A Wind in the Door*, Mrs. Murry's research allows the reader to learn about mitochondria (which really exist) and farandolae (invented by L'Engle), for example. Meg tells Mr. Jenkins that her mother's "*business* is facts" (*Wrinkle* 31). At some point, Meg wonders whether she is victim of her imagination, of a kind of hallucination (*Wind* 51) and it is Calvin's turn to doubt: "She thought she could sense disbelief" (54).

Throughout the *Time Quintet*, characters and readers are invited to suspend their critical faculties and believe the unbelievable, hence the use, by the characters themselves, of the phrase coined by Samuel Taylor Coleridge in Chapter XIV of *Biographia Literaria* (Wordsworth and Coleridge 4): "a willing suspension of disbelief"[3] (*A Wrinkle in Time* 56; *An Acceptable Time* 81). Interestingly, this is also one of MacDonald's sources, "for his understanding of the imagination was [...] Coleridge" (Waddle 2). As "the success of the sermon relies on the willingness of the congregation to exercise their own imagination" (Waddle 5), the success of the immersion in another world relies on the willing suspension of disbelief from characters and readers. Scientific explanations are neither enough, nor compulsory to make a fictional world believable. MacDonald did not use them, at least, not so explicitly. What seems to be essential is the writer's ability to make his/her characters and readers accept and recognize the existence of a mythical universe and make them aware of the difficulty of describing what happens there.

"I beg my reader to aid me in the endeavor to make myself intelligible—if here understanding be indeed possible between us," Mr. Vane asks (MacDonald, *Lilith* 12). In a similar way, Proginoskes (a cherubim), highlights the fact that he does not look like the baby pigs painted by earthling artists to represent cherubs (L'Engle, *Wind* 61). Because he is different from the most common representation of his species, the characters (and the readers) know that they are not dreaming and believe in him: "The thing that makes me think we're awake is that if I were to dream about a cherubim, it wouldn't look like that—that—" (62). Thus, through such devices, it is easier to believe that goblins, ogres, fairies, shadows, angels and giants or seraphim, nephilim, mammoths, unicorns, manticores and griffins also exist, at least in the imaginary world of the books.

There is no age limit to entering those mythical worlds and mixing with their creatures. Everybody is invited to travel. However, it is acknowledged, in a way, that "adults take longer at this kind of thing" (L'Engle, *Wind* 186), particularly because they are "years away from games of Make Believe and Let's Pretend" (190) played by most children. At some point, as she became an adult, Meg wondered: "I told Charles Wallace I'm out of practice in kything.[4] Maybe I've been settling for the grownup world" (L'Engle, *Swiftly Tilting* 52). Although she is married and pregnant, Meg has, apparently, kept her childlike heart since she manages to kythe with her brother during his journey into the past. Encouraging their characters and readers to keep a childlike heart seems to be another common point between the two authors. L'Engle initially did not like the fact that the *Time Quintet* was marketed for children or young adults, she wrote for readers of any age. The editors who rejected *A Wrinkle in Time* thought that "children would [not] understand it." "L'Engle found this amusing. She knew that children would understand her work perfectly well, and that it was the grown-ups who did not" (Baptiste 46). "If a book is not good enough for *everyone* to read, she believed, it certainly is not good enough for children" (Baptiste 90). As for MacDonald, he wrote: "For my part, I do not write for children, but for the childlike, whether of five, or fifty, or seventy-five" ("Fantastic Imagination" 7). It is worth noting that most people identifying with Meg Murry who sent letters to L'Engle were "16 on up to 80" years old (Rosenberg 77).

No matter how old they are, some people have more difficulty than others in suspending their disbelief and letting their imagination work. The writers do not leave them out. Doctor Louise Colubra and the scientists Alex and Kate Murry think that Bishop Nason is a bit mad, that his adventures are "beyond reason" (L'Engle, *Acceptable Time* 95). Sandy and Dennys are aware of being the rational and down-to-earth twins of the Murry family: "We've never had very willing suspension of disbelief. We're the pragmatists of the family" (L'Engle, *Many Waters* 24). Then, it is not surprising that they cannot believe in Meg's story about being within Charles Wallace even if Mr. Jenkins confirms it (*Wind* 234–235). Consequently, *Many Waters* is devoted to converting them. Transported through time to the Middle East just before the flood, Dennys tells the biblical Noah: "I am not as much of a skeptic as I used to be" (*Many Waters* 105) and he even wishes that he had a Bible to understand better what is going to happen. At the end of the story, the bet is won: Sandy and Dennys are "changed" (324). A similar phenomenon occurs at the end of *Phantastes*, Anodos's sisters see that their brother has changed too: Anodos is "instructed [...] by the adventures that had befallen [him] in Fairy Land" (MacDonald 204). The previously skeptical characters are now wiser.

This kind of growth affects everybody, readers included: "story can stretch us and change us and even make us heroic," L'Engle thought ("The Heroic" 126). G.K. Chesterton said that *The Princess and the Goblin* "made a difference in [his] whole existence": it "helped [him] to see things in a certain way from the start" (Hein). As for C. S. Lewis, he considered that *Phantastes* had "baptized" his imagination (146). Thus, L'Engle goes beyond "the semblance of truth" mentioned by Coleridge. Following MacDonald, she is able to create what J.R.R. Tolkien called "Secondary Belief" in his essay "On Fairy Stories."

L'Engle's fictional world and fictional world-within-the-fictional world are more than consistent, often relying on history or well-known legendary material. MacDonald's fictional worlds are also marked by history and by his own epoch. Both writers can be considered as witnesses of their time, although they did not live at the same time, so their books do not always reflect the same things or not in the same way. First, on account of their different countries and eras, they shed light on different ills. In *A Wind in the Door* and *Lilith*, allusions to Darwin can be found (78; 6, respectively). At MacDonald's time, Darwin's theory, developed in *On the Origin of the Species* (1859), was sometimes used to cast doubt on the Bible and some people abandoned their religion because of it. Scientific discoveries and biblical criticism, however, did not affect most people (Larsen), including MacDonald, who decided to talk about his vision of God in his books, fighting in a way against potential apostasy and showing that science and Scripture were not antithetical (Jeffrey Johnson, "Sacred Story").

Social injustice, poverty and alcoholism are also raised in MacDonald's work. In *At the Back of the North Wind*, one night, Diamond (a child) takes care of the drunken cabman's baby and what he says to him resembles an indictment against alcoholism and public-houses: "Baby's daddy takes too much beer and gin, and that makes him somebody else, and not his own self at all. Baby's daddy would never hit baby's mammy if he didn't take too much beer" (MacDonald 168).[5] Diamond's words have an impact on the cabman's behavior: "And for a whole week after, he did not go near the public-house, hard as it was to avoid it, seeing a certain rich brewer had built one, like a trap to catch souls and bodies in, at almost every corner he had to pass on his way home" (171). Nanny's Grannie, old Sal, drinks too: "She's worse when she's sober than when she's half drunk" (191). She is the only relation that Nanny has, but she behaves badly toward her: Nanny knocks at the door ("in a very dirty lane"), but she does not open it, so Nanny spends the night outside, in "an empty barrel" (48–50). Nanny is poor, wears rags, has many holes in her shoes and spends her time sweeping a crossing to earn a bit of money. She becomes so ill that she is brought to the Children's Hospital (195). Once better, Nanny comes to live with Diamond's family, who becomes short of money. The threat that they "shall all have to go to the workhouse" (300) hangs over them, highlighting another social evil.

Although, in L'Engle's books, some characters do not appear to have the best living conditions, the main ill seems to be the use of violence. The fear of a nuclear conflict during the Cold War is mirrored in *A Swiftly Tilting Planet*. Charles Wallace is in charge of preventing a nuclear war from happening. To achieve his aim, he has to alter history, so as to transform the present dictator Madog Branzillo into "a man of peace" (302). Even though *Many Waters* is a rewriting of Noah's story, before the Great Flood in the Book of Genesis, one of the major threats to the world today—terrorism—appears in it as well. Tiglah's father and brother are compared to "terrorists who hijacked a plane" (222). Thus, past and present meet. In *A Swiftly Tilting Planet*, through her direct allusions to the Salem witch trials (161), to a Welsh legend and to the Civil War, L'Engle demonstrates her amazing ability to intermingle the layers of time and stories. She did a lot of research to use history ("The Heroic" 125). The use of a legend in this book and of the Bible in *Many Waters* calls attention to intertextuality.

The fact that the Welsh legend really exists makes the story even more believable. Consequently, the reader can think that *The Horn of Joy*, a novel by Matthew Maddox (a character), exists too. This idea is given additional weight by the presence of this book among a collection of real ones in *An Acceptable Time*: "an assortment of novels, from Henry Fielding's *Tom Jones* to Matthew Maddox's *The Horn of Joy*, and on up to contemporary novels" (25). Furthermore, T. Gwynn Jones's poem about brothers killing each other (*A Swiftly Tilting Planet* 269), which is also mentioned, exists.

Intertextuality is a literary device used by MacDonald too, through which he invites "the reader into a deeper conversation" (Jeffrey Johnson, "Sacred Story"). In *At the Back of the North Wind*, the narrator shares his impression about Mr. Raymond's story, entitled "Little Daylight": "I cannot myself help thinking that he was somewhat indebted for this one to the old story of The Sleeping Beauty" (238). This reference to a well-known tale and to its influence on the man's work makes Mr. Raymond more real. Later, the narrator goes to Mr. Raymond's house, "built for Queen Elizabeth as a hunting-tower" (313), where he meets the main character of the book, Diamond: "I was then a tutor in a family whose estate adjoined the little property belonging to The Mound. I had made the acquaintance of Mr. Raymond in London some time before, and was walking up the drive towards the house to call upon him one fine warm evening, when I saw Diamond for the first time" (314). Thus, thanks to all these realistic details, the reader tends to think that Diamond is a real person, whose adventures with the North Wind are real.

In *Many Waters*, the twins talk about the biblical story in which they now take part. Sandy says that "it was a very patriarchal society" and Dennys adds: "Whoever wrote the Bible was a man. Men" (190). MacDonald also lived in a rather patriarchal society (Duby and Perrot 497). Even if he is sometimes seen as being ahead of his time—"a social reformer in the field of education" (Jeffrey Johnson, "Did You Know"), for example[6]—L'Engle appears, inevitably, as more modern, especially in her treatment of sex, love and women.

In this field, a generation gap is clear. In *Many Waters*, in particular, it is obvious that "the old ways are changing": Yalith's sister, Mahlah, stays at night with a man without being married to him (L'Engle 56). Eblis, a nephil, makes Yalith aware of her sexual maturity: he tells her that she is not a child anymore and he wants to teach her about "men's ways" (50–51). Tiglah is viewed as "an easy lay" by Dennys (212) and as a "slut" by Sandy (258). When Tiglah and Sandy are kissing in the desert, the reader can wonder whether they will go further or not. Sandy answers: "He knew what she wanted, and he wanted it, too; he was ready, but not, despite her gorgeousness, with Tiglah. Tiglah was not worth losing his ability to touch a unicorn" (228). Indeed, it is said that unicorns "will not let themselves be touched by anyone who is not a virgin" (28). Even if Tiglah is tempting him with pleasure, Sandy resists temptation and stops before it is too hard and too late. Rofocale does not care if she has sex with "the naked giant" as long as she stays his. Furthermore, he likes his "women to be experienced in the ways of lust" (232). Those direct references to sex would have been censored as inappropriate in the Victorian Age, but pose no problems to fifteen-year-olds in L'Engle's day.[7]

At MacDonald's time, women *experienced in the ways of lust* would have been considered as "fallen women" (Duby and Perrot 373). The Maid of the Alder-tree in *Phantastes* could belong to this category. However, in the novel, what happens between her and the knight, then between her and Anodos is only implied, although the implication is clear. The knight in his rusty armor is ashamed (MacDonald, *Phantastes* 42–43) and Anodos does not (want to) remember: "What followed I cannot clearly remember" (48). Similarly, menstrual periods, which make pregnancy possible, are alluded to in "Little Daylight," but they could not be discussed as they are in *An Acceptable Time* (194–195).[8] Girls had to remain innocent and ignorant on that subject. Some of them did not even know where the babies came from (Duby and Perrot 357), as in *Phantastes*: "they arrive no one knows how" (86). It left room for the imagination. In his "Dream," Diamond can see the naked little boy-angels but, like them, he can't see the probably naked girl-angels (MacDonald, *At the Back* 219–223). Irene is associated with one of these (MacDonald, *Goblin* 22–23). This parallel between a girl and an angel brings to mind the feminine ideal of this era, conveyed through a series of poems by Coventry Patmore: "The Angel in the House" (1854–1863). The perfect woman was a pure and domestic wife, devoted to her husband and children. Except when she travels from one place to another or goes to the seaside with her son, Diamond's mother seems to spend her time at home, in *At the Back of the North Wind*.

Her mission is to be a wife and mother. Besides, after her sweeping job, Nanny learns how to take care of a baby thanks to her.

In L'Engle's books, Mrs. Murry is not only called to motherhood, but also to a professional and scientific mission. The bonnet, which her daughter Meg puts on, is said to be "one of her mother's rare successful ventures into domesticity" (*Wind* 85). Times have changed, so woman's vocation appears less restricted and rather the result of a choice: "Women have come a long way" (*Acceptable Time* 41). "If a woman is free to choose a career, she's also free to choose the care of a family as her primary vocation" (40), and yet, it is not simple: "there will always be problems—and glories—that are unique to women" (41).

Meg Murry has her share of *problems and glories*, especially as a teenager, at the beginning of the *Time Quintet*. It is worth noting that this character is loosely based on L'Engle's own life history. "She was quite unpopular, and sometimes she was even bullied. Madeleine felt very solitary as an only child and without any friends at school" (Baptiste 16). At boarding school in Switzerland, L'Engle was called by the number 97 instead of her name (Baptiste 20). "She believed that taking away a person's name was to take away his or her reality. That brush with conformity left a bad impression on Madeleine" (Baptiste 20). The conformity she denounces via Camazotz in *A Wrinkle in Time* is still topical "in the way everyone dresses alike and listens to the same music and in peer pressure" (Baptiste 54). Throughout MacDonald's stories, the influence of his own life can be felt too, especially that of his previous career as a churchman.

Although she sometimes quotes the Bible directly, many readers discovered that L'Engle was a Christian writer only while reading her re-telling of Noah's story, according to the reviews, or when rereading the books (this was the case for Karin Snelson in Rosenberg). Accordingly, she is "one of the Christian authors listed on the Web site www.passageway.org" (Baptiste 96), and yet, she did not want to be considered as such: "I'm not a Christian writer. I resist and reject that kind of classification. I'm a writer, period" (L'Engle, qtd. in Baptiste 89–90). In contrast, MacDonald wanted to be a Christian writer. As a Congregational minister, he had to resign on account of his beliefs, judged as unorthodox: "he was forced out on charges of heresy by church leaders fearful of his sympathy with science and with German theology" (Waddle 1). However, he was convinced that "preaching" was "in part [his] mission in this world" (qtd. in Raeper 99), that is why he decided to go on through his writings. According to L'Engle, preaching was as natural to him as breathing" ("Nourishment" 113). This also seems to be the case for one of her characters, Bishop Nason Colubra, who, even though he is retired, cannot help preaching several times (*Acceptable Time* 93; 253). The following comparison could apply to MacDonald: "Nason, if you'd been a druid, you'd probably have been excommunicated for heresy, just like Karralys" (186). The character's answer is interesting: "Yesterday's heresy becomes tomorrow's dogma" (186). MacDonald would probably have liked it to happen. It is still possible, knowing that his ideas are still read and spread through his work and the work of others he influenced.

Whether they wanted to do this in the first place or not, both writers share their theological ideas. Throughout L'Engle's *Time Quintet*, more or less direct allusions to the Bible can be found. Calvin O'Keefe reads *Genesis* to Charles Wallace (*Wrinkle* 56). Christian songs are sung like "Dona nobis pacem" in *A Swiftly Tilting Planet* (13) and the "Kyrie eleison" in *An Acceptable Time* (215). After their reconciliation, Lamech says about Noah: "This my son was dead and is alive again, was lost and is found" (*Many Waters* 159). His words echo "The Parable of the Prodigal Son," one of the parables of Jesus in the Gospels (Luke 15.11–32).

In *A Swiftly Tilting Planet*, in the story-within-the-story, when Pastor Mortmain asserts that "storytelling is of the devil," Richard Llawcae replies: "How strange that you should say that, Pastor Mortmain. Scripture says that Jesus taught by telling stories. *And he spake many things unto them in parables* [...] *and without a parable spake he not unto them*. That is in the thirteenth chapter of the Gospel according to Matthew" (145). Thus, the character draws a parallel between the art of storytelling and what Jesus Christ did. In this way, the teaching power of stories and parables is put forward.

What their stories teach depends on the personal interests or beliefs of the writers. L'Engle quotes Emerson to illustrate this idea: "What you are speaks so loudly over your head that I cannot hear what you say" (*Circle* 156). L'Engle was particularly interested in science. She was fascinated by Einstein's theory of relativity or Planck's quantum theories (Baptiste 42–43). The Murry parents do research into time and space. Alex studies the macrocosm and Kate the microcosm (*Acceptable Time* 107). The two are interconnected: "everything and everyone everywhere interreacting" (*Swiftly Tilting* 16). For example, "the number of cells in the brain" corresponds to "the numbers of stars in the universe" according to Mr. Jenkins (*Wind* 206). What happens on a small scale has an impact on a larger scale. If something affects the farandolae, mitochondria are affected too. If the Earth were blown up, it would affect the solar system, which could affect the galaxy (*Swiftly Tilting* 16). The author is convinced that what you do as a human being has its consequences: "Everything that happens within the created Order, no matter how small, has its effect. If you are angry, that anger is added to all the hate with which the Echthroi would distort the melody and destroy the ancient harmonies. When you are loving, that lovingness joins the music of the spheres" (*Swiftly Tilting* 65). What matters is to keep the harmony of the music (the stars' song).[9] Thus, everybody has a part to play in the real created Order as in the fictional created Order.

This role can correspond to creativity, which is "the aspect of humanity that is most God-like," according to MacDonald (Waddle 3): "a repetition in the finite mind of the eternal act of creation," according to Coleridge (qtd. in Prickett with Trafton). Readers and writers are "sub-creators" (Tolkien's words), taking part in the co-creation thanks to their imagination (Baptiste 82). What L'Engle says about writers/teachers giving something of themselves works also for readers. MacDonald points out that "everyone [...] who feels the story, will read its meaning after his own nature and development" ("Fantastic Imagination" 7). This principle applies to the Gospel story too. MacDonald and L'Engle took the Bible as Truth (Jeffrey Johnson, "Sacred Story"; Baptiste 96) but, like Saint Augustine, they did not always interpret it literally (Waddle 6; Baptiste 96): "God allows for and even encourages a variety of interpretative responses to the language of scripture" (Waddle 6). The twins in *Many Waters* (190) echo what MacDonald says in "The Temptation in the Wilderness" (*Unspoken Sermons*)[10]: "the Bible contains the words of God, it nowhere claims to be *the* word of God," as Waddle sums it up (6).

For MacDonald, it is not reasoning but the power of imagination that can help people come to a true understanding of what is: "You cannot have such proof of the existence of God or the truth of the Gospel story as you can have a proposition in Euclid or a chemical experiment" (qtd. in Seper 62). However, he would certainly have agreed when L'Engle joins science and religion in this way: "All science can do is open up a wider understanding of the universe [...] God doesn't change, we change in what we believe" (Rosenberg 81). Following the idea developed by MacDonald in his essay "On Polish" and explained in Waddle's article, MacDonald and L'Engle can be said to *polish* the Scriptures through their writings. Indeed, their stories "reveal and reflect" (Waddle 3) their personal interpretations, what they imagine. "With the pen as his pulpit, George MacDonald used fiction to show the relevance of scriptural truth to the problems of his age" (Jeffrey Johnson, "Sacred Story"). Years later, it helped L'Engle too: "Meeting George MacDonald's writing when I was very young was a blessing to my understanding of God and creation and our own small but potentially beautiful place in it" ("Nourishment" 120). She consciously followed in his footsteps.

Both writers thought that readers read, not only to enjoy this "delight" (MacDonald, "Fantastic Imagination" 7) or "pleasure" (L'Engle, "The Heroic" 124), but also to get a better understanding of the loving and benign Maker (Rosenberg 79), of creation—their own real world—and of man's place in it. Consequently, they had many ideas in common. Assuredly, they convey the same "eternal verities and spiritual truths" (Alexander). As seen previously, L'Engle shows in her stories that "what *you* do is going to make a difference" (*Swiftly Tilting* 280), as one character declares. MacDonald agreed with this idea. People use their free will and choose what they want to do. For L'Engle, "it is the ability to choose which makes us human" (*Walking on Water* 22) because "free will involves fallibility" ("The Heroic" 123). Both authors remind their readers that people do not always make the right choice. Indeed, since the Fall of Man, when Adam and Eve (included in the "cast" of *Lilith*) made the wrong choice, everybody has been fallible. The Fall is evoked in *Many Waters*: "the hard labor that has come upon us because of the curse upon the ground [...] When our forebears had to leave the Garden [...] *You shall gain your bread by the sweat of your brow*" (L'Engle 98). Since then, many wrong choices have been made; fratricides and wars have happened repeatedly: "Over and over again we get caught in fratricide, as Bran was in that ghastly war. We're still bleeding from the wounds. It's a primordial pattern, left us from Cain and Abel, a net we can't seem to break out of. And unless it is checked it will destroy us entirely," as L'Engle's fictional Matthew points out (*Swiftly Tilting* 278).

As human beings, MacDonald and L'Engle's heroic characters are ordinary, not perfect, but fallible, and have to accept it: "human nature is human nature" (L'Engle, *Many Waters* 222). "It is fine to be fallible!" ("The Heroic" 123), L'Engle exclaims. MacDonald "also had a realistic view of the complexity of human nature" (L'Engle, "Nourishment" 114). Throughout their adventures, their characters learn from their mistakes, from pain and from the past (story and History). "We can learn from the past. We must, for it inevitably shapes our present and becomes the raw material for crafting better futures" (Alexander). "Give yourself a chance. We do learn from our mistakes" (L'Engle, *An Acceptable Time* 87). In *The Princess and Curdie*, Curdie experiences what is known since St. Augustine as a Fortunate Fall. Because he needlessly shoots a white pigeon (MacDonald 11), he ends up meeting the Mistress of the Silver Moon and realizes that he was doing wrong. Thanks to his fall, he will grow better (18).

MacDonald believed that through suffering and adversity, people could see better and become more beautiful inside. In *Paul Faber, Surgeon*, he wrote: "So sure am I that many things which illness has led me to see are true, that I would endlessly rather never be well than lose sight of them" (qtd. in Hein). L'Engle agreed with him (Baptiste 21–22). The fire of roses notably borrowed from Dante in *The Princess and Curdie* has this effect on the characters. The old lady tells Curdie: "it will hurt you terribly [...] but much good will come to you from it" (MacDonald, *Curdie* 38). L'Engle "came across" this kind of motif "in the work of famous scientists" too ("Nourishment" 114) and has recourse to it as well: "This fire is to help and heal" (*Swiftly Tilting* 29). It can destroy and create (29). According to Gaudior the unicorn, "Roses often burn. Theirs is the most purifying flame of all" (105); "fire is roses" (285). Along the same lines, in his *Unspoken Sermons*, MacDonald compares God's wrath to "the consuming fire of Love" through which people can be purified from their sins and saved.

From the fire, Curdie gets his ability to see the soul of someone while touching their hand. L'Engle identified with Curdie. She even felt the burning of the fire of roses on her own hands ("The Heroic" 121). This passage had an impact on her life: shaking hands was never the same afterwards ("The Heroic" 121). In her third novel about the Austin family, entitled *The Young Unicorns* (1968), one of her characters even refers to Curdie's gift: "Then Rob remembered how, in *The Princess and Curdie*, Curdie was given the great gift of being able to tell, when holding someone's hand, what he was really like inside" (210). As a result, he immediately knows that the Bishop is not to be trusted, because his hand resembles a hawk's talon. Curdie's gift is also analogous to that of Chuck in *A Swiftly Tilting Planet*, who can discern what people are like by their odor (193). The use of the senses is primordial to go beyond appearances: "people are more than just the way they look" (L'Engle, *Wrinkle* 55). Both writers insist on that point. The essence of a person is what matters. However, they do not have a dualist vision of reality: beauty can hide good or evil and the other way round. Aunt Beast is a creature with tentacles and no eyes. Meg "felt utter loathing and revulsion when it reached out a tentacle to touch her face," and yet this beast loved and healed her (*Wrinkle* 210). The Beast's awful looks remind us of MacDonald's Lina with her hideous appearance and beautiful soul (*Curdie* 35, 41). When Sandy meets Tiglah, he thinks that she is "the most spectacularly beautiful girl he had ever seen" (L'Engle, *Many Waters* 172), and yet, she is evil-minded. Conversely, the Wise Woman in MacDonald's eponymous tale can seem to act cruelly to put the lost girls back on the right track.

For both authors, nobody can remain on the wrong path forever. MacDonald and L'Engle announce the final victory of a Loving God. Because "people's hearts are turned to wickedness" (L'Engle, *Many Waters* 109) or "sank toward their old wickedness" (MacDonald, *Curdie* 131), something will happen to change things: the flood in *Many Waters* or the final destruction of the city in *The Princess and Curdie*. The fall of Gwyntystorm can be compared to that of Sodom or Gomorrah (Isa. 1.9). "Literary critics have worried and puzzled over the ending of Curdie for decades (an ending that bothers few children) and yet the source and explanation lies firmly ensconced in Isaiah" (Jeffrey Johnson, "Sacred Story"). L'Engle reflects this anxiety and puzzlement. Taking a step back because of his knowledge of the future, her character, Sandy, also puzzles over the flood and he considers that it did not work: "Wiping out all those people, and then starting all over again. People are taller, and we do even worse things to one another because we know more" (*Many Waters* 224). MacDonald "wants his readers—whether they are aware of it or not—not only to understand Isaiah better, but to learn how relevant the text remains to the troubles of their very own age" (Jeffrey Johnson, "Sacred Story"). Both writers, first, make their readers aware of the everlasting struggle of good against evil to, then, better bring hope: one day, good shall triumph: "Good and not Evil is the Universe. The battle between them may last for countless ages, but it must end" (MacDonald, *Lilith* 142). An analysis of this great outcome will be made in the light of another part of Isaiah. "They shall not hurt nor destroy in all my holy mountain: for the earth shall be full of knowledge of the Lord, as the waters cover the sea" (Isa. 11.9).

"The people that walked in darkness have seen a great light: they that dwell in the land of the shadow of death, upon them hath the light shined" (Isa. 9.2). The opposing realities mentioned before must be reconciled for people to live in harmony. On the journey home, Mr. Vane observes: "It had ceased to be dark; we walked in a dim twilight [...] The microcosm and macrocosm were at length atoned, at length in harmony" (MacDonald, *Lilith* 230). Darkness must be the friend of light: that is what Charles Wallace learns within Harcels (L'Engle, *Swiftly Tilting* 69). In the same book, the moon is personified and is said "to join, briefly, her brother, sun" (104). At the end of "The History of Photogen and Nycteris," by MacDonald, "all is well" because the two characters (standing for day and night, sun and moon) are united too (340). So, masculine and feminine are together as they are in the God in which MacDonald believed. L'Engle too explains: "God made man in El's own image, male and female" ("Nourishment" 120).

The former pastor developed his perception and emphasized the loving aspect of God. His *alter ego*, L'Engle's "Bishop Colubra, too, believed in a God of total love" (*Acceptable Time* 274). Consequently it may be assumed that L'Engle had the same point of view. As a matter of fact, the character of the Old and Wise Woman is an expression of their vision of God and/or of His helpers. Irene's "great-great-grandmother" (MacDonald, *Goblin* 14) has the face of "a woman of three-and-twenty" (112) because the "right old age means strength and beauty" (121). In "The Wise Woman," the eponymous character folds her cape round the girls to protect them. The same characteristics can be found in some of L'Engle's books: "The age or sex" of Mrs. Whatsit "was impossible to tell" (*A Wrinkle in Time* 17); "the great wings of Mrs Whatsit folded round her [Meg] and she felt comfort and strength pouring through her" (90). With Mrs. Who and Mrs. Which, Mrs. Whatsit forms a trinity, described as "guardian angels," "Messengers of God" by Calvin (231). What's more, the wind blowing on Gaudior and Charles Wallace while they travel (*Swiftly Tilting*) recalls the North Wind—wrongly called "Mister" by Diamond the first time they meet (MacDonald, *At the Back* 14–15)—and can be linked to the Holy Spirit. The old women often accompany, physically or spiritually, the characters: "grandmothers are marvelous" (L'Engle, *Acceptable Time* 123). These grandmothers are sometimes linked to the eternal Sophia (through The Wise Woman)[11] or Mother Nature (*Phantastes* 73) in MacDonald's work. The Mother occupies a prominent place in the culture of the prehistoric people in *An Acceptable Time* too (L'Engle 46–47). She is described as "a loving birth-giver" (161). She "speaks in the dark, in the waters, in the womb of the earth" to "*Her* children" (160). "The moon goddess. And the Mother, the earth" (168) are not really separate gods, but "all One Presence, with many aspects" (250). The fact that *the Presence* can take different aspects is underlined in MacDonald's work too.¹² Through the words of characters from the two time periods in *An Acceptable Time*, the vision of God developed by L'Engle is similar to that of her predecessor. God/The Presence is "The One who is more than the Mother, or the Goddess. Starmaker, wind-breather, earth-grower, sun-riser, rain-giver. The One who cares for all" (103); "a God of love and compassion, a God who was mysterious and tremendous […] A God who cared about all that had been created in love" (273). Love is the cement. "Everything is connected by the love of the creator" (311). This sentence could be linked to the "unity and wholeness in God's creation" claimed by Wordsworth (Prickett with Trafton). MacDonald rejoiced in this "Christian pantheism."

Christians believe that, on account of his love for men, Christ offered himself as a sacrifice. Like MacDonald (Dearborn), Bishop Colubra sees Christ as "the alpha and omega" (L'Engle, *An Acceptable Time* 252–253). His birth is announced in Isaiah (7.14; 9.6). According to the Scriptures, he shed his blood to save men from death: "He will swallow up death in victory […] we have waited for him, and he will save: this is the Lord; we have waited for him, we will be glad and rejoice in his salvation" (Isa. 25.8–9). Louise Colubra takes the example of a blood transfusion to explain to Polly that he did not sacrifice himself unwillingly (*An Acceptable Time* 195–196). Following his example, Mrs. O'Keefe in *A Swiftly Tilting Planet* gives her life out of love. Thanks to the rune (a prayer) she gives to Charles Wallace, Mrs. O'Keefe helps him to change the course of events and save the planet. Here, L'Engle throws light upon the fact that everybody has still the Old Music in them. One day, everybody shall go back to God, even The Queen of Hell or The Great Shadow (as in MacDonald's *Lilith*): "All flesh [shall] come to worship before me, saith the Lord" (Isa. 66.23). L'Engle concurred with MacDonald's rejection of the traditional doctrine of eternal punishment (Baptiste 97). She thought that everybody would eventually repent and, like MacDonald, believed in universal salvation: "He was excommunicated from his church because he refused to believe that a God of love would wipe out two-thirds of the planet as being unworthy of his attention. And I think that's fine. I agree" (Rosenberg 79).

At the beginning of the story, talking about Mrs. O'Keefe, Mrs. Murry asserts that there is "more to her than meets the eye" (L'Engle, *A Swiftly Tilting Planet* 4; 25; 33). At the end, Meg and the reader understand what Mrs. Murry meant: "You're more than right about Mom O'Keefe, Mother, more right than any of us could possibly have imagined." (304). "As a Christian, MacDonald obviously believes that there is much more to the world than meets the eye" (Hart). Going beyond what meets the eye seems to be a key to true understanding. "Truth about God" seems to lie in "an attitude leading to right actions" (Waddle 6). While waiting for the happy ending, characters and readers are invited to adopt a childlike attitude, characterized by faith and innocence. "If ye be willing and obedient, ye shall eat the good of the land" (Isa. 1.19). They have to obey and believe without seeing or understanding. Irene is "obedient to the guiding thread" (MacDonald, *Goblin* 155). Curdie cannot see the thread, so he has trouble believing what Irene says. He "must believe without seeing" (170). L'Engle's Meg guesses that she will "just have to accept it without understanding it" and her mother answers: "Maybe that's really the point I was trying to put across" (*Wrinkle* 56). "For the things which are seen are temporal. But the things which are not seen are eternal," Aunt Beast explains (225), quoting the Scriptures (2 Corinthians 4.18). Meg's brother Sandy had "to see things to believe in them." Through his adventure, he realizes that "some things have to be believed to be seen" (*Many Waters* 290). This acknowledgment is even said to have become his "favorite quotation" in the last volume of the *Time Quintet* (*Acceptable Time* 143). Thus, MacDonald and L'Engle agree with Paul, the Apostle: "we walk by faith and not by sight" (2 Cor. 5.7), but the step of faith may lead to seeing.

Faith allows people not to fear death. Both writers did not see death as an end; consequently it was not a problem for them to raise this topic in their work. Death is often explored by MacDonald: *At the Back of the North Wind* even ends with the death of the main character, Diamond, who is still a child. In *An Acceptable Time*, L'Engle makes clear that one of Zachary's problems is that he is afraid of death, certainly because he does not "believe in God" (365). Unlike Zachary, Diamond is not afraid at all. He is even looking forward to what is coming next, having had a glimpse of life "at the Back of the North Wind." Thus, throughout the book, he is waiting to be taken with joy because he knows that "the best thing to do is wait and be patient for a while" (to use L'Engle's words in *A Wind in the Door* 33). When it finally happens, Diamond's death is not viewed as an end but rather as the beginning of his afterlife and of an endless happiness: "They thought he was dead. I knew that he had gone to the back of the north wind" (*At the Back* 346), the narrator concludes.

Despite the eschatological pictures offered by MacDonald in *Lilith*, what is beyond death and the end of the world remains mysterious, hence the title of its last chapter "The 'Endless Ending'" (237). The characters, and the readers who identify with them, are left waiting for the "great good" which "is coming" (MacDonald, *Phantastes* 205; *Lilith* 231). Once they come back home from their other world, Sandy is "homesick" and Dennys feels the same (L'Engle, *Many Waters* 352). As for Mr. Vane, he waits hopefully for the final and real waking: "I wait; asleep or awake, I wait" (*Lilith* 238).

To conclude, the technique L'Engle uses to invite her readers to follow her characters in their physical and spiritual journey is similar to MacDonald's. She adopts the same symbolism of light versus darkness and relies on the use of imagination too, so as to win over the same target audience, that is to say the childlike and not just children. Her own particular way of writing seems to bring her even closer to her "grandfather." Indeed, her use of science, not only makes her fictional worlds more real, but also shows how it can help to understand God and Creation better. Both writers fully believed that the discoveries of science in their eras did not weaken the truth of the Gospel story. Even if allusions to the Scriptures are present in both corpora, on account of MacDonald's preaching aim or L'Engle's Christian faith, they can go unnoticed by their readers and are not necessary to enjoy their stories, which are often based on history or legend. As mirrors of their times, their books hint at a few differences because of the gap between the two generations. However, their own answers to the preoccupations of their fellow citizens or their own interpretations of the Bible match, certainly because they shared the same convictions: they believed in the power of Love, which leads to the victory of good, in a transient form of divine punishment and in Christian Universalism. Thus, it is not surprising that they spread the same message in their fiction: even if some things go wrong during their life on earth (problems, ills, suffering, bad decisions) as part of a pattern since the original Fall, each person should learn through pain, not care about appearances, do his best to adopt the right attitude[13] and believe that the outcome will be good even if what it is hidden "at the Back of the North Wind" can only be imagined. This essay will not end with the traditional proverb "All is well that ends well" but with a hopeful assertion from one of L'Engle's characters, which could equally well have been formulated by MacDonald: "All shall be well. Wait. Patience. Wait" (*Many Waters* 318).

Notes

1. The three fairy tales in question are: *At the Back of the North Wind* (1871), "The Wise Woman, or The Lost Princess: A Double Story" (1874) and "The History of Photogen and Nycteris: A Day and Night Mährchen" (1879).

2. This literary influence is acknowledged by Madeleine L'Engle and by literary critics: MacDonald's fairy tales "stand not only in their own right but as the forerunners of many such writings by G. K. Chesterton, C. S. Lewis, Charles Williams, J. R. R. Tolkien, and Madeleine L'Engle," Hein underlines in "Life and Religion Are One."

3. "a semblance of truth sufficient to procure [...] that willing suspension of disbelief for the moment, which constitutes poetic faith," Coleridge, quoted in the introduction to Wordsworth and Coleridge's *Lyrical Ballads* (4).

4. "Kything": a kind of "telepathic communication" used in L'Engle's *Time Quintet*.

5. Diamond's speech goes on as follows:
He's very fond of baby's mammy, and works from morning to night to get her breakfast and dinner and supper, only at night he forgets, and pays the money away for beer. And they put nasty stuff in the beer, I've heard my daddy say, that drives all the good out, and lets all the bad in. Daddy says when a man takes to drink, there's a thirsty devil creeps into his inside, because he knows he will always get enough there ... And he says, too, the only way to make the devil come out, is to give him plenty of cold water and tea and coffee, and nothing at all that comes from the public-house [*At the Back of the North Wind* 168–169].

6. Moreover, MacDonald's friendship with "Victorian Visionaries" such as F. D. Maurice or Octavia Hill is discussed by Prickett, Woodruff Tait, Philip Newell and Johnson in their article.

7. In *The Victorian Frame of Mind*, Walter E. Houghton shows that the prudery of the time was accompanied with a mass censorship of what was considered as "shameful" (356–357).

8. Polly and Dr. Louise's conversation about menstrual periods:
"What about blood?"
"Well, I know that blood is important in all cultures. And in lots of Eastern religions women have to be set apart, away from everybody else, during their menstrual periods, because they're thought to be unclean."
"Maybe not unclean as you're thinking of it," the doctor said. "Remember, sanitary napkins and tampons are inventions of this century." Polly looked at her questioningly. "My grandmothers, and women before them, used old sheets, any old linens. Back in the Stone Age there weren't any cloths to use. Having women set apart during their periods was a simple sanitary measure, and a ritual that was often looked forward to, when women could be together and rest from the regular backbreaking work. It was a time of rejuvenation, of peace and prayer."
"I hadn't thought about that," Polly said. "I guess I took a lot for granted. But weren't men convinced that women were—I think I read somewhere—separated from God at that time?"
Dr. Louise smiled [*An Acceptable Time* 194–195].

9. The stars' song in the *Time Quintet* can be linked to the stars' song in the *Book of Job* in the Bible: "When the morning stars sang together, and all the sons of God shouted for joy?" (Job 38.7). This parallel was drawn by Suzanne Bray, for instance, in her article on Evil in the *Wind Trilogy* ("Disperser l'antique terreur : Le mal et comment le vaincre dans la trilogie du Vent de Madeleine L'Engle" 88).

10. In one of his *Unspoken Sermons* (from "Series One"), entitled "The Temptation in the Wilderness," MacDonald explains what he sees as the Word of God:
What I must say is this: that, by "the Word of God," I do not understand "The Bible." The Bible is "a" Word of God, the chief of his written words, because it tells us of The Word, the Christ; but everything God has done and given man to know is a word of his, a will of his; and inasmuch as it is a will of his, it is a necessity to man, without which he cannot live: the reception of it is man's life. For inasmuch as God's utterances are a whole, every smallest is essential: he speaks no foolishness—there are with him no vain repetitions. But by "the word" of the God and not Maker only, who is God just because he "speaks" to men, I must understand, in the deepest sense, every revelation of Himself in the heart and consciousness of man, so that the man knows that God is there, nay, rather, that he is here. Even Christ himself is not The Word of God in the deepest sense "to a man," until he is this Revelation of God to the man,—until the Spirit that is the meaning in the Word has come to him,—until the speech is not a sound as of thunder, but the voice of words; for a word is more than an utterance—it is a sound to be understood. No word, I say, is fully a Word "of"

God until it is a Word "to" man, until the man therein recognizes God. This is that for which the word is spoken.

11. Katharine Bubel discusses this parallel in her article entitled "Knowing God 'Other-wise.'"

12. In MacDonald's books, the Old Woman/North Wind can appear under different aspects. For example, in *At the Back of the North Wind*, she turns into a wolf to frighten a drunk and wicked nurse (37–38) and then she explains: "Good people see good things; bad people, bad things" (39). In *The Princess and Curdie*, she says the same thing to Curdie: "Shapes are only dresses, Curdie, and dresses are only names. That which is inside is the same all the time [...] it is one thing what you or your father may think about me, and quite another what a foolish or bad man may see in me" (31). In the Bible, the aspect of Jesus's face or of his clothes is not fixed. In the Gospel according to St. Luke, it is written: "And as he prayed, the fashion of his countenance was altered, and his raiment *was* white *and* glistering" (9:29).

13. To give another example of what it is meant by "the right attitude," L'Engle actually invites people to follow Edward Nason West's definition of agapé: "a profound concern for the welfare of another without any desire to control that other, to be thanked by that other, or to enjoy the process" (*A Circle of Quiet* 158–159).

Works Cited

Alexander, Jonathan. "Late L'Engle: The Wrinkles of Time, Redeemed by Jonathan Alexander." *Los Angeles Review of Books (LARB)*. 16 Aug. 2015. Web.

Baptiste, Tracey. *Madeleine L'Engle. Who Wrote That?* New York: Chelsea House, Infobase Publishing, 2009. Print.

Bray, Suzanne. "Disperser l'antique terreur : le Mal et comment le vaincre dans la Trilogie du Vent de Madeleine L'Engle." *L'Enigme du Mal en Littérature de jeunesse. Cahiers Robinson* 37. Arras: Artois Presses Université (2015): 87–98. Print.

Bubel, Katharine. "Knowing God 'Other-wise': The Wise Old Woman Archetype in George MacDonald's *The Princess and the Goblin, The Princess and Curdie* and 'The Golden Key.'" *North Wind: Journal of the George MacDonald Society* 25. De Pere: St. Norbert College (2006): 1–17. Web.

Dearborn, Kerry. "Love at the Heart of the Universe: For George MacDonald, Belief in God and Obedience to God Went Hand in Hand." *Christian History & Biography Magazine* 86: "George MacDonald: Writer Who Inspired C.S. Lewis." 2005. Print.

Dickens, Charles. *Hard Times*. 1854. Oxford: Oxford University Press, 2006. Print.

Duby, Georges, and Michelle Perrot. *Histoire des Femmes en Occident, vol. IV : Le XIXe siècle*. Paris: Plon, 1991. Print.

Ellison, Robert H. "A Born Preacher: George MacDonald's Sermons Passed the Victorian Tests of Earnestness and Practicality with Flying Colors." *Christian History & Biography Magazine* 86: "George MacDonald: Writer Who Inspired C.S. Lewis." 2005. Print.

Hart, Trevor. "The Wise Imagination: George MacDonald's Legacy Is His Reminder That We Are Creative Beings Because We Are Made in the Image of the Creator." *Christian History & Biography Magazine* 86: "George MacDonald: Writer Who Inspired C.S. Lewis." 2005. Print.

Hein, Rolland. "Life and Religion Are One: George MacDonald Embraced All Experiences, Both Joys and Hardships, as Vehicles of Grace—and Inspired Others to Do the Same." *Christian History & Biography Magazine* 86: "George MacDonald: Writer Who Inspired C.S. Lewis." 2005. Print.

The Holy Bible, King James Version. New York: Meridian, 1974. Print.
Houghton, Walter E. *The Victorian Frame of Mind, 1830–1870*. New Haven: Yale University Press, 1957. Print.
Jeffrey Johnson, Kirsten. "Did You Know? Interesting and Unusual Facts About George MacDonald." *Christian History & Biography Magazine* 86: "George MacDonald: Writer Who Inspired C.S. Lewis." 2005. Print.
_____. "Sacred Story: With the Pen as His Pulpit, George MacDonald Used Fiction to Show the Relevance of Scriptural Truth to the Problems of His Age." *Christian History & Biography Magazine* 86: "George MacDonald: Writer Who Inspired C.S. Lewis." 2005. Print.
Larsen, Timothy. "The Power of Books: For the Victorians, Reading Could Be the Doorway to Doubt—or to Faith." *Christian History & Biography Magazine* 86: "George MacDonald: Writer Who Inspired C.S. Lewis." 2005. Print.
L'Engle, Madeleine. *An Acceptable Time*. 1989. New York: Square Fish, by Farrar, Straus and Giroux, 2007. Print.
_____. *A Circle of Quiet* (1972). San Francisco: Harper and Row, 1972. Print.
_____. "George MacDonald: Nourishment for a Private World." *Reality and Vision*. Ed. Philip Yancey. Dallas: Word Publishing, 1990. 111–121. Print.
_____. "The Heroic in Literature and in Living," *The Lion and the Unicorn* 13, Number 1. Baltimore: Johns Hopkins University Press (June 1989): 120–128, Web.
_____. *Many Waters*. 1986. New York: Square Fish, by Farrar, Straus and Giroux, 2007. Print.
_____. *A Swiftly Tilting Planet*. 1978. New York: Square Fish, by Farrar, Straus and Giroux, 2007. Print.
_____. *Walking on Waters: Reflections on Faith and Art*. 1980. Tring: Lion Publishing, 1982. Print.
_____. *A Wind in the Door*. 1973. New York: Square Fish, by Farrar, Straus and Giroux, 2007. Print.
_____. *A Wrinkle in Time*. 1962. London: Penguin Books, 2014. Print.
_____. *The Young Unicorns*. 1968. London: Hodder & Stoughton, 1970. Print.
Lewis, C.S. *Surprised by Joy: The Shape of My Early Life*. 1955. London: Fount Paperbacks, HarperCollins, 1991. Print.
MacDonald, George. *At the Back of the North Wind*. 1871. New York: Alfred A. Knopf, a division of Random House, 2001. Print.
_____. "The Fantastic Imagination." 1893. *The Complete Fairy Tales*. London: Penguin Books, 1999. 1–10. Print.
_____. "The History of Photogen and Nycteris: A Day and Night Mährchen." 1879. *The Complete Fairy Tales*. London: Penguin Books, 1999. 304–341. Print.
_____. *Lilith: A Romance*. 1895. New York: Dover Publications, 2008. Print.
_____. *Phantastes: A Faerie Romance*. 1858. New York: Dover Publications, 2005. Print.
_____. *The Princess and Curdie*. 1883. Radford: Wilder Publications, 2008. Print.
_____. *The Princess and the Goblin*. 1872. London: Puffin Books, 1964. Print.
_____. *Unspoken Sermons*, Series I, II, III. 1867, 1885 and 1889. Project Gutenberg Association, Oct. 2005, 10th edition. EBook *online*. Web.
_____. "The Wise Woman, or the Lost Princess: A Double Story." 1874. *The Complete Fairy Tales*. London: Penguin Books, 1999. 225–303. Print.
Prickett, Stephen, with Jennifer Trafton. "A Faith That Feels: Samuel Taylor Coleridge and William Wordsworth Translated Romantic Ideals into the Language of Christian Experience." *Christian History & Biography Magazine* 86: "George MacDonald: Writer Who Inspired C.S. Lewis." 2005. Print.

———, Edwin Woodruff Tait, J. Philip Newell, and Rachel Johnson. "Victorian Visionaries: George MacDonald's Friends Worked to Reform Society, Challenge the Church, and Inspire the Imagination." *Christian History & Biography Magazine* 86: "George MacDonald: Writer Who Inspired C.S. Lewis." 2005. Print.

Raeper, William. *The Major Biography of George MacDonald: Novelist and Victorian Visionary*. 1987. Tring: Lion Publishing, 1988. Print.

Rosenberg, Aaron. *Interview with Madeleine L'Engle* (conducted by Karin Snelson at Amazon.com). New York: Rosen Publishing, 2006. 76–81. Print.

Seper, Charles. *C.S. Lewis Called Him Master: Exploring the Life & Adult Fantasy Works of George MacDonald*. Chicago: Victor, Broadstreet and Johnson, 2007. Print.

Tolkien, J.R.R. "On Fairy Stories." *Essays Presented to Charles Williams*. Oxford: Oxford University Press, 1947. 1–27. Print.

Waddle, Keith. "George MacDonald and the Homiletics of Religious Imagination." *North Wind: Journal of the George MacDonald Society* 18. De Pere: St. Norbert College (1999): 1–11. Web.

Wordsworth, William, and Samuel Taylor Coleridge. *Lyrical Ballads* (1798). London: Routledge Classics, 2005. Print.

Madeleine L'Engle
An Anti-Romantic Romantic?

Gregory G. Pepetone

This essay examines three aspects of Madeleine L'Engle's outlook and sensibility that place her squarely within the tradition of early nineteenth-century Romanticism: (1) her devotion to the so-called Art Religion, (2) her contribution to the Romantic Cult of Childhood, (3) her imaginative synthesis of science, spirituality, and politics.

The Murky Inanities of the Art Religion

Madeleine L'Engle's strong association with orthodox Anglicanism is well-known. It accounts, in large measure, for her popularity in America and elsewhere during a period marked by what is sometimes referred to in retrospect as a modern Evangelical revival. In the 1970s and 1980s, though controversial among most conservative Christians, she was widely viewed as a champion of the cause. This is ironic in that the distinguishing feature of L'Engle's spirituality is precisely her avoidance of this theologically narrow expression of religious primitivism that, for a time in the United States, came to define Christianity itself, despite the efforts of progressive Christians such as Jim Wallis to reclaim the faith from the religious Right. What Madeleine L'Engle offers instead is an authentic Evangelicalism whose roots can be traced backward to the Alexandrian Church Fathers and forward to a cluster of post–Enlightenment thinkers and artists known collectively as the Romantic generation. She is even sometimes, incorrectly, associated with the famous group of British Romantic Christians called the Inklings. Nineteenth-century European Romanticism is widely misrepresented as an attempt to accommodate Judeo-Christian concepts and values to the secular humanism that prevailed in Western culture after the revolutions—political, scientific, and technological—of the late eighteenth-century. However, it would be quite as appropriate to view Romanticism, at least in the first half of the nineteenth century, not as a secularization of the spiritual but as the spiritualization of the secular—an attempt to rehabilitate secular humanism by promoting the fine arts as a spiritual project. According to this view, the aesthetic disciplines—literature, painting, and preeminently music—may be seen as a Western cultural yoga suited to filling the emotional and intellectual void created by Enlightenment skepticism and its aftermath.

It has been said that the Romantic imagination is a capacity to perceive the extraordinary in the ordinary, one bound up inextricably with the Gothic imagination, another somewhat nebulous term that has been more ponderously defined as, "that which gives expression and meaning to life's darkly mysterious, painful, frightening, and seemingly irrational experiences by embracing them as a potential source of insight and transcendence" (Pepetone, *Gothic* 22). The premise of this article is that L'Engle was a mid-twentieth-century purveyor of Gothic story-telling whose outlook was rooted in a deeply Romantic sensibility, a sensibility she shared with many of the artists she most admired as well as some that she did not. A good example of the latter is the German Romantic composer, Richard Wagner. Writing of Wagner and Romantic music generally, she says:

> My parents, who were in their thirties at the time of the First World War, loved Romantic music, Chopin, Wagner—how they loved Wagner! But Wagner has little to say to me [...] My generation, and my children's, living in this embattled and insane period, find more nourishment in the structure of Bach and Mozart than in the lush romanticism of Wagner. Wagner is fine if the world around one is stable. But when the world is, indeed, in chaos, then an affirmation of cosmos becomes essential [*Walking* 49].

This aesthetic pronouncement is remarkable in several respects: Firstly, in denouncing the relevance of Wagner to the times in which she lived, she tacitly assumes a quintessentially Romantic understanding of art, namely that it is an affirmation of cosmos over chaos. That is a view to which few, if any, exponents of twentieth-century modernism would subscribe either in theory or practice. L'Engle's anti–Romantic Romanticism mirrors that of one of modernity's greatest musical exponents, Igor Stravinsky, the same Stravinsky who lashed out at what he termed "the murky inanities of the nineteenth-century art religion" (Taruskin 471). As a composer, he is remembered today for his neo-Baroque/neo-Classical style, though his eclecticism also embraced post–Romanticism, primitivism, and even atonality. He rejected any metaphorical or programmatic understanding of music famously declaring that "music is essentially powerless to express anything at all, whether a feeling, an attitude of mind, a psychological mood, a phenomenon of nature [...]

Expression has never been an inherent property of music" (Stravinsky 53–54). Paradoxically, as Leonard Bernstein remarks, Stravinsky's musical scores are nevertheless laced with emotive terms such as "*expressivo*" (399). By all accounts, he was also a closet admirer of Tchaikovsky—the lushest of the lush where Romantic music is concerned. Nor is this phenomenon unique to modern writers and composers. Frédéric Chopin, who many (including L'Engle, apparently) would regard as the quintessential Romantic, was notoriously critical of his contemporaries such as Robert Schumann, and even dismissive of paintings by his Romantic friend and confidant, Delacroix. His musical role models were the same two that L'Engle signals out, J. S. Bach and Mozart. In truth, the values that both Chopin and L'Engle associated with the well-ordered worlds of Bach and Mozart, as well as those associated with the ostensibly disordered worlds of the Romantics, are merely a matter of emphasis. All significant art displays a synergy of Classical and Romantic values without which the former would be sterile and the later unintelligible.

The historical origins of the Art Religion can be traced to a cluster of German Romantic poets and philosophers such as Goethe, Schiller, Kant, and Hegel. Writing of this loosely allied group, cultural historian Jacques Barzun says, "Although the 'death of God' was not proclaimed until the mid-nineteenth century, it was implied, felt, and acted on fully a hundred years earlier, during the century of Reason, the Enlightenment." Speaking of Rousseau's belief in "the Sublime" (understood as nature's capacity to invoke numinous qualities of awe and fear traditionally associated with religion), Barzun goes on to say "With that revelation, Rousseau opened the way to artists and thinkers known as Romanticists, who undertook the task of reconstruction after skepticism. They did not abandon Reason, but demanded its compliment. It turned out to be the religion of art" (26). It goes without saying that wild and untamed nature, i.e., sublime nature, as a source of spiritual renewal is a leitmotif in the writings in L'Engle's stories. Some of her books, such as *The Moon by Night* are largely travel logs in which she records the effects of nature on her characters. Seething oceans, dizzying vistas, and vast tracks of uninhabited, or sparsely inhabited terrain serve as the Romantic backdrop against which Vicky Austin's tumultuous journey from adolescence to adulthood is set. Indeed, her proximity (and that of her Byronic suitor Zachary Grey) to the eruption of a mountain caused by seismic disturbance is not only a dramatic climax to this what-I-did-last-summer narrative, but a fitting metaphor of the spiritual upheaval experienced by them both. Writing of art in terms that reflect this Romantic predilection for the Sublime, L'Engle says, "Artists have always been drawn to the wild, wide elements they cannot control or understand—the sea, mountains, and fire. To be an artist means to approach the light, and that means to let go of control, to allow our whole selves to be placed with absolute faith in that which is greater than we are" (*Walking* 161).

The synthesis of the arts as a homogeneous enterprise and divine inspiration as the source of artistic inspiration were common assumptions during the early Romantic era. Writing as Florestan (his journalistic pseudonym for the more extroverted side of his creative persona), Robert Schumann says in one of his many Novalis-like aphorisms, "The aesthetic principle is the same in every art; only the materials differ [...] Great thoughts often make the round of minds in similar words and tones" (44–46). Although, like all Romantics, he gave primacy to music as the ideal art form, he was himself torn between a career in music or literature. Ultimately, he reconciled these two interests, not only as a successful writer about music, but through the creation of a "musico-literary" art that draws upon literary techniques such as quotations of self and others, structural blue-prints modelled on literary templates, and musical cyphers that spell out or otherwise allude to names and places dear to the heart of this most representative of all Romantics. To judge from her non-fiction as well as her fictional works, L'Engle shared a similar view of "the arts." From *A Wrinkle in Time* onwards she constantly invokes the great musicians, painters, and authors. The names Shakespeare, Goya, Dostoevsky, the Brontë sisters, and especially Johann Sebastian Bach appear as icons of art conceived as an incarnational activity. "We look at a painting, or hear a symphony, or read a book and feel more named," writes L'Engle. "'Named,' in her private lexicon is a synonym for existential affirmation (*Walking* 46)—"The purpose of the work be it story or music or painting is to further the coming of the kingdom, to make us aware of our status as children of God, and to turn our feet toward home" (163).

One of the cardinal tenets of the Romantic Movement was the supremacy of music in the Pantheon of the fine arts. Referring to the widely held view that that music was the doyen of the arts, the art to which all others aspired, author Roger Cardinal speaks of the "the extraordinary rise of Romantic music, which of course the Romantics themselves, from Wackenroder on, insisted was the superior art form" (22). Music plays a significant role in the writings of L'Engle, who was herself a competent pianist and classical music enthusiast. In her science fiction fantasy, such as *A Wind in the Door* and *A Swiftly Tilting Planet*, the presence or absence of cosmic music—as conceived by philosophers from Pythagoras, Boethius and beyond—is a central metaphor. It also figures prominently in her non-fiction book on the relationship between faith and art entitled *Walking on Water*. Her negative assessment of Chopin and Wagner (and by extension the music of other Romantics), as well as her positive assessment of music belonging to the Baroque and Classical eras, has already been mentioned, but there is one composer, more than any other appealed to L'Engle's taste. J.S. Bach, whose highly structured, elaborately contrapuntal music was heard by her as perhaps the nearest earthly approximation of the cosmic Music of the Spheres, is frequently cited as a source of spiritual renewal. Second century Alexandrian theologians, such as Clement and Origen, had equated this kind of supermundane music with the divine *logos* (Pepetone, *Angels* 154–61). References to Bach's music are sprinkled plentifully throughout L'Engle's writings. Particular pieces by Bach named by L'Engle include his keyboard fugues, two-part inventions, Brandenburg concerti, and sacred choral compositions, especially the *St. Matthew Passion*.

Once again there is an element of irony involved here, in that L'Engle's view of Bach is very much in the Romantic tradition. It was Romantics such as Mendelssohn and Schumann who led the Bach revival of the nineteenth century and who seized upon his contrapuntal style as a symbol of a transcendent reality to which they both aspired. It was, after all, Mendelssohn who rescued the *St. Matthew Passion*, a work that L'Engle terms "an icon of the highest quality," from oblivion. Commenting on this choral work she writes:

> The St. Matthew Passion is [...] an open door into the realm of the numinous. Bach, of course, was a man of deep and profound religious faith, a faith which shines through his most secular music [...] There is nothing so secular that it cannot be sacred, and that is one of the deepest messages of the Incarnation [*Walking* 50].

Nearly all of the great nineteenth-century composers, with the exception of Berlioz and Wagner, regarded Bach as a seminal influence. Mendelssohn's *Preludes and Fugues for Piano*, Op. 35 are modelled on the forty-eight preludes and fugues from Bach's *Well-Tempered Klavier*; and, in his late neo-Baroque cycles for piano, such as *Gesänge der Fruhe*, Op. 133 and *Seven Character Pieces in the form of Fughettas*, Op 126, Schumann explicitly imitates the textural clarity and intricacy of Bach's polyphonic music. In the embattled and insane final stages of his life, this troubled composer latched onto the intellectual rigor and logic of Bach's Baroque style as a potential remedy for his advancing dementia. But much earlier in his life, Bach served him as a musical role-model. In a letter dated January 31, 1840, written to a correspondent critical of the new Romantic generation's alleged indifference to the discipline of Bach's music, Schumann responds by saying, "Mendelssohn, Bennett, Chopin, Hiller—in fact the whole so-called Romantic School [...] is far nearer to Bach in its music than Mozart ever was; indeed, I myself make a daily confession of my sins to that mighty one, and endeavor to purify and strengthen myself through him" (93). In much the same way, Madeleine L'Engle would later turn to the intricately patterned cosmos of Bach as a refuge from the chaos of the world:

> Along with reawakening the sense of newness, Bach's music points me to wholeness of body, mind, and spirit, which we seldom glimpse, but which we are intended to

know. It is no coincidence that the root word of whole, health, heal, holy, is hale (as in hale and healthy). If we are healed, we become whole; we are hale and hearty; we are holy [*Walking* 57].

Not only did the first Romantic generation of artists respond to Bach in much the same way as Madeleine L'Engle, they did so for much the same reasons. It was the Romantics who first spoke of him as a religious mystic, a high priest of the Art Religion of wholeness to which they all subscribed.

In *The Moon by Night*, Vicky Austin's artist uncle, Douglas, attempts to bring his teenage niece out of her dark mood, a mood occasioned by her encounter with Zachary Grey, a handsome, intelligent, and decidedly reckless young man made cynical by uncaring parents, the brutalities of the world in the age of atomic weapons, and his own medical condition (which prefigures the possibility of an early death). Zachery both mocks and envies Vicky's innocence and religious conviction. While her own faith is not seriously undermined by his taunting remarks, she does have simmering questions concerning the fairness of life and the reliability of God in times of trouble that are brought to a boil when she and Zachery attend a theatrical presentation of *The Diary of Anne Frank*. Like millions before and after her (including Madeleine L'Engle) Vicky agonizes over the tragic outcome of a vital young woman's encounter with the radical evil of Nazism. Where, she wonders, was God when Anne Frank was most in need of him? Her uncle first reminds her that God's ways are not those of man and that Nazism represented a choice freely undertaken by millions of misguided Germans—a choice that by no means mirrored the will of God. He goes on to point out that selfishness, not righteous indignation, often lies at the core of our anger at God, "When you're yelling at God, what you're doing is saying, Do it MY way, God, not YOUR way, MY way" (*Moon by Night* 167). In short, he offers the standard arguments of theodicy, which for Vicky as for most of us, are not entirely satisfying. He next tries a metaphor in an attempt to appeal to imagination rather than reason. Life, he asserts, is like a picture puzzle with missing pieces. Only God can see the completed puzzle, because only He has access to all of its component parts. At that moment, Vicky's Aunt Elena, a concert pianist by profession who has been practicing finger exercises in the background, breaks into a Bach fugue. This prompts her opportunistic husband to remark, "It's like a fugue too [...] Elena and I are the lucky ones. She has music and I have painting. They give form and shape to everything we do" (*Moon by Night* 172). The intricate interweaving of independent melodic parts in such a way as to avoid an unintentionally discordant whole is the essence of a Bach fugue.

It is also a compelling metaphor of what St. Augustine called the City of God and what Martin Luther King, Jr., more recently termed the Beloved Community. L'Engle's merger of the spiritual with the aesthetic—inane and murky though Stravinsky might have found it—is one with which Schiller, Hegel, Schumann, Delacroix and every other exponent of the early nineteen-century Art Religion would have concurred. Where L'Engle distances herself from this Romantic legacy, with the benefit of historical hindsight, is in her awareness of the need to separate the artist from the art. Schumann wrote, "I do not like the man whose life is not in harmony with his work." L'Engle writes, "My mother used to sigh because her beloved Wagner was such a nasty man [...] How do we reconcile atheism, drunkenness, sexual immorality, with strong, beautiful poetry, angelic music, transfigured painting? We human beings don't and that's all there is to it" (*Walking* 125). Granted, but, she also equates holiness with wholeness, the Romantic ideal toward which Schumann was pointing (and that prompted her mother's sigh). "I do not need to be 'qualified' to play a Bach fugue on the piano," writes L'Engle, "and playing a Bach fugue is for me an exercise in wholeness" (*Walking* 71).

In her preference for Bach and Mozart over Chopin and Wagner, L'Engle ignores one half of musical Romanticism which divided into two schools of thought and practice, each of which pursued quite different artistic agendas: the Leipzig School of "conservative" Romantics comprised of Schumann, Mendelssohn, Sterndale-Bennet and Brahms, and the more radical, avant-garde Paris/Weimar School comprised of Chopin, Liszt, Berlioz, and Wagner. Their philosophical and aesthetic differences led, in the second half of the nineteenth century, to a schism that is sometimes referred to as the "War of the Romantics" (see the epilogue to Jan Swafford's *Johannes Brahms: A Biography*). Essentially, the Leipzig School sought to maintain stylistic, formal, and generic continuity with the past of Bach, Mozart, and Beethoven, while the Paris/Weimar School did not. Adopting Liszt's biblical motto, "new skins for new wine" (60), the radical Romantics set out to devise novel forms and genres with which to express their ideas. In retrospect, this division was not as absolute as it appeared at the time, but certainly the spirit that emanated from each is noticeably different and, as Swafford maintains, the cultural victory of the Paris/Weimar aesthetic led to an unanticipated outcome in the twentieth-century, viz. the regrettable chasm that to this day separates classical from popular culture.

The sentimentality and nationalism of Chopin and Wagner as well as the programmatic literalism of Berlioz and Liszt are not really informed by the aesthetic outlook implicit in Schilling and F.W.A. Froebel (philosophy) William Blake and Wordsworth (literature), Schumann (music), and Phillip Otto Runge (painting). Similarly, the loose, programmatically informed musical syntax of the radicals (Chopin excepted) differed sharply from the structural integrity and musical logic practiced by Brahms. This now largely forgotten *guerre de plume* between advocates of programmatic vs. absolute music is only relevant in this context because L'Engle, like many of her generation, painted musical Romanticism with too broad a brushstroke, thereby rejecting aspects of early nineteenth-century thought and feeling that find eloquent expression in her own writings. Not that the wildly passionate, awe-inspiring side of Romanticism made no appeal to L'Engle's imagination. As noted above, she was obviously stirred by the Sublime in Nature and supernature (as her conception of angels attests). Indeed, this aspect of Romanticism is one that in the nineteenth century was shared by conservatives and radicals alike. Nevertheless, her essential outlook and sensibility are more consonant with the transcendental poetry of Wordsworth than with the pessimism of Byron or the fatalism of Tennyson. The Romantic cult of personality with its strong-man ethic—a cult that achieved its apotheosis in the Wagnerolatry of the late nineteenth-century—is fundamentally at odds with the Christian ethics advocated by L'Engle. My point is that her gentle and loving genius has more in common with that of the early German Romantics in literature, painting, and music. The connection between her work and theirs seems quite strong.

Madeleine L'Engle and the Cult of Childhood

When the English Romantic poet William Wordsworth called childhood the seed-time of the soul, he was contributing to a cluster of ideas that would find practical expression in the Kindergarten movement of the German educationist Froebel. What Wordsworth and Froebel have in common is an underlying conception of childhood as a privileged space and of the inner life of children—imaginative and emotional as well as intellectual—as an organic growth. Like a plant, a child's mind and spirit must be nurtured in the educational environment to which it is best suited. For Wordsworth this was nature itself, whereas for Froebel it was an environment that encouraged "spontaneous play and productive activity" as opposed to rote learning. "It is for us," writes Froebel "to see that the child develops, from the first, freely and independently, as complete in himself, and yet as a harmonious part of a larger whole" (Schenk 19). It was this new, more holistic attitude towards children that gave rise to the Romantic Cult of Childhood in literature, music, and painting.

In literature and philosophy, the governing concept was that of the *Bildungsreise*, a German term for the circular journey of education. Cultural historian and literary critic M. H. Abrams writes, "Coleridge said that if we see that 'the nurture and evolution of humanity is the final aim,' we recognize that its course is that of a circuitous journey'" (191). Moreover, just as the maturity of humanity itself describes an ascending spiral in which we are led through progressive cycles of repetition that bring us back to a more enlightened version of where we started, so too does a child negotiate the difficult transition from childhood to adulthood through a series of repeated experiences. According to this paradigm, maturity is seen not in terms of a linear progression in which past experience is discarded as mere stepping stone, but rather our childhood experience accompanies us as a source of information as well as inspiration throughout our adult lives. This series of recurrent episodes is determined by individual character (character, according to the Romantic poet Novalis, is destiny). It is our ideally ever-more nuanced and appropriate response to them that is the measure of our maturity. Meg Murry and Vicky Austin are characters who frequently find themselves precipitated into crises dictated by their own intemperate natures.

Learning to face the often painful consequences of their reckless words and actions is the substance of their *Bildungsreise*. It is worth noting that some of L'Engle's favorite authors, judging from the frequency with which they are mentioned and referenced in her writings (e.g., the Brontë sisters, Charlotte and Emily) construct plots that describe such circuitous journeys. The opening chapters of both *Jane Eyre* and *Wuthering Heights* depicts the actions and characters of their heroines and villains as children, thereby establishing a reference point against which their progress toward maturity (or the lack of same) can be measured. Similarly (and long before Freud) novels by Dickens, such as *David Copperfield* and *Great Expectations*, traced the *Bildungsreise* of their central characters to childhood traumas. Indeed, it is their ability or inability to transcend these traumas, by integrating them into their adult lives that marks their personal development and growth. Gothic heroes often follow a trajectory that leads from trauma to either transcendence or what the Swiss psychoanalyst C. G. Jung termed *Enantiodromia* (the reversal into the opposite). In supernatural Gothic narratives, such as *Frankenstein* or *The Strange Case of Dr. Jekyll and Mr. Hyde* this reversal occurs when the principal character can no longer control the process of transformation from human into monster. In each instance, as Uncle Douglas says to Vicky Austin with reference to the Holocaust, "Man exercised the freedom of choice to do wrong, and innocent people paid for it…" (*Moon by Night* 169).

Originally, the Cult of Childhood found expression in the fairytales and folktales by authors such as the brothers Grimm, Hans Christian Anderson, and Goethe. These *Hausmärchen*, or household fairytales as they were called in German, were soon supplemented by narratives in the manner of fairytales, or *Kunstmärchen* (artistic fairytales for adults) such as Dickens's holiday classic, *A Christmas Carol*. This generic distinction may be found in the music as well as the literature of the Romantic era. Robert Schumann (1810–1856) composed both *Scenes from Childhood* and *The Album for the Young*. The former was the musical equivalent of *Jane Eyre*, i.e., a pianistically sophisticated attempt to capture the inner life of children as filtered through adult memory. Hence, this cycle of thirteen short character pieces with programmatic titles such as "a Child Falling Asleep" is a musical *Kunstmärchen* intended for performance by adults, while the *Album for the Young* (a collection of forty-three programmatic character pieces intended for performance by children) is a musical *Hausmärchen*. Speaking of this musical Cult of Childhood, Schumann's biographer Marcel Brion asks rhetorically, "Is it possible to speak to children without at the same time speaking to the child that lies buried in in oneself?" (48). L'Engle would clearly answer in the negative. Addressing this very topic she writes:

> I need not belabor the point that to retain our childlike openness does not mean to be childish. Only the most mature of us are able to be childlike, and to be childlike involves memory; we must never forget any part of ourselves. As of this writing I am sixty-one years old in chronology. But I am not an isolated, chronological numerical statistic. I am sixty-one, and I am also four, and twelve, and fifteen, and twenty-three, and thirty-one, and forty-five ... and ... and.... Jesus told his friends and disciples over and over again that not only were they to let the little children come to him, but that they were to be like little children themselves [*Walking* 74].

Brion also touches on the connection between the Romantic Cult of Childhood and Christianity when he writes, "Happy childhood, enthusiastic childhood so ready to be touched [...] by that sacred language in which all things and beings speak direct to the child-heart, the Word becoming God" (13, 50). This remark suggests that the origin of the Romantic Cult of Childhood can be traced to those biblical passages in which Christ signals out children as role-models for all who would enter the Kingdom of God.

In summary then, most of L'Engle's books for and about young people are *Kunstmärchen*, artistic fairytales designed to appeal both to the young as well as the young at heart. "When I am grappling with ideas which are radical enough to upset grownups," writes L'Engle, "then I am likely to put these ideas into a story which will be marketed for children, because children understand what their parents have rejected or forgotten" (*Walking* 110). Another modern master of the adult fairy tale genre, J. R. R. Tolkien has some pertinent things to say about it. His conception of art, like that of L'Engle, is anchored in religious faith. A devout Catholic, Tolkien believed that human creativity was one of humanity's highest, most God-like attributes. Just as God created the primary world we all inhabit, humans possess the ability to create secondary worlds of fantasy and fairytale with words, sounds, and colors. These, in turn, provide three basic and useful functions: escape from the brutalities of "what man has made of man," consolation for the sense of loss to which our fallen human nature inevitably gives rise, and recovery of the world as it is meant to be, i.e., the world as God intended it to be (*Tolkien Reader* 55–73). It is one of the core tenets of Christianity as well as of the Romantic imagination that the world is neither as it appears to be, nor as it should be. Through engagement with stories that spring from the baptized imaginations of creative authors such as L'Engle and Tolkien, we are reminded of our potential for redemption, to affirm the divine pattern by correcting the grotesque distortions of that pattern that result from the inappropriate application of free will. In all of her work, but in her science fiction fantasies especially, L'Engle makes explicit use of this concept of sin as a deviation from a cosmic pattern. Through having her young hero Charles Wallace travel on the back of the unicorn Gaudior in *A Swiftly Tilting Planet* to different "Whens," Wheres," and "Might-Have-Beens," L'Engle is able to track wrong or dangerous choices made over millennia to their outcome—in this instance, the imminent threat of thermonuclear war posed by a mad South American dictator.

An argument can be made that the Romantic Cult of Childhood, like the Art Religion to which it belonged, was corrupted by some of its late exponents in the second half of the nineteenth century. The notion of the child-mind, in the hands of writers such as James Barrie, turned into something else entirely. Peter Pan represents not an escape to a saner, healthier alternative reality—a temporary respite from the brutalities and inequities of the world as well as a compass that points to necessary course corrections on our journey from youth to maturity—but rather a nostalgic flight from adulthood, a narcissistic refuge from responsibility. Peter Pan is an archetype, not of the Child Within, but of a sentimental yearning to avoid the pain that the process of maturation inevitably entails. Sentimentality is not excessive or insincere emotion so much as it is inappropriate emotion. Both the Art Religion and the Cult of Childhood recognized the legitimacy of trans-rational modes of perception such as intuition, revelation, artistic afflatus, and powerful emotion. The Romantic child—as a literary archetype—by virtue of its innocence, vulnerability, imagination and sense of wonder, is often portrayed as enjoying access to radical possibilities that those preoccupied with the limiting rationalities of science, capitalism, technology, and realpolitik are apt to deny. But the authentic exponents of this archetype (including L'Engle) never use it to suggest a rejection of the ethical responsibilities that maturity implies. On the contrary, the character of Sporos, the recalcitrant farandola in *A Wind in the Door*, typifies the selfishness of those who, like Peter Pan, desire to assert their individuality at the expense of the common welfare as well as their own development.

Sporos, this microscopic creature, in its refusal to join the dance, i.e., to affirm God's cosmic pattern, can perhaps be understood as a commentary on the counter-culture of the 1960s with its understandable, if lamentable, excess of hedonism, drugs, artistic primitivism, anti-intellectualism, and anarchist politics. This anti-war sub-culture devolved from the naïve pacifism of "flower power" and a facile interest in Zen Buddhism into the pointless self-indulgence now associated with the "Woodstock Generation." Indeed, it has been argued by social critics such as Christopher Lasch that American culture has progressively given way to a Sporos-like condition of radical narcissism with adults seeking to emulate the fads and fashions of youth. What else are we to make of modern pop-culture's preoccupation with sexuality, the aesthetic banality of its music, and its use of drugs—to name only a few of the less savory legacies of the youth counter-culture of the 1960s. Madeleine L'Engle first achieved international recognition during a time when a generation inspired by the leadership of JFK recognized and challenged this anti-democratic shift—a challenge that failed for reasons that by now should be obvious. In her adolescent science fiction—*A Wrinkle in Time, A Wind in the Door,* and *A Swiftly Tilting Planet*—she addresses obliquely the political issues that shaped her America from a unique, though not—as we will see—an unprecedented, perspective. It is a perspective that—while recognizing not only the horrors of war but those that lead to war—also affirms that "if love is stronger than hate [and according to L'Engle it is], then war is not all there is" (*Walking* 53).

The Premature Death of Wonder: L'Engle's Romantic Synthesis of Science and Religion

One of the seldom discussed casualties of war is language. Writing of this, L'Engle says, "In time of war language always dwindles, vocabulary is lost, and we live in a century of war [...] Dante, writing in exile when dukedoms and principalities were embroiled in wars, was forging language as he wrote his great science-fiction fantasies" (*Walking* 38). So too was L'Engle attempting to repair the depredations of a century of war in her own science-fiction fantasies. Presumably what she had in mind in alluding to Dante was his great epic poem, *The Divine Comedy*. Her characterization of this artistic and theological masterpiece as science-fiction may give some readers pause, but of course the dividing line between science and religion was not as sharply drawn in Dante's time as it would later become. The atheistic materialism and mechanistic reductionism so often associated with science is historically a product of nineteenth- and early-twentieth-century thinking. The famous Oxford debate in 1860 between Huxley and Wilberforce was in retrospect probably the decisive cultural moment at which religion's claim to intellectual parity with science was routed. From then until the mid–twentieth century, when the dark side of science was revealed at Hiroshima and Nagasaki, the negative view of religion popularized during the Enlightenment (i.e., religion as an obsolete relic of a pre-scientific era) was the consensus view adopted by Western intellectuals.

Needless to say, such was not the case in antiquity, when both science and religion were widely viewed as complementary approaches to understanding a cosmos whose divine origin was assumed. Increasingly over the centuries, however, science and religion came into conflict as the Cartesian dichotomy of mind/matter leading to Sir Isaac Newton's clockwork universe gained credence. The scientific world view ended up, at the start of the twentieth century, with a universe comprised of dead matter governed by laws without a law giver. As for human consciousness, an inconvenient truth that didn't conform to this model of reality, "Well," it was reasoned, "the brain secretes thoughts the way the liver secrets bile and let's just leave it at that." Such a consensus left little room for the trans-rationality of Romantic heroes, the painful mysteries of the Gothic imagination, or the wonderment of childhood. Indeed, there were those who believed that empiricism and materialism combined would soon provide a comprehensive answer to the ultimate question of the Universe, All, and Everything (though alas, "42," as Douglas Adams asserts in his burlesque science fiction *The Hitchhiker's Guide to the Galaxy* wasn't it). A corollary of this belief was an *a priori* certainty that the "more things in heaven and earth" of which Hamlet dreamt were nonexistent. According to such self-styled agnostics as Thomas Huxley, what could not be proven by empirical science was either unreal or unimportant. Unfortunately, those who subscribed to this circular line of reasoning failed to realize that a Jewish mathematician residing in Switzerland was about to point out that energy equals mass times the speed of light squared, thereby shattering the prevailing consensus. Pondering this revolutionary equation and its implications for our understanding of time, L'Engle's Polly O'Keefe in *An Acceptable Time* wonders, "What did Einstein's equation really mean?" (312). The plot of *A Wind in the Door* links the potentially terminal illness of young Charles Wallace Murry to a "cosmic scream" emitted by vanishing stars in galaxies, stars that are being "Xed" by Echthroi (the cosmic forces of negation). In L'Engle's universe, as in that of early German Romantics such as Schelling, microcosm and macrocosm are inseparably linked. But can matter be annihilated? According to Einstein's theorem the answer is no, as Mrs. Murry explains. Energy can be converted into matter and vice versa, but not destroyed. "Einstein's law has never been disproved," says Mrs. Murry. "But it's coming into question." "Nothingness," exclaims her skeptical son Dennys, "That's impossible." "One would hope so," his mother replies" (*Wind* 38).

Whatever else Einstein's mystifying formula might mean, it meant to succeeding generations of scientists that there most certainly were more things in heaven and earth—more at any rate than the late-nineteenth century consensus was prepared to admit. As Einstein and those who followed him into the mysterious worlds of astrophysics and Quantum physics demonstrated, the imminent demise of wonder proclaimed by those who anticipated the immanent omniscience of science was woefully premature. In *Walking on Water*, L'Engle says:

> We simply do not understand time [...] Lewis Carroll expressed a profound truth when he had the Mad Hatter say, "If you know time as well as I do, you wouldn't be talking about wasting it"[...] Lewis Carroll was a story-teller, an artist as well as a mathematician, and artists often have a more profound sense of what time is all than do scientists [*Walking* 95–96].

Elsewhere in the same book she writes, "Non-linear space/time is more easily understood by poets and saints than by reasonable folk" (87). In thus linking the trans-rationality of poets and saints with the mathematical genius of Einstein, she underscores an age-old connection between the spiritual, the aesthetic, and the scientific (in the highest sense) that was, for a time lost to Western civilization, a connection that, following the Enlightenment, was first rediscovered by early-nineteenth century Romantics such as the German writers and philosophers such Friedrich Schelling. As Papegeno (Seth Cook) says in *Troubling a Star*, "It is a good and chastening thing that the human being knows a great deal less than we thought we did a hundred years ago" (173). It is ironic that at a time when science has, in part, overcome its late nineteenth-century hubris, a reactionary strain of Christianity has reasserted the hubris of religion.

Writing of Schelling, cultural historian Roger Cardinal says, "Schelling's Nature Philosophy was an invitation to scientists to translate phenomena into coherent meaning by elucidating, as it were, the deeper syntax beneath the confused calligraphy of the surface" (34). He goes on to quote a passage from *The Apprentices at Sais*, an unfinished novel by Novalis, in which the author discusses the interconnectedness of all things in a way that might have come straight from the pages of L'Engle:

> That marvelous secret writing that one finds everywhere, upon wings, egg-shells, in clouds, in snow, crystals, and the structure of stones, on water when it freezes, on the inside and outside of mountains, of plants, of animals, of human beings, in the constellations of the sky, on pieces of pitch or glass when touched or rubbed, in iron fillings grouped about a magnet, and in the strange conjunctions of chance [34–35].

Commenting on this passage, Cardinal notes, "It is as though the macrocosm were composed of an infinite number of perfect microcosms" (35). This, of course, is precisely the point of L'Engle's adolescent science fiction. In the space/time adventures of Meg Murry, Charles Wallace, Polly O'Keefe, their parents and grandparents, the reader enters a world in which the barriers that seem to separate times, places, and accepted categories of reality are erased. Through the tesseract, vast expanses of space are bridged, Mrs. Whatsit, now a person, was once a supposedly inanimate object (a star). Events that occurred in the distant past relative to the temporal setting of the principal characters influence the present and vice versa. Events that transpire at a cellular level affect the fate of galaxies and the destiny of earth (the shadowed planet) hinges on the loving and moral character of a young woman (age doesn't matter) willing to risk being "Xed," by Echthroi in order to "name," (i.e., affirm) a punctilious and seemingly insignificant school administrator (worldly rank and position don't matter) with an indispensable part to play in upholding the divine pattern. In L'Engle's world—a world in which "creative scientists and saints expect revelation and do not fear it. Neither do children" (*Walking* 76). No one, including Mr. Jenkins, is insignificant.

Writing of science during the early Romantic age, Richard Holmes says, "Romanticism as a cultural force is generally regarded as intensely hostile to science [...] but I do not believe that this was always the case." He goes on to say:

> The notion of an infinite, mysterious Nature, waiting to be discovered or seduced into revealing all her secrets, was widely held [...] There was too, a subtle reaction against the idea of a purely mechanistic universe, the mathematical world of Newtonian physics, the hard material world of objects and impacts. These doubts, expressed especially in Germany, favored a softer 'dynamic' science of invisible powers and mysterious energies, of fluidity and transformations, of growth and organic change [xvii-xviii].

In short, Romantic science, in its embrace of wonder, anticipated the post–Einstein paradigm shift toward the "holographic universe" of physicist David Bohm. In Bohm's theory, with its "implicate orders of reality," the world of nature functions like a holographic image. In such a world, William Blake's intuition that there is a universe implicit in a grain of sand is scientifically justified. "Indeed," as author Michael Talbot affirms, "Bohm believes that our almost universal tendency to fragment the world and ignore *the dynamic interconnectedness of all things* [emphasis added] is responsible for many of our problems, not only in science but in our lives and society as well" (49). It is this modern paradigm upon which L'Engle draws for many of her theological insights. She does so unapologetically, citing Archbishop William Temple to the effect that "it is a great mistake to think that God is chiefly interested in religion" (*Walking* 132). She was, however, by no means unaware of the mechanistic, pre–Einstein paradigm and the dangers it posed. In her own words:

> It strikes me that perhaps I am elevating scientists and down-grading theologians, and that is not true, nor fair. For the few scientists who live by revelation there are many more who are no more than technicians, who are terrified of the wide world outside the laboratory, and who trust nothing they cannot prove. Amazing things may happen in their test tubes and retorts, but only the rare few see the implications beyond the immediate experiment. They cannot trust further than their own senses, and this lack of trust is often caught by the rest of us [*Walking* 76].

This is the dark science of nuclear, biological, and psychological warfare that—together with the ever more sophisticated technologies of surveillance—has threatened human survival and undermined democracy.

The Unity of Art, Spirituality and Politics

I recount these developments in this context because Madeleine L'Engle, who grappled obliquely with the rise of a national security culture, was, in her own loving and thoughtful way, a counter-cultural voice. What this has to do with historical Romanticism will be explained presently. *A Wrinkle in Time*, for instance, deals with a journey undertaken by Meg Murry and her younger brother Charles Wallace (together with Meg's future husband Calvin O'Keefe) to Camazotz, a distant planet presided over by a personification of evil identified simply as IT. Meg's scientist father is being held prisoner in the bowels of a sprawling, high-security labyrinth known as the C.C.I. (an acronym for CENTRAL Central Intelligence). C.C.I. obviously invites comparison with another well-known acronym within the intelligence community just as Camazotz itself gives rise to an unavoidable comparison with American society during the Cold War era. It's not a flattering portrayal. Indeed, in defiance of the prevailing norms that governed children's literature at the time it was written, *A Wrinkle in Time* sounds all of the themes that define the political Gothic imagination: conspiracies, subversive narratives, abusive power, and the correct balance between ends and the means used to achieve them. Camazotz may be a corruption of Camelot—mythical home to the fabled King Arthur as well as a convenient shorthand for a nominally democratic political order threatened with dissolution. The society presided over by IT, a disembodied brain of the sort popularized in numerous science-fiction films of the 1950s, is a dystopian nightmare of conformity in which all houses are identical to one another and children play in the same way at the same time each day. Conformity is mandatory and those who fail to comply are promptly dealt with by agents of the C.C.I.

In combating IT's attempt at brainwashing, Meg loudly recites the Declaration of Independence to which her young brother (temporarily possessed by IT) replies, "But that is exactly what we have on Camazotz. Complete equality, everybody exactly alike." In a sudden moment of insight, Meg replies triumphantly that "like and equal are not the same thing at all!" (146). Meg's Jeffersonian insight proves short lived however. Resentful of a father whom she had assumed would relieve her of responsibility, she lashes out at his alleged betrayal and the unfairness of life generally. Spiritually damaged by an encounter with the evil Black Thing, Meg is revived by the loving ministrations of a tentacled, highly maternal monster named Aunt Beast who remarks wisely, "She was almost taken by the Black Thing. Sometimes we can't know what spiritual damage it leaves even when physical recovery is complete" (171). Whatever the damage, Meg ultimately volunteers to risk the terror and pain of the Black Thing once again in order to rescue her brother. This act of sacrificial love (a quality possessed by Meg that IT utterly lacks) is also ultimately an act of freedom understood as a spiritual as well as a political value. Her sacrifice is undertaken despite intense terror and against the dictates of reason because, as L'Engle points out in quoting from St. Paul, "The foolishness of God is wiser than men; and the weakness of God is stronger than men" (182). In comparing such freedom to an act of artistic creation, viz., the writing of a sonnet, Mrs. Whatsit (one of her guardian angels) says, "You're given the form, but you have to write the sonnet yourself. What you say is completely up to you" (179). By thus conflating the political, the artistic, and the spiritual, L'Engle exhibits once again her Romantic commitment to an agenda having to do with atonement (at-one-ment), i.e., the reintegration of categories that were separated and compartmentalized culturally by the analytical mentality of the Enlightenment.

Conclusion

Though the early Romantic Movement was not homogeneous in its politics, it did represent a concerted, if short-lived, counter-culture to that spawned by post–Enlightenment developments in science and industry. Speaking of what he terms "the Victorian Compromise," whereby the political revolutions that shook America and Europe were averted in England, G. K. Chesterton writes of, "the trend of the English Romantics to carry out the revolutionary idea not savagely in works, but very wildly indeed in words" (201). Though political revolution did break out in Germany in 1848, what was true of England in the first half of the nineteenth century was also true of Germany. It was the German Romantics in literature, music, and painting who sought to realize through their art the freedom of mind and spirit that had inspired revolution in America and France prior to the oppressive era of Prince Metternich. Like L'Engle, early German Romantics such as Novalis sought a spiritual rebirth that might, at least, have mitigated the ravages of war to which nationalist ideology gave rise. In his prophetic essay *Christendom or Europe*, Novalis writes:

> Who knows whether there has been enough of war? But it will never come to an end unless someone grasps the palm branch, which a spiritual power alone can offer. Blood will wash over Europe until the nations perceive the fearful madness which is driving them about in a circle; until, arrested by *holy music* [italics mine], and soothed, they approach former altars in multi-hued fusion and undertake works of

peace; until a great feast of love is celebrated as a festival of peace amid hot tears upon smoking battlefields [...] The other continents await Europe's reconciliation and resurrection in order to join with it and become fellow citizens of the heavenly kingdom [...] Christendom must come alive again and be effective, and, without regard to national boundaries, again form a visible Church which will take into its bosom all souls athirst for the supernatural, and willingly become a mediatrix between the old world and the new [...] It will, it must come, that sacred time of endless peace [61–63].

Making allowances for the differing styles of eloquence applicable to the different eras in which they lived and the bitter experience of history that separated them, Novalis's Romantic hymn to peace, progress, and the reintegration of the religious with the artistic and the political is essentially identical to that of L'Engle. The political idealism of Enlightenment thinkers soon gave way, however, to a strong tide of nationalism. The Enlightenment focus on "inalienable human rights" was replaced by a new spirit of tribalism according to which individual worth was conflated with national identity and patriotism replaced loyalty to the cosmopolitan ideals of liberty, equality, and fraternity. Thus, a short-lived season of liberal hope spawned by Enlightenment thinkers (and later, as Chesterton affirms, sublimated by Romantic artists) was suppressed by reactionary monarchist forces in Europe and preempted by a growing wave of tribal sentiment in favor of king and country. This pattern would be repeated in modern American history. In his famous American University Address in 1963 Kennedy, echoing the words of Novalis, asked: "What kind of peace do we mean and what kind of peace do we seek? Not a *Pax Americana* enforced on the world by military weapons of war [...] not just peace in our time, but peace for all time" (460). A very different vision for America and the world prevailed after Dallas. My point is that the traumatic decades of the 1950s and 1960s followed by a sudden, violent turning to the Right in America were revisiting a pattern that characterized European cultural and political history in the first half of the nineteenth century.

"The sickness of the shadow that darkened the earth," so vividly described in *A Wrinkle in Time* (83) is more oppressive and opaque than ever. As during the period of early European Romanticism, the aspirations of those who sought to dispel it by promoting a peaceful and integrated culture in which people would live in peace and harmony with God, nature and one another were frustrated. They made the attempt not by political but by artistic means. Writing in 1974, cultural historian Jacques Barzun points to the parallels between the early Romantic creed and the Romantic resurgence of the 1960s counter-culture. William Blake summarizes the Romantic creed as follows:

The Eternal Body of Man is The Imagination, that is God himself [...] It manifests itself in Works of Art. Where any view of money exists, Art cannot be carried on, but War only. A Poet, a Painter, A Musician, an Architect: The Man or Woman who is not one of these is not a Christian. Christianity is Art and not Money. Money is its curse. The Whole Business of Man Is the Arts [...] Art is the Tree of Life [...] Science is the Tree of Death.

Commenting on this litany, Barzun observes, "The doctrine has a familiar ring to those who have listened to the rebel young in these latter years. At the 1968 demonstrations in Chicago, the main group uttered a program in 25 articles of which two were: "The abolition of money and 'Every man an artist'" (36). Though she would certainly have disagreed that only artists can be Christian, Madeleine L'Engle, though not an overtly political writer, once again used the art of story-telling on behalf of realizing a similar vision of what she calls the "coming kingdom" and what Martin Luther King referred to as "the beloved community."

The Romantic Art Religion against which Stravinsky railed and that L'Engle rejected was associated with Wagner. But this nationalistic, egotistical, and racist expression of late Romanticism had little in common with the idealistic spirit and extravagant optimism of first generation Romantics such as Schumann, Mendelssohn, Caspar David Friedrich and Novalis. True, a darker strain of pessimism and Gothic pain is to be found in early Romantics such as Lord Byron, Chopin and Delacroix, but such pain is an inevitable corollary of living in a world that is neither as it appears to be nor as it should be. As L'Engle asks, "Could Beethoven have written that glorious paean of praise in the Ninth Symphony if he had not had to endure the dark closing of deafness?" (*Walking* 62). To the Romantic imagination, trauma is a catalyst to introspection and critical self-examination, both of which are necessary to transcending our Gothic dilemmas. Just as the resurrection presupposes the cross, the price of spiritual renewal following our violations of the divine pattern presupposes suffering. No tenet of Christianity is more difficult to sustain at times than the faith that even the most excruciating pain can serve a deeper good, depending upon our response to it; and that the burden of transforming—through a combination of memory and imagination—pain into self-knowledge is perhaps our highest spiritual calling.

The mystery and incomprehensibility of the human psyche—that we are fundamentally strangers to one another as well as ourselves—is the foundation of Gothic psychology. In Romantic art this idea is often conveyed through imagery that makes use of masks, as in a masquerade ball. Indeed, the masked ball or carnival is a central image in the musico-literary art of Robert Schumann as well as in novels such as *Villette* by Charlotte Brontë and short stories such as Poe's *The Mask of the Red Death*. Writing of this Romantic theme, L'Engle says, "Our identity is hidden, even from ourselves [...] the doctrine that we are made after the image of God proclaims that the human being is fundamentally a mystery [...] Complicated creatures we are, aware of only the smallest fragment of ourselves" (Walking 129–131).

It is on this basis—rather than some sentimental and unrealistic notion of philanthropy—that we are enjoined to refrain from casting stones and to turn the other cheek. Both Romanticism and Christianity acknowledge the Jekyll and Hyde duality of mankind. For all his many defects as well as his admirable qualities, Zachary Gray in *An Acceptable Time* deserves our compassion because his fate, i.e., his transformation from man to monster, is potentially one that any of us might experience. That transformation, and the process by which it occurs, can overtake societies as well as individuals.

In *A Swiftly Tilting Planet*—which is perhaps L'Engle's most complex and incarnational representation of the unity of art, spirituality and politics—she has an anguished veteran of the Civil War say, "I went to war thinking of myself as Galahad, out to free fellow human beings from the intolerable bondage of slavery. But it wasn't as simple as that. There were other, less pure issues being fought over, with little concern for the souls which would perish for nothing more grand than political greed, corruption, and conniving for power.... Oh God, it was brother against brother, Cain and Abel all over again" (243). Obviously, L'Engle shared with Jim Wallis a belief that "Christ commits Christians to a strong presumption against war" (Wallis 153). Indeed, there are those such as Tolstoy, Dominic Crossan, David Ray Griffen, and James W. Douglas who either affirm or else imply that Christ's opposition to violence was unconditional. As we can infer from the death of Ron James in *The Other Side of the Sun*, L'Engle was not an absolutist in her stance against violence.

The peace-loving counter-culture of Romanticism in the early part of the nineteenth century and the peace-oriented counter-culture of the 1960s were incarnational moments in Western cultural and political history. Both affirmed human creativity as a divine gift by means of which we might hope to counter demonic influences. In this respect, Madeleine L'Engle, who contributed to the mini-Romantic revival of the Kennedy era, was what Romantics such as Goethe and Schumann called a "kindred spirit." Her rejection of Wagner, like her embrace of Bach and Mozart, were to some extent simply a reflection of the anti–Romantic age in which she lived. Just as emotionalism of nineteenth-century art is best understood as a reaction against the excessive emotional restraint of eighteenth-century art, twentieth century advocates of modernism sought to define themselves in relation to their Romantic predecessors. Nevertheless, all art worthy of the name is an affirmation of cosmos over chaos. All artists in moments of decision try to make what seems to be the most loving, the most creative decision (*Walking* 153). But what anti–Romantic Romantics like L'Engle recognized, and many first generation Romantics did not, is that the creative imagination can be not only the antidote to a narrow rationality but a tool for the promotion of evil.

In his essay on the fairy tale, Tolkien identifies what he terms the *Eucat-*

astrophe as a defining characteristic of the genre. The *Eucatrastrophe* is the unexpected happy ending, in opposition to the expected unhappy endings of Greek tragedy. In as much as the story of Christ is one that is fraught with trials, hardships, and suffering but ends in an unexpected triumph, it is—as many of its staunchest critics contend—a fairy tale. The faith of which Madeleine L'Engle speaks is precisely an existential decision to live as if life were a true fairy tale, to be child-like enough to search out underlying patterns to the seeming chaos of life, as if, to cite one of her favorites, Lady Julian of Norwich, "All shall be well and all shall be well and all manner of things shall be well." L'Engle's heroine Vicky Austin, is a child/adolescent whose faith enables her to explore the uncharted waters of the Antarctica, because, "A Child is not afraid of new ideas, does not have to worry about the status quo or rocking the boat, is willing to set sail in uncharted waters" (*Walking* 117). That is why, according to L'Engle, "the opposite of sin can only be faith and never virtue" (*Walking* 148) and why Christianity, for L'Engle, is ultimately a choice between hope and cynicism. Writing of the importance of hope, Jim Wallis says, "Most important of all is the spiritual power of hope, which may be the only thing that can finally overcome our too characteristic cynicism. Hope vs. cynicism is the key moral and political choice of our time" (7). For Christians such as L'Engle, belief in God is an existential choice, because, as one of her characters expresses it, "there isn't any point to life without him" (*Moon by Night* 169). At the very conclusion of *Troubling a Star*, a Celtic harpist sings a lilting, somewhat humorous poem by Vicky Austin, dealing with the ability to see the extraordinary in the ordinary. It might serve as Madeleine L'Engle's final commentary on faith, story, life, and death:

> *If it has feathers I give you my word*
> *It won't be a dolphin, it won't be a whale.*
> *It may be an angel, it may be a bird;*
> *Whatever it is, it can tell us a tale.*
> *It may be a penguin, it won't be a seal,*
> *It may point to a place where a song is dwelling.*
> *If it's an angel I'm sure its real*
> *And will give us a story worth the telling*
> *It gives us no answers, it promises naught*
> *Except that we all have a say in the words,*
> *If it has feathers, we've all been taught*
> *It may be the most unexpected of birds!*

WORKS CITED

Abrams, M. H. *Natural Supernaturalism*. New York: W.W. Norton, 1971. Print.
Barzun, Jacques. *The Use and Abuse of Art*. Princeton: Princeton University Press, 1975. Print.
Bernstein, Leonard. *The Unanswered Question*. Cambridge: Harvard University Press, 1976. Print.

132 Dimensions of Madeleine L'Engle

Blake, William. "Appendix to the Prophetic Books" (from Blake's Engraving of the Laocoön). *Poetical Works* (1908). Bartelby.com. Web.
Brion, Marcel. *Schumann and the Romantic Age*. London: Collins, 1956. Print.
Byron, George Gordon. *Byron's Poetry* "Manfred," Act 1, Scene 1. New York: W.W. Norton, 1978. Print.
Cardinal, Roger. *German Romanticism in Context*. London: Cassell & Collier Macmillan Publishers, 1975. Print.
Chesterton, G.K. *The Everyman Chesterton*, "The Victorian Age in Literature." New York: Alfred A. Knopf, 2011. Print.
Holmes, Richard. *The Age of Wonder: How the Romantic Generation Discovered the Beauty and Terror of Science*. London: HarperCollins, 2008. Print.
Kennedy, John F. *Public Papers of the Presidents of the United States: John F. Kennedy, 1961–1963*, vol. III. Washington, D.C.: Government Printing Office, 1964. Print.
L'Engle, Madeleine. *An Acceptable Time*. New York: Farrar, Straus, Giroux, 1989. Print.
_____. *The Moon by Night*. New York: Bantam Doubleday Dell, 1963. Print.
_____. *A Swiftly Tilting Planet*. New York: Bantam Doubleday Dell, 1978. Print.
_____. *Troubling a Star*. New York: Farrar, Straus, Giroux, 1994. Print.
_____. *Walking on Water: Reflections on Faith and Art*. New York: Bantam Books, 1980. Print.
_____. *A Wind in the Door*. New York: Bantam Doubleday Dell, 1973. Print.
_____. *A Wrinkle in Time*. New York: Bantam Doubleday Dell, 1962. Print.
_____. *The Young Unicorns*. New York: Farrar, Straus, Giroux, 1968. Print.
Lewis, Sinclair. *It Can't Happen Here*. New York: Penguin Books, 1935. Print.
Liszt, Franz. "Berlioz und seine *Harold-Symphonie*" (1882). *Aus des Annalen des Fortschritts. Konzert und –kammermusikalischen Essays*. Leipzig: Breitkopf und Härtel, 1978. Print.
Novalis, *Hymns to the Night and Other Selected Writings*. Tr. Charles E. Passage. Indianapolis: Bobbs-Merrill, 1960. Print.
Pepetone, Gregory G. "Angels, Echthroi, and Celestial Music in the Adolescent Science Fiction of Madeleine L'Engle." *Religion and Science Fiction*. Ed. James F. McGrath. Eugene, OR: Pickwick Publications, 2011. 154–16. Print.
_____. *Gothic Perspectives on the American Experience*. New York: Peter Lang, 2003. Print.
Schenk, H.G. *The Mind of the European Romantics*. Oxford: Oxford University Press, 1979. Print.
Schumann, Robert. *On Music and Musicians*. New York: W.W. Norton, 1946. Print.
Stravinsky, Igor. *An Autobiography*. New York: Simon & Schuster, 1936. Print.
Talbot, Michael. *The Holographic Universe*. London: HarperCollins, 1991. Print.
Taruskin, Richard. *Music in the Early Twentieth Century*. Oxford: Oxford University Press, 2010. Print.
Tolkien, J.R.R. *The Tolkien Reader*. New York: Ballantine, 1966. Print.
Wallis, Jim. *God's Politics: Why the Right Gets It Wrong and the Left Doesn't Get It*. San Francisco: HarperCollins, 2005. Print.

Discarded Image and Expanding Universe
The (Meta)physics of C.S. Lewis and Madeleine L'Engle

NAOMI WOOD

Madeleine L'Engle's classic young adult novel *A Wrinkle in Time* (1962) depicts a universe infinitely large and yet navigable. Vastness coexists with the minute; "retired stars" Mrs. Whatsit, Mrs. Which, and Mrs. Who counsel human children Meg and Charles Wallace Murry and Calvin O'Keefe in their quest to rescue the Murrys' father. Theoretical physics provides the model for traveling, but motive and soul is emotive: love is the ground of the cosmos. In L'Engle's sequel *A Wind in the Door* (1973), Meg enters her brother's infinitesimal mitochondria, where she witnesses the dance of life mirroring cosmic order. Though based on contemporary science, L'Engle's images frequently share marked similarities to the scientifically discredited Ptolemaic model of the universe beloved of medieval and renaissance thinkers—and of C.S. Lewis. Lewis's space trilogy, beginning with *Out of the Silent Planet* (1938) and the *Chronicles of Narnia* (1950-56) depict planets and stars as conscious, their movement ordered by reason as well as gravity. Both L'Engle and Lewis conceive of sublime order behind apparent disorder, meaning emerging out of meaninglessness, music and life animating the depths of space.

L'Engle acknowledged Lewis as an inspiration for her own writing, and the two writers shared interests in music, fantasy, metaphysics, and apologetics. Their differences, though, are perhaps even more significant. They highlight the challenges of faith during a secular era, especially of articulating the significance of humanity's place in the universe. Lewis's work promotes a view of the universe chosen for its beauty over its scientific validity. He criticizes science's hubristic aspects, especially its efforts to analyze, break apart, and control the inner workings of nature. Humanity's refusal to submit to natural limits, Lewis warns, can lead to no good. L'Engle, by contrast, imagines scientists as heroes and scientific research as encouraging religious wonder and awe. In her Newbery Award acceptance speech L'Engle enthusiastically referenced Hoyle's theory of the universe "in which matter is continuously being created, with the universe expanding but not dissipating" ("Expanding" 258). For her, science opens the way to religious belief, first by asking the questions posed by children and philosophers and saints, such as "Why am I here? Does my life have any meaning?" (Wintle 256); and second by answering them in complex and powerful ways that recognize the magnitude of the universe and the mystery of matter and energy. In a 1979 interview with the Evangelical monthly magazine *Christianity Today* she says, "Reading Einstein and Eddington [...] opened up a world where I could conceive of a loving God who really could note the fall of every sparrow and count the hairs on every head" ("Allegorical" 17).

This essay compares the metaphysical science fiction and fantasy of C.S. Lewis and Madeleine L'Engle by contextualizing their common themes and imagery. While critics have long noted the similarities between the two authors (see, for example, Carter, Hein, Patterson, Steem), their differences have not been as extensively considered. L'Engle is much more than an American follower of C.S. Lewis's tradition of Christian fantasy, even if both have been embraced by the Evangelical community. Joined by church affiliation and aesthetic sensibility, Lewis and L'Engle nonetheless differ significantly in their depictions of science, their understanding of humanity's place in the universe, and their epistemologies; these differences have consequences for individual, social, and political ethics.

The Cultural Work of Science and Religion

Though Lewis began his academic life as an atheist, his philosophical interests led him to idealism and thence to theism and Christianity (Lewis, *Surprised*; McGrath). He returned to the Anglican Church in 1930. Having determined to his own satisfaction that the supernatural did exist and was logically consistent with his other beliefs about reality, Lewis did not trouble about scientific proof. Ensconced at his beloved Oxford and having achieved academic distinction, Lewis added apologetics and fiction to his impressive body of work. (Ironically, these activities served to discredit his academic work for some.) Lewis distrusted his contemporaries' enthusiasm for applying scientific theories to social problems, such as what he saw as the "hijack[ing]" of "scientific theories about evolution [...] by those with social and cultural agendas" (McGrath 47). He chose to embrace a deliberately archaic persona that found truth in Western humanism before the Renaissance ("De Descriptione")

L'Engle's journey from agnosticism to theism transpired when, as a young mother in a small rural Connecticut town trying to establish a career as a writer, she sought intellectual and spiritual inspiration in the writings of Arthur Eddington, Albert Einstein, and other physicists and mathematicians (qtd. Hettinga 21). She remarked in a 1974 interview that she resisted outright conversion and claimed that *A Wrinkle in Time* was actually "a violent rebellion against Christian piety," a "fumbling toward something that wasn't an offence to my instincts and to my mind" (Wintle 254). L'Engle frequently alludes to scientists' influence not only on her world-view but also on her spiritual growth. Notwithstanding L'Engle's frequent protests that she found God in science, Peter Bowler's history of the clashes between science and religion in the twentieth century contends that many of the writers L'Engle most frequently cites (Arthur Eddington, James Jeans, J.W.N. Sullivan) at times underplayed the differences and overstated points of connection between scientific and religious thought. Christians in the 1920s and '30s perceived Eddington, Jeans, and Sullivan as allies, but Albert Einstein never made claims for a personal God. L'Engle appears to have read these works primarily for what they offered her imagination—she found the German theologians she had been given turgid and uninspiring (Wintle 254). Still, L'Engle's imaginative fusion between science and religion has not only inspired other fantasy writers, but also scientists such as astronaut Janice Voss (Lyden 2007). And as Marek Oziewicz has shown, L'Engle's imaginative syntheses frequently anticipate later scientific theories and discoveries (Oziewicz 2008).

Thus, despite their contrasting social, educational, and national identities, both Lewis and L'Engle expressed congruent ways of understanding the cosmos and humanity's place in it, seeking intellectual, imaginative, and aesthetic satisfaction in available models. Both adopted or rejected models primarily on their capacity to express beauty. Both, thus, conceive of the universe in humanistic terms and use metaphors drawn from music and dance to describe its qualities and workings. Both could be described as having a Classical—as opposed to Romantic or Gothic—affinity for balance, structure, and symmetry. Fully aware that the Ptolemaic model of the universe is not true, Lewis adopted it in the *Chronicles of Narnia* for its pleasing qualities, as Mary Frances Zambreno has shown. Lewis described it approvingly as "vast in scale, but limited and intelligible. Its sublimity is not the sort that depends on anything vague or obscure. It is [...] a classical rather than a Gothic sublimity. Its contents, however rich and various, are in harmony. We see how everything links up with everything else" (*Discarded* 12). L'Engle had a similar appreciation for classical structures; she preferred Bach and Mozart to the "lush Romanticism of Wagner," according to Gregory Pepetone (160). L'Engle's frequent allusions to Bach and Brahms suggests that she might agree with Pepetone's proposition that Western classical music "reflect[s] more accurately the cosmic pattern than other kinds of music" (159). In similar fashion, Lewis's writing depicts a harmonious and decorous cosmos, notwithstanding his keen Romantic sensibility and appreciation for Romantic literature and music. Lewis's *Perelandra*, his revision of the Fall, depicts the planetary spirits of Venus and Mars, Venus's Adam and Eve, and the human hero Ransom conversing in the manner of a fugue, which develops into a great dance: "like the parts of a music into which all of them had entered as instruments" (*Perelandra* 198). In *The Magician's Nephew*, Aslan sings the world of Narnia into being, and then is joined by stars with "more voices than you could possibly count," all in harmony with his initiating melody (*Magician's* 107). In *Prince Caspian*, the titular hero wonders if the conjunction of two planets will result in their collision, but is assured by his tutor that "the great lords of the upper sky know the steps of their dance too well for that" (*Prince* 50).

For Lewis, the medieval model offers "splendor, sobriety, and coherence" (Lewis qtd. Zambreno 264); its pomp—a Lewisian term of approbation—amplifies classical values of dignity, balance, and symmetry. Contributing to this sense is the very human-scale and human-centered concepts of space and time also adopted by Lewis in his fantasies. Zambreno has shown how the Narnian Chronicles' bounded geography and temporality express medieval concepts of space and time: history is defined by the human record and delimited by God. Just as humans have a natural lifespan that may be truncated by accident or malice, so too planets and solar systems are allotted a "certain amount of time" that may be "ended prematurely by the misdeeds of the world's inhabitants, but—and this is the most important point—it cannot be extended" (Zambreno 256). This "fact of an ending" (257) rendered as the deaths not only of likeable characters but even of Narnia itself in *The Last Battle* is one of the more controversial aspects of the Chronicles.

Lewis's insistence upon the limits of life-spans responded to contemporary science fiction writers, such as H.G. Wells and Olaf Stapledon, who imagined infinite human evolution, guided by scientists for the goal of infinite expansion into the universe (Schwartz 29). Not so concerned with human origins as with human *telos*, Lewis condemned the "conceptual apparatus that consigns other human beings to subhuman status, or summons up an 'evolutionary imperative' to legitimate the suspension of time-honored ethical norms" (Schwartz 6). In Narnia, the worst characters are also the most "modern": officials and managers and petty tyrants whose language and demeanor echo twentieth-century bureaucracy. "No interviews without appointments except between nine and ten p.m. on second Saturdays," says the slave-dealing governor of the Lone Islands before he is abruptly relieved of his office by King Caspian (*Voyage* 56). No need for an election.

Such types receive even harsher treatment in Lewis's adult novel *That Hideous Strength*, which exhibits the cliques and cabals of academic power struggles over appointments, space, and funding; the petty betrayals of personal loyalty to obtain favor with the "in" crowd. Mark Studdock, in his attempts to join the "inner circle," must conform. He falsifies news columns and participates in the destruction of old monuments and communities in the name of hygiene and efficiency; he adopts a mindset that sees the poor, the mentally inferior, or anyone not "in the know" as an object with no rights. Finally, Mark must kill his "instinctive preferences" for ethics, aesthetics, and logic by being trained in what the diabolical National Institute for Coordinated Experiments (N.I.C.E.) calls objectivity (*That Hideous* 296–98). Beginning with exposure to creepy surrealist art and progressing to acts of obscenity and other degradation, the treatment is designed to estrange Mark from his humanity. It culminates, tellingly, in an act of artistic and religious vandalism: Mark is asked to spit on and violate a crucifix (*That Hideous* 334–35). The antagonists of *That Hideous Strength* eventually worship the decapitated head of a murderer they themselves animated, perfectly encapsulating the solipsistic scientific naturalism Lewis decries. Human control over the evolution of the species, Lewis implies, produces only monstrosity. In this book and in many essays, Lewis protests against those advocates of "eugenics and other forms of social control" and against "science as an agency by which humans try to dominate the world and each other" (Bowler 319).

L'Engle shares a great deal with Lewis in her opposition to modern pressures toward conformity: her dystopian planet Camazotz enforces complete conformity and submission by means of a gigantic brain called IT. The planet's dreary city-scape has often been interpreted as "a cautionary tale about soviet communism or totalitarianism" (Voiklis 219). However, L'Engle herself described Camazotz as a version of American suburbia: the idea, she claimed,

> sprang mostly from seeing Camazotz round the country. When you leave New York tonight you'll be flying over Camazotz—house after house after house, the people in them all watching the same television programs, and all eating the same things for dinner, and the kids in their mandatory uniforms [Wintle 257–58].

L'Engle locates conformist pressures in schools and community institutions—Meg contends not with evil scientists but with her school principal Mr. Jenkins and the gossipy village postmistress. Both Lewis and L'Engle depict schools as hostile environments particularly hard on children who are different or gifted (Avakian). L'Engle's Camazotz presents a picture of scientific social programming and technological control that recalls the literal/figurative Head of the N.I.C.E. in *That Hideous Strength*, its "enlightened" methods of re-education, and its preference for utility over beauty. On Camazotz, there is no need for actual flavor in food—it can all be done by manipulating the mind (*Wrinkle* 124). The little boy who doesn't bounce his ball correctly is painfully coerced into replicating the mandatory rhythm; "after today he'll never desire to deviate again," IT chortles through IT's temporary mouthpiece, Charles Wallace (*Wrinkle* 137). This rational society culls the unfit by "annihilat[ing] anyone who is ill" or handicapped or different (*Wrinkle* 133), all in the pursuit of "happ[iness] and efficien[cy]" (*Wrinkle* 136); no one can ever disagree because there is only one mind (*Wrinkle* 136). In her Newbery Acceptance Speech, L'Engle decries standardization as "the limited universe, the drying, dissipating universe" ("Expanding" 260).

As an alternative to these projections of technologically aided totalitarianism, L'Engle proposes an order imagined as cosmic music and dance. When Meg, Charles Wallace, and Calvin visit the planet Uriel, they witness great winged beasts flying, singing, and making music in "a kind of dance," with an entire planet as its stage (*Wrinkle* 62). In *A Wind in the Door*, L'Engle turns to the sub-microscopic level. Here, mitochondria are participants in the dance; a mitochondrion is "a self-replicating organelle [...] acting as the major site of cellular respiration and energy production" (OED), and yet it also plays an essential role in the cosmos. L'Engle proposes the dynamic between structure and free will is like a sonnet: Calvin asks, "you're comparing our lives to a sonnet? A strict form, but freedom within it?"—"Yes [...] You're given the form, but you have to write the sonnet yourself. What you say is completely up to you" (*Wrinkle* 191). Like the classical music that inspired both L'Engle and Lewis, sonnets demand submission to the form, but offer freedom of expression and choice within those constraints. Both writers found this a beautiful and satisfying way of understanding cosmic order.

Anthropocentrism and an Expanding Universe

Though Lewis and L'Engle agree in their aesthetic appreciation for the universe as metaphorically ordered by music and dance, they part company in their account of humanity's place. The Ptolemaic cosmos was organized as a series of concentric spheres, with the earth in the middle. From there, expanding circles denoted higher orders of being and responsibility until one attained the sphere of God himself. There is no center in an expanding universe. This difference has significant consequences for Lewis and L'Engle's approach to humanity and its relation to other sentient creatures.

Just as the medieval model was anthropocentric, so the action in the Narnian Chronicles centers on the characters and deeds of "sons of Adam and daughters of Eve" brought out of their own world to serve the often mysterious purposes of Aslan, King of Beasts. Aslan, as Christ-figure in that world, created it and sacrifices himself for it. But although Aslan is preeminent, Lewis uses other elements from the medieval model, including the hierarchical chain of being, with humans—sons of Adam and daughters of Eve—raised to rule and responsibility, followed by an array of semi-humans, nature spirits, talking animals, and dumb animals. Aslan produces Narnia's geography and inhabitants out of song, so society is not seen as a dynamic system but as a set composition, either happily in balance or unhappily out of it. According to Zambreno, the medieval model of history was less interested in "progress" or "evolution" than in images of great deeds and glorious heroes. Narnia exhibits "a splendid permanence throughout the ages of a purely human (or at least intelligently inhabited) history" (Zambreno 258). The good is in the past, to be remembered for imitation. A place gains significance because of the deeds there accomplished. So Narnia is at the center of its world "because it is where Aslan stood to create the world and because (like Jerusalem) it is where his Death and Resurrection occurred" (Zambreno 259–60).

This anthropocentric notion of geography is supported by tacit human exceptionalism. Lewis, like his medieval predecessors, rejoices in nature deities and other half-human or nonhuman sentient creatures. Whether *hrossa* and *seroni* on Mars, or naiads, river-gods and fauns in Narnia, Lewis imagines many different ensouled beings, all exhibiting distinctive personalities, preoccupations, and talents. Many times these creatures are superior in virtue, courtliness, and beauty—Ransom's mentor the hross Hyoi (*Silent*); the mouse Reepicheep (*Prince, Voyage*); the Unicorn Jewell (*Last*) come to mind. Still, humans are special. In *Perelandra* humans are said to be distinguished because of Christ's human incarnation (99). The logic of anthropocentrism manifests even in Lucy's first acquaintance of Narnia, when Mr. Tumnus asks if she is a "Daughter of Eve": in an impossible, magical world, human identity and priority is still a given. Even in this magical world, only "Adam's flesh and Adam's bone" can rule legitimately (*Lion* 81). Continually "bent" by willful and rebellious desires or by fear and cowardice, humans nonetheless possess the divine potential to choose good, characterized as obedience to Aslan's word. This struggle pervades the Narnian Chronicles as the child protagonists are required to follow instructions without necessarily knowing the reason for or the outcome of their quests: in *The Lion, the Witch, and the Wardrobe*, Mr. Beaver rebukes Peter's plan to approach the White Witch instead of going straight to Aslan; in *Prince Caspian* Lucy demands her reluctant older siblings follow Aslan's lead, even if they can't see him; *The Silver Chair*'s Eustace and Jill must follow Aslan's "signs" even if they don't make sense; in *The Magician's Nephew* Digory must pick an apple of life for Narnia rather than for his dying mother. Human choice and human action is both central to a world's well-being but also completely subordinate to a larger, often ineffable, plan.

L'Engle, while acknowledging the role of people in "bringing light" to the world through music, art, and discovery, does not place them at the center of creation in the same way that Lewis does. Appropriate to her cosmic model of expansion, L'Engle peoples the universe with a wide array of fantastic creatures, some drawn from mythology and others more recognizably science-fictional. If she uses recognizable unicorns, pegasi, cherubim, and angels, she also invents inhabitants for mitochondria and confronts us with tentacled aliens, albeit in a much different mode from Lovecraft's Chthulhu. Appropriately for an Einsteinian universe, size difference is relative: it does not inhibit communication and connection between the microscopic and the cosmic. As Marek Oziewicz has helpfully explained, L'Engle's reading in the theories of relativity and quantum theory provide justification for her liberties with size, distance, and time-frame ("Integrating" 186–89). Lewis, by contrast, uses size to convey radical orders of otherness and rank, as in his account of the planetary guardians of the solar system in his space trilogy. L'Engle's universe does not emphasize obedience or hierarchy based on species, size, age, or location.

L'Engle's articulation of cosmic order rests less on human centrality and more on recognition of interconnectedness between Others. This theme is powerfully rendered in *A Wind in the Door,* which charts a homology between galactic disturbances and cellular malfunction. On the one hand, Mr. Murry, the physicist, has been studying a "cosmic scream" that produces "a small rip in the galaxy" and cause stars to disappear (*Wind* 37); on the other, Mrs. Murry, the biologist, identifies "farandolae" in the ultra-microscopic mitochondria that disrupt the crucial respiratory functions of the cell and thence of the organism. These unbalancing phenomena turn out to be related, as Meg learns, and products of menacing entities called "Echthroi," nihilistic forces that seek to exterminate and negate creation by "X"ing it (*Wind* 84). The characters opposing this force are suitably heterogenous and challenge any lingering anthropocentrism on the reader's part. Here the central struggle takes place inside the interior of a mitochondrion, in interactions with "farandolae," an invention of L'Engle's. These organisms are "so tiny that they can only be postulated" (Oziewicz, "Integrating" 185) and look like small mouse-like, shrimp-like creatures in their youthful "spore" stage. In maturity they root themselves to become tree-like beings called "farae" A single farandola's individuality becomes the focus of the conflict and L'Engle's extended metaphor about relativity, interconnection, and choice.

To prepare Meg and her companions for their journey into the mitochondrion, an alien giant named Blajeny, transports them to a "postulatum" called Metron Ariston (Greek for "moderation is best"). Blajeny explains that the postulatum "makes it possible for all sizes to become relative. Within Metron Ariston you may be sized so that you are able to converse with a giant star or a tiny farandola" (*Wind* 127). The inference is that all beings are morally equal, without regard to size. Meg's "class" includes Calvin, her boyfriend; Mr. Jenkins, a mediocre school principal; Louise the Larger, a snake; Proginoskes, a cherubim; and Sporos, a farandola from one of her brother's mitochondria. Blajeny explains that just as the tininess of human beings in the cosmos does not prevent them from being conscious and aware of the galaxy, so the farandolae may be conscious of their place in the cosmos even though they are "as much smaller than you [Meg] are as your galaxy is larger than you are" (*Wind* 129). Calling the school a "postulatum" suggests that the effort of learning is not only experiential but also a work of the creative imagination, an ability to theorize; the humans cannot "comprehend anything that huge, that macrocosmic" and are told "Don't try to comprehend with your mind. Your minds are very limited. Use your intuition" (*Wind* 128). Through the postulatum, "we can almost do away with variations in size, which are, in reality, quite unimportant" (*Wind* 129); all that is necessary is that we "make believe" (*Wind* 134). L'Engle's model of the expanding and yet connected universe affirms progress and recommends curiosity and imagination to underscore their importance in learning, development, maturity.

At the same time as size and age are not as important as we may imagine, individual choice is elevated to great consequence, because any choice has ramifications. In the well-known metaphor of the butterfly effect—what L'Engle described as a "beautiful and imaginative concept" that postulates that a butterfly's death might be registered "in galaxies thousands of light years away" (qtd. Hettinga 24). The smallest action may have manifold and enormous consequences, as L'Engle illustrates with the old nursery rhyme about how the "want of a nail" loses a kingdom (*Wind* 179). As is typical of L'Engle, scientific concepts inspire literary and artistic responses. *A Wind in the Door* affirms that individuals, even if they are not at the center of the universe, still have a role in the great dance of the cosmos. In Charles Wallace's mitochondrion, Meg listens to the song of the farae and learns that "they are rooted, yet never separated from each other, no matter how great the distance. We are the song of the universe," they chant, "[...] The farae and the stars are the singers. Our song orders the rhythm of creation" (*Wind* 180). But if an individual may participate in this great order, this great dance, she may also violate and compromise it. Charles Wallace's mysterious illness in *A Wind in the Door* is traced to the malfunctioning of his mitochondria, specifically, an individual farandola's refusal to mature, which drains energy from the farae and, by extension, from Charles Wallace, whose increasing difficulty in breathing is depicted in short vignettes as Meg's quest proceeds (Filmer 116). Meg and her friends must convince these wild, pleasure-seeking farandolae that giving up their "irrational tarantella" to "deepen" and become part of the cosmic order is worth it.

This episode might suggest that L'Engle, like Lewis, adopts a hierarchical notion of cosmic order, but L'Engle is post–Einsteinian, not Ptolemaic. Rather than including an overarching, universally ordering deity or positing absolute relations among creatures and creation, L'Engle posits that *all* creation, no matter what size or dimension, contributes to order or disorder. L'Engle's work appeared in a period remarkable for its paradigm-shifting manifestoes: Rachel Carson's *Silent Spring* (1962), an exposé of the environmental costs of the proliferation of chemical attempts to control nature; Thomas Kuhn's *Structure of Scientific Revolutions* (1962), which defied the conviction that scientific discovery could be separated from culture and consciousness and coined the term "paradigm shift"; and L'Engle's Smith College classmate Betty Friedan's *Feminine Mystique* (1962), which demolished the myth of the happy 1950s housewife. As Marek Oziewicz characterizes L'Engle's context, "an increasing number of Americans were growing uneasy about their consumer society, about where its economy was going, and about the political, environmental, social, and psychological costs of affluence available only to some" (Oziewicz, "Time Quartet" 216). L'Engle both employed and defied this spectrum of revolutionary thought: her enthusiasm for the possibilities theorized by physicists and mathematicians persisted, as did her conviction that science offered an intellectually compelling and consolatory theology. Rather than being dismayed by the demolition of the anthropocentric model, L'Engle "envisions spirituality as a way of life and attitude akin to the spirit of genuine scientific inquiry, thus suggesting that science and spirituality [...] complete each other" (Oziewicz, "Integrating" 182). This small planet provides "lights to see by": Jesus, Leonardo, Michelangelo, Shakespeare, Bach, Pasteur, Mme. Curie, Einstein, Schweitzer, Gandhi, Buddha, Beethoven, Rembrandt, St. Francis, Euclid, Copernicus (*Wrinkle* 85–86). L'Engle's genealogy of "fighters" for the light, is progressive for its time: this mid-twentieth-century pantheon of multidisciplinary achievement mentions one woman and three non–Western men in its list of religious founders, artists, musicians, scientists, and physicians.

The Epistemologies of Sight and "Kything"

Among the most significant differences between Lewis and L'Engle is their depiction of epistemology: Lewis prefers the clarity of sight imagery, while L'Engle invokes intuition and empathy in "kything," a word she resurrected from an old dictionary. Lewis endorsed the truth-value of metaphor: "Imagination, producing new metaphors or revivifying old, is not the cause of truth, but its condition [...] [A]ll our truth, or all but a few fragments, is won by metaphor" ("Bluspels" 157, 158). Worth registering, however, is that Lewis's favorite metaphors for knowledge were visual: Alister McGrath writes that Lewis "draws extensively on the language of sight and vision for [his] metaphors of truth and meaning" (84). For Lewis, all the wisdom central to human purpose has already been conveyed in the person of Jesus Christ and the revelation of scripture, and by means of their light do we see. This perspective orients Lewis's elevation of "logic," as Professor Kirke is always saying, as a ladder towards truth, especially the Platonic understanding that our ideas must be copies of greater, more real, Truth. Thus, Lewis is an aficionado of sight. The sight metaphor for knowledge premises that the best way to understand something is to stand apart from it, to observe it from multiple angles, and to establish visual control. Lewis saw divine light as something *by means of which* we see, which implies correct point of view and an incorrect one (Ward 17). Lewis's apologetics and philosophical passages frequently reduce problems to either-or propositions that stylistically mimic visual clarity, as Professor Kirke does in *The Lion, the Witch and the Wardrobe* when he demolishes Peter's and Susan's concerns about Lucy's sanity.

Perhaps because she was guided by her reading interests, and had no allegiance to a particular school of thought, L'Engle's epistemology relies on a heterogeneous frame of reference, including mathematics, quotations from world literatures in multiple languages (German, Spanish, French, Latin, Greek), and intuitive empathy. In *A Wrinkle in Time*, Mrs. Who and Mrs. Whatsit describe the titular "tesseract," by offering a quotation from Cervantes, a visual aid, and a mathematical analogy (*Wrinkle*, 72–75), which Meg intuits without being able to explain (*Wrinkle* 75). L'Engle's other-worldly characters frequently comment on the limits of human language and consciousness and civilization. The eyeless tentacled Beasts of the planet Ixchel who tend to Meg and her companions after their traumatic encounter with IT on Camazotz have much different sensory apparatus from sight. Aunt Beast, Meg's caregiver, demolishes the priority of sight: "We do not know what things *look* like, as you say [...] we know what things *are* like. It must be a very limiting thing, this seeing" (*Wrinkle* 174).

In place of the distancing objectifying function of sight, L'Engle offers "kything," an empathic entry into the perspective and mindset of another fuelled by love. Taken from a medieval English word, to make known "in words," "by action," "to show," "to exercise," it encompasses ways of knowing beyond vision (OED). As described in *A Wind in the Door*, kything is "how cherubim talk. It's talking without words" (*Wind* 88). It's also how the farae of a mitochondrion communicate with galaxies and participate in the cosmic dance. To understand through kything is to "Name," to truly apprehend the Other, which is one of Meg's tasks, and which cannot take place from the vantage point of distanced objectivity. L'Engle has already used the spacetime continuum of the theory of relativity to question conventional notions of distance and size; she now offers empathy as a key epistemological tool.

To amplify her emphasis on intuition and empathy, L'Engle draws on the images and symbols of analytic psychology and Gnosticism, affirming that to know the universe one must know the self. L'Engle's epistemology draws from traditions of imaginative and interior knowing, such as Gnosticism. In *A Wind in the Door,* Meg is lessoned by creatures who are emblems of Gnostic wisdom traditions (Pagels 30–31). The cherubim Proginoskes is first described as "dragons" because of his many eyes, wings, and fiery breath. And Meg is warned and encouraged by a large black snake, whom the children have named "Louise the Larger," after the doctor Louise Colubra attending Charles Wallace in his illness. Both colubras (the Latin feminine for snake) and Proginoskes, from the Greek "progignoskein," "to know" (Patterson 198) are teachers and helpers as Meg works to save her brother's life. Another key part of knowing is receptivity—listening to the Other as well as one's self. As Cara-Joy Steem has noted of *A Swiftly Tilting Planet* (1980), L'Engle constitutes listening as a "heroic action," one that "shatter[s] traditionally idolized qualities of autonomy, distinctive ability, and desire for power; and, in their place, emphasize[s] a mythic sense of interconnection, childlike wonder, humble cooperation, and sacredness of life" (36).

Meg naturally kythes with those she loves—her brother Charles Wallace, her boyfriend Calvin—but in *A Wind in the Door* she must recognize, Name, and kythe with her quotidian nemesis Mr. Jenkins. From the beginning of *A Wrinkle in Time*, Mr. Jenkins is characterized as an unsympathetic and small-minded principal, a bureaucrat who wants nothing more than to quash Meg's difference and enforce conformity in his school. Meg's conflicts with him set the scene in *A Wrinkle in Time* and get worse in the following book. In *A Wind in the Door*, Mr. Jenkins has been unable to manage the unruly teenagers at the high school and been demoted to the local grade school where Charles Wallace is enrolled as a first grader. To Meg, Mr. Jenkins is the dour embodiment of petty tyrant, administering discipline without empathy. His looks are as unpromising as his personality: he's bespectacled, business-suited, always with "a small snowfall of dandruff on his shoulders" (*Wind* 93). Mr. Jenkins makes Meg feel "the least [herself]" (*Wind* 79). Meg's first challenge is to "Name" Mr. Jenkins, which is defined as understanding "who people are, and who they are meant to be" (*Wind* 97). Donald Hettinga has characterized the challenge in Christian terms: Meg's lesson "highlights the existential dimension of agapic love" (35). In less specifically Christian terms, it might be understood as accepting the Other, recognizing the inherent value of Mr. Jenkins, recognizing his psychic pain and discomfort and its affect upon his ability to love and be loved. Meg learns that despite his antagonism toward her and her family, Mr. Jenkins is capable of kindness—he noticed Calvin had no athletic shoes and bought him new ones, disguised as used. Like Meg's own, Mr. Jenkins's feelings of inadequacy impede positive relationships with others, and he struggles to accept the demands of kything and the time-space-and-size disorientation. However, Mr. Jenkins also offers key support in the struggle, drawing on his adult experience and knowledge, avoiding the anti-intellectual implication that all we need is a little child to lead us.

Good, Evil, and Responsibility in an Expanding Universe

I have stressed the ways L'Engle parts ways with Lewis scientifically and theologically, and have suggested that their contexts contribute to those differences. In their formulation of the conflict as between good and evil, L'Engle and Lewis sometimes characterize evil as external, sometimes as internal. Both feared that modern progress advanced at the cost of individuality and freedom; L'Engle in particular related increasingly unstable environmental and social forces to Evil in the abstract. For Lewis, a good Augustinian, evil was distorted good that resulted from our inability to choose rightly. In *Out of the Silent Planet*, the unfallen Malacandrians translate "evil" as "bent." Evil results from a choice not to do the will of God, not to obey. L'Engle's account of evil draws strongly on notions of a "shadow," of "nothingness," of nihilism. Her evil characters in *Wrinkle* are those who have given up free will for security; in *Wind* they are those who seek to eradicate connections. Meg's weapons in the fight against IT are her "faults" (*Wrinkle* 96), her disinclination to cooperate with authorities. The conflict in *Wind in the Door* focuses on individuals who refuse to cooperate with cosmic order. The contrast between the anti-conformist theme of *Wrinkle in Time* (1962) and the plea for maturity, stability, and "rooting" in *Wind in the Door* (1974) bears traces of the era's culture wars—the rise of the counter-culture and its rejection of social norms and conventions as "fuddy-duddy" impositions on personal autonomy and freedom (*Wind* 190). *Wind* also manifests the era's anxieties about school violence, drug abuse, and environmental degradation (85–87). The farandola Sporos, whose name emphasizes his immaturity, is depicted as a rabble-rouser in thrall to powerful forces of unreason and negation. Sporos threatens the survival of the wise Senex (literally, old man), a rooted fara. Though Sporos defies its role in the mitochondrion by refusing to root, to "deepen" and to mature, Senex explains the difference between the free movement of the farandolae and the rooted farae: "Now that I am rooted, I am no longer limited by motion. Now I may move anywhere in the universe. I sing with the stars. I dance with the galaxies" (*Wind* 190). In the second novel, L'Engle almost seems to come round to Lewis's notion of the chain of being and the Fall. In later books of the Time sequence, such as *A Swiftly Tilting Planet* (1978), L'Engle employs more orthodox accounts of both the cosmic Fall (referenced in *Wind*) and of the Fall of Man.

Nonetheless, their depictions of appropriate response to evil are quite distinct and suggest radically different approaches to the conflict. Lewis almost inevitably stresses physically violent negation of the forces of evil. The children (the boys, at least) in Narnia are given swords and expected to kill; in *Perelandra*, Ransom decides he cannot defeat the demon-possessed Unman by words, and resorts to fists. L'Engle by contrast calls for love. Meg imagines "if she could give love to IT, perhaps it would shrivel up and die" (*Wrinkle* 200); in *Wind* Meg must love not only Mr. Jenkins but even, in a way, the terrifying Echthroi who seek to negate everything. In the climactic scene, Meg draws upon the kything connection she has with all her comrades to Name (that is, to recognize and affirm) even the Echthroi. "You are not to X me, Echthroi. I fill you," she sings, almost succumbing before Proginoskes helps her to fill the void by giving himself up (*Wind* 201–02). In her final effort, Meg calls on all creation and Names it, joining with the song and the cosmic dance to defy nihilism and affirm order. Though Proginoskes is lost in the fight, his love remains and Meg and Charles Wallace "know that somehow or other, he's all right" (*Wind* 210). Some critics are uncomfortable with the mystical and Christian overtones of this conflict, but its resolution is consistent with L'Engle's notion of the universe as a vast yet interconnected web of being and purpose. In this, she anticipates and affirms "biologist Margulis's idea of symbiogenesis—networking and cooperation rather than competition as the basic principle of life" (Oziewicz 191). For L'Engle, denying these connections and insisting upon responsibility-free autonomy causes cosmic disruption.

Lewis and L'Engle ultimately affirm participation in larger cosmic structures, but they characterize that action differently. Their contrasting conservative and progressive mindsets embody conflicts about meaning and ethical action that continue to be debated in religious and nonreligious contexts. L'Engle, in her openness to new ideas, her creative engagement with scientific frontiers of knowledge, offers ways of spiritual knowing that don't require adherence to outmoded models and static dogma. Nor does her synthesis require giving up humanist heritage and aesthetic pleasure. L'Engle is Lewis's science fictional heir because she becomes the poet of our most current models of the cosmos in both her works' imaginative strengths and, let it be said, their weaknesses. L'Engle's Christian universalism and her humanism is undoubtedly and significantly limited by class and cultural blinders. The problematic status of culture heroism embodied in her list of fighters for the "light"; her tendency to racialized color-coding (especially in *Swiftly Tilting Planet* and *An Acceptable Time* [1989]); her reliance on elite "white savior" figures; all deserve critical attention. So do her soft-pedaling of socioeconomic disenfranchisement, classism, racism, homophobia, and the problematics, for women especially, of an ethic of sacrifice. All these remain open questions about her *oeuvre*. But in these first two books of the Time sequence, in her depiction of the imaginative and spiritual benefits of scientific metaphors, L'Engle offers the hope that readers can develop an ethics of imagination that creates "explosive material capable of stirring up fresh life endlessly" ("Expanding" 260), a program appropriate for small yet significant inhabitants of an expanding universe.

Works Cited

Avakian, Tanya. "The Wildness of Christianity: The Legacy of Madeleine L'Engle." *Commonweal* 134.18 (26 Oct. 2007): 8. *Literature Resource Center.* Web. 29 Feb. 2016.
Bowler, Peter J. *Science and Its Conceptual Foundations: Reconciling Science and Religion: The Debate in Early-Twentieth-Century Britain.* Chicago: University of Chicago Press, 2010. Print.
Carter, M.L. "The Cosmic Gospel: Lewis and L'Engle." *Mythlore* 30 (Winter 1982): 10–12. Project Muse. Web.
Filmer, Kath. *Scepticism and Hope in Twentieth Century Fantasy Literature.* New York: St. Martin's, 1992. Print.
Hein, Rolland, *Christian Mythmakers: C.S. Lewis, Madeleine L'Engle, J.R.R. Tolkien, George MacDonald, G.K. Chesterton and Others.* Chicago: Cornerstone, 2002. Print.
Hettinga, Donald R. "Quests in Time," *Presenting Madeleine L'Engle.* New York: Twayne, 1993. 21–46. Print.
L'Engle, Madeleine. "Allegorical Fantasy: Mortal Dealings with Cosmic Questions [Interview]." *Christianity Today* 23 (8 June 1979): 14–20. Print.
_____. "The Expanding Universe." August 1963. Rpt. *A Wrinkle in Time*, Fiftieth Anniversary Edition. 257–62.
_____. *A Swiftly Tilting Planet.* New York: Farrar, Straus and Giroux, 1978. Print.
_____. *A Wind in the Door.* New York: Farrar Straus Giroux, 1973. Print.
_____. *A Wrinkle in Time.* 1962. Fiftieth Anniversary Edition. New York: Farrar Straus Giroux, 2012. Print.
Lewis, C.S. "Bluspels and Flalansferes: A Semantic Nightmare." *Selected Literary Essays.* Ed. Walter Hooper. Cambridge: Cambridge University Press, 1969. 251–65. Print.
_____. "De Descriptione Temporum." *Selected Literary Essays.* Ed. Walter Hooper. Cambridge: Cambridge University Press, 1969. 1–14. Print.
_____. *The Discarded Image: An Introduction to Medieval and Renaissance Literature.* 1964. Cambridge: Cambridge University Press, 1967. Print.
_____. *The Lion, the Witch, and the Wardrobe.* 1950. Fiftieth Anniversary Edition. New York: HarperTrophy, 2000. Print.
_____. *The Magician's Nephew.* 1955. Fiftieth Anniversary Edition. New York: HarperTrophy, 2000. Print.
_____. *Out of the Silent Planet.* 1938. London: Pan Books, 1956. Print.
_____. *Perelandra (Voyage to Venus).* 1943. London: Pan Books, 1953. Print.
_____. *Prince Caspian.* 1951. Fiftieth Anniversary Edition. New York: HarperTrophy, 2000. Print.

_____. *Surprised by Joy: The Shape of My Early Life*. London, Harcourt Brace & Co, 1955. Print.

_____. *That Hideous Strength: A Modern Fairy-Tale for Grown-Ups*. 1945. New York: Scribner, 1997. Print.

Lyden, Jacki. "L'Engle's Fiction Inspired Real Science." *Weekend All Things Considered*. 8 Sept. 2007. Literature Resource Center. Web. 28 Jan. 2016.

McGrath, Alister E. *The Intellectual World of C.S. Lewis*. Malden, MA: John Wiley & Sons, 2014. Print.

Oziewicz, Marek. "Integrating Science and Spirituality: Madeleine L'Engle's Time Quartet (1962–1986)." *One Earth, One People: The Mythopoeic Fantasy Series of Ursula K. Le Guin, Lloyd Alexander, Madeleine L'Engle and Orson Scott Card*. Critical Explorations in Science Fiction and Fantasy, 6. Jefferson, NC: McFarland, 2008. 171–97. Print.

_____. "The Time Quartet as Madeleine L'Engle's Theology." *Journal of the Fantastic in the Arts* 17.3 (2006): 211–22. Print.

Pagels, Elaine. *The Gnostic Gospels*. 1979. New York: Vintage Books, 1989. Print.

Patterson, Nancy-Lou. "Angel and Psychopomp in Madeleine L'Engle's 'Wind' Trilogy." *Children's Literature in Education*. 14.4 (1983): 195–203. Print.

Pepetone, Gregory. "Angels, Echthroi, and Celestial Music in the Adolescent Science Fiction of Madeleine L'Engle." *Religion and Science Fiction*. Ed. James McGrath. Cambridge: The Lutterworth Press, 2011. 154–68. Print.

Prickett, Stephen. *Narrative, Religion, and Science: Fundamentalism versus Irony*. Cambridge: Cambridge University Press, 2002. Print.

Schwartz, Sanford. *C.S. Lewis on the Final Frontier: Science and the Supernatural in the Space Trilogy*. Oxford: Oxford University Press, 2009. Print.

Steem, Cara-Joy. "Listening as Heroic Action in L'Engle's *A Swiftly Tilting Planet*." *Mythlore* 32.1 (2013): 35–53. Proquest. Web. 1 Feb. 2016.

Voiklis, Charlotte Jones. "Afterword." *A Wrinkle in Time: 50th Anniversary Edition*. New York: Farrar Straus Giroux, 2012. 207–222. Print.

Ward, Michael. *Planet Narnia: The Seven Heavens in the Imagination of C.S. Lewis*. Oxford: Oxford University Press, 2008. Print.

Wintle, Justin. "Madeleine L'Engle." *The Pied Pipers: Interviews with the Influential Creators of Children's Literature*. Ed. Justin Wintle and Emma Fisher. New York and London: Paddington Press, 1974. 249–62. Print.

Zambreno, Mary Frances. "A Reconstructed Image: Medieval Time and Space in the Chronicles of Narnia." *Revisiting Narnia: Fantasy, Myth and Religion in C.S. Lewis's Chronicles*. Ed. Shanna Caughey. Dallas: BenBella Books, 2005. 253–66. Print.

A Problematic Sense of Place
Madeleine L'Engle's "White in the Moon the Long Road Lies"

Gérald Préher

>Ah, Destiny! Why must we ever go
>Away from the Florida beach?
>—Constance Fenimore Woolson, "The Florida Beach"

Madeleine L'Engle did not write a lot of short stories and she never put together a collection out of the fourteen or so that were published in periodicals or anthologies. Nevertheless, the coherence of her fictional world can gain from a look at those texts that very often feature characters or places she uses in longer works. Born in New York, L'Engle spent her early years in the Big Apple before her parents moved to France and sent her to a boarding school in Switzerland. Upon the family's return to the United States, the decision was made to settle in Florida which many relatives already called home and which L'Engle herself had visited many times on vacation as a small child. L'Engle attended a boarding school in Charleston, South Carolina and subsequently moved north where she enrolled and later graduated from Smith College.[1] The South is not a predominant place in L'Engle's fiction—she writes about it in *Ilsa* (1946) and *The Other Side of the Sun* (1971), and also in two stories, "White in the Moon the Long Road Lies" (1939) and "Poor Little Saturday" (1956). Nonetheless, as the dates of publication suggest, L'Engle regularly returned to the South throughout her career and, just like the South of France, she clearly knew this region "with her senses" (*A Circle of Quiet* 94). Her depiction of the South and its customs rings true and suggests that she would probably have subscribed to Eudora Welty's comment that "[l]iterature does belong in essential ways to place, and invokes place to speak in its fullest voice. To Southerners that assumption is so accepted, lies so deep in the bones, as never to have needed stating among themselves" (*Place* 548–49).

As an outsider, originally coming from the North, L'Engle might have been as out of place in the South as the Rolls-Royce that opens *The Other Side of the Sun* and leads to the introduction of the central character: Stella, a British lady who has married a Southerner and relocated in Florida while her husband is on a diplomatic mission. The British car mirrors Stella's position in the South: she is trying to move along its roads though keeping her identity as a foreigner. L'Engle probably experienced the same feeling of estrangement upon discovering what Stella calls "this strange, wild land" (25) but she too had a reason to explore this place: the family moved to Florida because "Madeleine's grandmother fell ill" (Bray, "Transforming Memories" 139), and because, as one of her characters puts it, "in the American South [...] kin mattered" (*Other Side* 28). According to Robert O. Stephens, family in the South, "function[s] as the individual's link with the past" (247). In *The Other Side of the Sun*, Stella is made to explore this link by reading the journals of one of her husband's ancestors and listening to family stories. As is often the case in Southern literature, the past looms over the present: "the past doesn't ever seem to be past. It moves up and intrudes into the present. And it threatens the future" (*Other Side* 71). This is one of the many faulknerian comments to be found in the narrative, suggesting stability and continuity more than they do change.

Aunt Olivia is one of the voices from the past and she makes its presence clear: "It's strange how vividly I remember the past. It's all so clear to me, clearer than the present. It's not so much that I'm living in the past, as that the past is moving up to meet and engulf the present" (140). Olivia's concerns echo what Allen Tate has called "historical imagination." Tate coined this expression after World War I and L'Engle's novel does match his idea that after this specific war, the "South reentered the world—but gave a backward glance as it stepped over the border: that backward glance gave us the Southern renascence, a literature conscious of the past in the present" (545). *The Other Side of the Sun* owes much to that tradition as it explores the ramifications of the past in the present and makes L'Engle a Southern writer for, as Marjorie Kinnan Rawlings observes in a 1940 essay: "Regional writing may be done either by outsiders or insiders" (384). Like L'Engle, Rawlings was born in the North and she moved to Florida where she found inspiration for her stories.

For Rawlings, regional writing reflects "the approach of the sincere creative writer who has something to say and who uses a specialized locale—a region—as a logical or fitting background for the particular thoughts or emotions that cry out for articulation" (385). It is the impact of place on the self that triggers the creative impulse which, more often than not, stems from the senses. A similar effect can be traced in the writings of an earlier woman writer: Constance Fenimore Woolson. Born in New Hampshire, Woolson "spent seven winters in St. Augustine, Florida, where she wrote novels, short stories, and travel sketches while tending to her invalid mother" (Lowe 92). Despite being an outsider, Woolson is nonetheless a Southern writer who is "drawn to the sensual and mysterious elements of the tropical sublime" (Lowe 109) that both "attract and repel" (Lowe 90).[2] Woolson's feelings for the South—and especially Florida—are summarized in the last two lines of her poem "The Florida Beach" used as the epigraph of the present essay: the speaker is on a boat that is sailing away from the coast of Florida and wonders whether there is a point in leaving a place that seems so perfect for anyone to blossom.

L'Engle's early story, "White in the Moon the Long Road Lies," is imbued with a similar anxiety as regards the future. L'Engle uses the heat as an indicator of her main character's inner development implying that staying in the South could lead to irreversible entrapment. The story appeared in *Opinion*, the literary section of the Smith College weekly, in 1939. L'Engle—then Camp, only a sophomore at the time—was one of the assistant editors and she managed to place a few of her own short stories there. While L'Engle is actually younger than her protagonist in the story, she had experienced leaving the South a couple of years earlier when she left Florida to attend Smith College in Massachusetts. Writing stories enabled her to express something of her mixed emotions about the region. As Eudora Welty puts it: "Fiction provides the ideal texture through which the feeling and meaning that permeate our own personal, present lives will best show through" (*Eye* 117).

Although it would have been appropriate, "White in the Moon the Long Road Lies" does not borrow its title from Woolson's poem but from one of the English poet and classicist A. E. Housman's signature works, *A Shropshire Lad* (1896). As John B. Vickery explains, in Housman's poem the "hollowness of hope for regaining what is lost is caught in the conventional injunctions of travelers" (416). In L'Engle's story, it is the perspective of a move to the North that leads Selina, the central character who has accepted a teaching position there, to think about a "narrow path" (4) rather than about a "long road" (Housman "XXXVI"). L'Engle takes up the image of the white moon leading her character "*from* [her] love" (Housman "XXXVI," emphasis added) but there is more hope in her story than there is in Housman's poem because Selina eventually imagines a "broad white horizon" (4) ahead. The story is set in Florida, as the descriptions of the landscape make clear and, throughout the narrative, Selina keeps wondering about her connection to place—other characters perceive her as a free spirit who does not belong anywhere, but she constantly tries to define her own sense of place as her departure approaches. The Housman intertext helps grasp Selina's fears about love and place; she feels that once she has left home, she may never find it again—a concern that Thomas Wolfe had explored a few years before L'Engle's story was published. Selina is not a lost lady, though; she is ready to take risks and become her own driver on that journey to selfhood.

Selina's "Meteorological Sensibility"

In *One Writer's Beginnings*, Mississippi writer Eudora Welty looks back at the importance of childhood memories on her fiction. She remembers her father bringing a barometer to the family house and telling the children how to behave should they ever lose their way "in a strange country" (*Beginnings* 4). His advice is that they "[l]ook for where the sky is brightest along the horizon" (*Beginnings* 4). Her father's instructions on how to interpret the weather are also central for what Welty has called her "meteorological sensibility" (*Beginnings* 4) which, she feels, fueled her creative imagination and "atmosphere took its influential role from the start" (*Beginnings* 4). The weather certainly has a specific function in Southern literature. In Faulkner's famous story "Dry September," the uncontrollable violence leading up to the lynching of a black man is closely related to the heat which another of his characters tries to account for: "That's the one trouble with this country: everything, weather, all, hangs on too long. Like our rivers, our land: opaque, slow, violent; shaping and creating the life of man in its implacable and brooding image" (*As I Lay Dying* 30).

The hot weather in L'Engle's story does not give way to physical violence but it mirrors Selina's state of mind. At the garden party that has been organized in town to celebrate her appointment as a history teacher, "the air had been heavy and the sun had beaten down upon the garden" (1). As opposed to the "cool sound of ice clinking in tall glasses," the narrator mentions the "warm buzz of 'good-byes,' a buzz of mosquitoes, the buzz of the lawn mower next door, the buzz of a telephone ringing incessantly inside the house" (1). The accumulation of noises adds to the idea of suffocation resulting from the high temperature: it is not only the air that is saturated because of the heat, the way people behave at the party also confines Selina in a specific role. The narrator reports that she "felt she had never been so 'deared' and 'darlinged' before […] and all the while she had been smiling and shaking hands and letting unintelligible words come out of her mouth in answer to those she had heard" (1). The party seems to mark the beginning of Selina's estrangement from the community—she uses "unintelligible words," words that come to her automatically and are deprived of meaning.

"The afternoon," the narrator observes, "had *dr*agged on interminably, and Selina felt little *drops* of moisture trickling down her back" (2, emphasis added). Weather and time are inextricably linked as the alliteration makes clear—the temperature makes Selina feels that the party is never going to end, which becomes painful. It can also be assumed that perspiration is related to Selina's rejection of the South which accounts for her attempt to find a way to escape. Time seems to have come to a standstill, leading her to wonder whether she had "somehow been dropped into an air-pocket of time where there would be anything but tired shrill voices and thick heat" (2). Again, the situation is reminiscent of Faulkner's observation that "time *is*, and if there's no such thing as *was*, then there is no such thing as *will be*" (*Faulkner in the University* 139). At the party, Selina is trapped in a present that encapsulates the values she learned in the past and prevents her from envisioning the future.

Although there is an upsurge of violence in Selina resulting from the heat, it is very different from faulknerian violence: Selina means to "scream [...] really yell," hoping that "[t]he heavy superlatives would be suspended in mid-air and the sun would loose[n] its hold on the hot afternoon" (2). Her plan is never acted out but its potential effect is clarified: "There would be a moment of nothingness after the flash, and then the low mumble of voices again" (2). The consequence Selina envisions for her scream shows the depth of her desire for a fresh start. However, in her mind, the voices do not hush for long and the cacophony is soon revived, suggesting that there is no room for change in such a place. The South, as Selina sees it, is doomed: "It's stagnant *and* old *and* narrow-minded [...] no one has survived the Civil War [...] I want to get out" (2, emphasis added). She perceives the presence of the past in the present as confining—she does not want to get away from the South but "out" of it before it closes in on her. Her reaction echoes the commonly accepted fact that the Civil War is a—not to say *the*—moment that defines the region's identity and which, instead of initiating change in the Southerners' way of life, has given way to an idealization of the past more akin to myth than anything else. Selina's use of a ternary rhythm also hints at her rejection of Southern culture as a whole and, as a history teacher, she certainly has the necessary distance to judge her region. By saying that "no one has survived the Civil War," Selina comes close to Mr. Compson's comment in Faulkner's *Absalom, Absalom!*: "Years ago we in the South made our women into ladies. Then the War came and made the ladies into ghosts. So what else can we do, being gentlemen, but listen to them being ghosts?'" (9). Both Selina and Mr. Compson use present tenses, making it clear that the injuries of the war left more than scars, what remain are "traces," in the derridian sense of the term. In *On Touching*, Derrida notes that

> Where the taking-place of the event doesn't find its place, a gaping locus, indeed, a mouth—except in *replacement*; where it doesn't find room except in replacement—isn't that trace the trace of metonymy or the technical prosthesis, and the place for

the phantasm as well, that is to say, the ghostly revenant (*phantasma*), at the heart of (self-) feeling? The revenant, between life and death, dictates an impossible mourning, an endless mourning—life itself [35, emphasis original].

When the narrator in L'Engle's story refers to people's farewell words to Selina, the individuals are not named because metonymically their voices stand for the community's reaction to the young woman's departure: "[…] are you really leaving tomorrow […] don't forget us 'way down here in the South'" (1). Selina does not want to forget about the South as place but the Southern state of mind—or frame of mind—clearly does not match hers. All the stories she has heard loom over a present she wishes to be rid of for, unlike Faulkner, she longs for a *will be*.

Defining Self through Space

Selina's impending departure from the South is made clear at the very beginning of the story when she leaves the house to take a walk on the beach and "[t]he door slammed behind [her]" (1). Nevertheless, leaving the party is the first real step towards her future. Significantly, she asks Bill, her brother, to let her drive the car home—a means for her to take control of the situation. While driving, Selina starts wondering if she has made the right decision when she accepted the job. She makes efforts to sound normal, "steady[ing] the alarm in her voice" (2) but even then, the environment seems to parallel her state of mind: "Do you think I'm wrong?' she whispered at last as the sun became a molten ball behind the pines and a faint salt breeze reached them from the ocean" (2). It is as if the South were trying to claim her, to keep her there. The conversation that follows centers on Selina's sense of belonging to this place. Her brother tells her that once she is gone she "won't belong here anymore" and he adds that she "never [has], really" (2): "You're part of the beauty, Selina, but it's because it's the only beauty you've had. You've clung to the ocean and all its moods because it's really the only thing you've had to cling to, except the family […]" (2). Bill points out the limitations of life in the South, as the repetition of "only" suggests, and hints at the life his sister will experience outside of it. More importantly, in a way that is reminiscent of the title of Thomas Wolfe's novel *You Can't Go Home Again*, Bill implies that Selina's Southernness will forever be altered after she has been exposed to the North.

Bill's words cut deep into Selina's heart and they force her to express her apprehension: "it's part of me–I feel as though I were tearing myself up—I'm breaking myself off at the roots—just going away for this year" (2). Although she is not gone yet, she sees her departure as a kind of self-destruction for she is the agent of change. The reference to her roots shows how much she identifies with place—the known—and is afraid of what lies ahead. The use of dashes to render her hesitation as she speaks makes obvious the fragmentation within her that is established in the phrasal verbs she has selected—"tear up," "break off," "go away." The process has started and cannot be controlled. This metaphorical disintegration comes full circle when she enters her bedroom: "bare, with all her books and papers gone from the desk and tables, and her suitcases on the chairs and about the floor" (2). The emptiness of the room mirrors the void that has settled within her and yet she tries to conquer this lost space by scattering her clothes around: "she was pulling her wilted dress above her head, tossing it in a crumpled heap in the corner, flinging her shoes under the bed, her stockings in the middle of the floor" (2). Selina's dress was mentioned during the party in relation to the heat and to the feeling of discomfort that was developing in her—"her linen dress wilting and clinging to her" (1). Taking it off also means that she is getting rid of an identity she was not happy with.

Unlike the place where the party was held, the family house looks like a shelter: "Inside the house it was dim and cool, and her heavy tiredness from the heat and nerves fell away" (2). The activity there revolves around Melly, obviously the black help, who also worries over Selina. Her voice fills the air and punctuates a conversation Selina has with her parents. Melly's words appear within brackets, making her presence in the background and her place within the family circle very clear. The situation presented as such on paper adds to the Southern flavor of the story. Melly appears as "a powerful figure within the white family" whose presence "has been chosen to explain and reflect upon life, particularly on the ways of Southern segregation" (Tucker 94, 96). Selina's sense of place is also dependent on Melly: "It would be a long time before she would hear Melly's voice again, Selina thought, and tried to shake off her recurring homesickness for the things she had not yet left" (3). In spite of herself, Selina is listing the places, the things and the people making up her South. Her story illustrates Louis D. Rubin's theory which, by extension, clarifies L'Engle's status as a Southern writer: "what makes the oft-remarked Sense of Place in Southern writers so important is the vividness, the ferocity even, with which it implies social and community attitudes. This is because the writer's own experience of a place has involved those attitudes so pervasively that for the writer to evoke place is to confront the community's values" (33).

On the beach, she observes her surroundings as she takes a "farewell walk" and wonders: "how could one say good-bye to the ocean and the great stretch of silver beach, the white dunes and leaping wind?" (3). It is clear that Selina here resembles L'Engle herself who noted that "the ocean is so strong a part of my childhood memories and of my own personal mythology. If I am away from the ocean for long, I get a visceral longing for it" (*Summer*

208–9). A sense of loss grows inside her though she tries to retain her place in that very space: "Selina let the soft dry sand near the dunes sift through her toes, ran down the beach to the cool wet sand, ran into the water and splashed it high ahead of her, made deep foot-prints and watched the slow wet sand sift into them" (1). Her attempt to leave an imprint is unsuccessful but the message, though she is not ready to accept it, is clear: a new page in her life is about to be written over the old ones, the sand covering her foot-prints provides fresh ground for a new story. Likewise, when she is described "trac[ing] odd figures in the sand with her finger" (1), the use of the adjective "odd" mirrors her feeling of dismemberment. When she tries to reassure herself about her kinship to place, the narrator also suggests that it cannot be fully defined: "this was something that was part of her, something that she could never leave without leaving part of herself behind, and she knew now that it was a part of her which she would have to leave forever, no matter how long it would take the wound to heal" (3). The construction of the sentence with the repetition of "part of her" in the two clauses surrounding one in which a "part of herself" is mentioned reinforces the reflexivity of the pronoun and stresses the change Selina is undergoing.

The Sense of an Ending

Finding her Southern self coincides with Selina's parting with it. However, the South is not the only thing she is leaving. When she sets out to go home from the party, her brother mentions the absence of Peter and asks her whether she really wants to go—a question that echoes her decision to move North and which she understands as such: "Of course, I want to go […] I want to get out" (2). Bill understands that his sister's desire to leave the South is inextricably linked with something else: the burdensome presence of the past in everyday life is "not really why [she] want[s] to go" (2). The fact that Peter is omnipresent when people inquire about the party points to him as another reason leading up to Selina's choice—the two of them were probably lovers. When he eventually appears on the beach, she realizes "she had refused to admit to herself that she had been hurt because he had not come to the garden party to say good-bye to her" (3).

Peter's appearance leads to the story's denouement and, as often in a short story, the narrative comes full circle. He tells Selina that she should not let her future experience "'narrow [her] horizon'" because "'[i]t is broad'" (3). Unlike Bill, he feels that she "'belong[s] down here in the sun, with the wind and the waves'" (3). As is the case in L'Engle's *Ilsa*, the horizon reveals the presence of a boat: in the novel, the narrator explains that he "longs to be on it, to run away from [the] words" of another character (121); in the short story, the narrator only hints at Selina's hopes by using imagery that evokes light: "The beam from the light boat swung around, brighter with every turn as the last light faded and the stars came out, one by one, white and blue and yellow, throbbing above the ocean and the beach" (3). As soon as Peter tells her goodbye and disappears, she notices that "[t]he gleam from the lightship made a white arc across the sand, and the moon seemed to leap above the ocean's edge" (3). The presence of the moon—a symbol of feminine power—hints at the change that is happening in Selina and it is not surprising that later on she observes that "[t]he narrow path on the ocean became broader and brighter as the moon climbed higher [...]" (4).

The time she spends on the beach brings her two selves together and helps her come to terms with her real identity. The first farewell comes from nature itself as "strangely [Selina] seemed to hear in the recurrence of the breakers a new note, to feel in the wind an adequacy of farewell that could never be attained by words" (3). The second one is Peter's and it comes right after her southern self has symbolically been acknowledged by nature. Peter's presence almost seals her acceptance of a future outside the South and when she whispers "'Good-bye Selina'" (3), it is her former self that she is letting go. This is even clearer when she adds "'Introducing *Miss* Williams, instructress of history'" (3). The emphasis on "Miss" suggests that it is not in relation to Southern manners that she is calling herself this way but rather that she is gaining a new status: as a woman and as a respected teacher.

After spending a day wondering whether leaving the South was the right decision, Selina eventually comes to terms with it and realizes its necessity. Again, it is while looking at the landscape that she feels justified because "[a]head of her, rolling over the edge of the horizon, the gleaming highway of water stretched wide and clear" (4). The comparison of the ocean to a highway emphasizes the range of possibilities Selina will be able to choose from and her newly acquired wisdom. In addition, she has regained an identity she thought lost when "for a moment she was fused into the solitary splendor of wind and wave and sky. It was as though her soul was being branded with a talisman of the night" (3). The adjective "solitary" confirms that Selina may now strike out on her own—she has appropriated the strength of her surroundings which the ternary rhythm also designates as indivisible. Selina's understanding of space echoes L'Engle's own observation that "anybody who hasn't grown up on sulphur water is apt to find it distasteful; perhaps it does smell like rotten eggs, but to me it is good and healthy, redolent of sun and wind and sea" (*Summer* 206). Acceptance is the key to both Selina and L'Engle's take on the South—like Faulkner's Quentin Compson, they might have claimed that they did not hate it, though their stories draw a picture that proves the duality of their feelings.

Writing about the South, L'Engle seems to subscribe to Welty's comment that "[t]he essential landscape remains one to induce the kind of meditation from which real writing springs" (*Place* 548). In the texts she devotes to this singular region, her characters are often bemused by a place they wish to understand but that remains opaque to them. They are inside outsiders rather than insiders because they keep moving on the margins of its peculiar civilization. By deciding to move, Selina follows in the footsteps of many Southerners who felt the need to distance themselves so as to give a fairer account of their native region. The path Selina has chosen to tread on is not foreign to "[t]he road [that] seemed to be a dividing line between life and death" in *Ilsa* (173): leaving the South after she has been accepted by it proves her endurance and her desire to move on with her life. As a history teacher, she might be looking backward but as a human being she is glancing forward.

Notes

1. Biographical details derive from Bray, "Transforming Memories," and Hettinga.
2. Reading L'Engle's *The Other Side of the Sun* in this light would prove simulating for Stella's reactions upon discovering the South are closely related to the sublime and, by extension, to the uncanny.

Works Cited

Bray, Suzanne. "Transforming Memories: Madeleine L'Engle's Literary Recreation of Her Childhood Experience in France and Switzerland." *A View from Elsewhere*. Eds. Marcel Arbeit and Roman Trušník. Olomouc: Palacký University, 2014. 135–54. Print.
Derrida, Jacques. *On Touching—Jean-Luc Nancy*. Trans. Christine Irizarry. Stanford: Stanford University Press, 2005. Print.
Faulkner, William. *Absalom, Absalom!* 1936. *Novels 1936–1940*. Eds. Joseph Blotner and Noel Polk. New York: The Library of America, 1990. 1–315. Print.
_____. *As I Lay Dying*. 1930. *Novels 1930–1935*. Eds. Joseph Blotner and Noel Polk. New York: The Library of America, 1985. 1–178. Print.
_____. *Faulkner in the University*. Eds. Frederick L. Gwynn and Joseph L. Blotner. Charlottesville: University of Virginia Press, 1959. Print.
Hettinga, Donald R. *Presenting Madeleine L'Engle*. New York: Twayne, 1993. Print.
Housman, Alfred Edward. *A Shropshire Lad and Other Poems*. 1896. London: Penguin, 2010.
Jackson, Robert. *Seeking the Region in American Literature and Culture: Modernity, Dissidence, Innovation*. Baton Rouge: Louisiana State University Press, 2005. Print.
L'Engle, Madeleine. *A Circle of Quiet*. New York: Farrar, Straus and Giroux, 1972. Print.
_____. *Ilsa*. New York: The Vanguard Press, 1946. Print.
_____. *The Other Side of the Sun*. 1971. New York: Ballantine, 1987. Print.
_____. "Poor Little Saturday." 1956. *Witches: Wicked, Wild and Wonderful*. Ed. Paula Guran. Germantown: Prime Books, 2012. 227–41. Print.
_____. *The Summer of the Great Grandmother* (Volume 2 of *The Crosswicks Journals*). New York: HarperCollins, 1974. Print.

_____. "White in the Moon the Long Road Lies." *Opinion: The Literary Section of the Smith College Weekly* 7.3 (June 1939): 1–4. Print.

Lowe, John W. "Nineteenth-Century Southern Writers and the Tropical Sublime." *Southern Quarterly: A Journal of the Arts in the South* 48.3 (2011): 90–113. Print.

Rawlings, Marjorie Kinnan. "Regional Literature of the South." *College English* 1.5 (February 1940): 381–89. Print.

Rubin, Louis D. "From Combray to Ithaca: On the 'Southernness' of Southern Literature." *The Mockingbird in the Gum Tree: A Literary Gallimaufry*. Baton Rouge: Louisiana State University Press, 1991. 21–35. Print.

Stephens, Robert O. "Family." *The Companion to Southern Literature: Themes, Genres, Places, People, Movements, and Motifs*. Eds. Joseph M. Flora, Lucinda H. MacKethan and Todd Taylor. Baton Rouge: Louisiana State University Press, 2002. 247–250.

Tate, Allen. "The New Provincialism." 1945. *Essays of Four Decades*. New York: William Morrow, 1968. 535–46. Print.

Tucker, Susan. "The Black Domestic in the South: Her Legacy as Mother and Mother Surrogate." *Southern Women*. Ed. Caroline Matheny Dillman. New York: Hemisphere Publishing Corporation, 1988. 93–102. Print.

Vickery, John B. "Bridges and Housman as Elegists: The Modern Threshold." *English Literature in Transition (1880–1920)* 48.4 (2005): 404–19. Print.

Welty, Eudora. *The Eye of the Story: Selected Essays and Reviews*. New York: Random House, 1977. Print.

_____. *One Writer's Beginnings*. 1984. New York: Warner Books, 1985. Print.

_____. "Place and Time: The Southern Writer's Inheritance." *Mississippi Quarterly: The Journal of Southern Cultures* 50.4 (Fall 1997): 545–551. Print.

Of God and Women
The Evolution of Theology in L'Engle's Biblical Reimaginings

Emily Louise Zimbrick-Rogers

"After Annunciation"
This is the irrational season
When love blooms bright and wild.
Had Mary been filled with reason
There'd have been no room for the child.
—*The Weather of the Heart* (45)

In Madeleine L'Engle's poem about the Annunciation, she hints at a theme that pervades her stories about biblical characters and narratives—reason and rationality cannot fully explain the workings of God and humans. While L'Engle is not primarily known as a biblical fiction writer, a handful of her books use fiction to re-imagine biblical stories. However, engaging with L'Engle's biblical reimaginings[1] is important, because these narratives model her theology and dialog with Scripture and God. Through an analysis of L'Engle's biblical retelling oeuvre, we gain insights into their author, into ourselves, into the nature and character of God. Working out her own theological struggles and musings on the nature of Scripture, L'Engle returns again and again to two primary themes in her biblical reimaginings, the nature and character of God (including God's name) and gender. She accomplishes this most often through retelling and expanding the stories and narratives of the Hebrew Torah, and in particular Genesis, which is similar to the Jewish practice of midrash.[2]

Midrash is the ancient rabbinic method of biblical exegesis, filling in fissures and expanding interpretations of the scriptural texts.[3] In rabbinic Judaism, rabbis engaged in biblical exegesis and then wrote commentaries on their study of Torah or the Mishnah (Oral Torah), often to explain an obtuse passage or to make Torah more applicable to the community of faith as they often did in homilies. Midrash both explains the biblical text and also addresses "social, cultural, religious, polemical, and apologetic concerns" (Kalmin 133). The Institute for Contemporary Midrash characterizes midrash as that which "fills in the cracks [...] puts flesh on the bones [...] reinterprets stories and characters [...] gives a voice to those in the story who have no voice." According to compilers of midrash, midrashic methods nourish "the mind as well as the soul, the intellect as well as the imagination" (Ginzberg x) and "have ever proven an unfailing spring with the power to refreshen and renew, sustain and strengthen the Jew athirst for the word of the Living God" (Epstein xix). In L'Engle's published writings, she does not refer to what she does as midrash, although her long-time friend, co-author, and editor Luci Shaw said that L'Engle did use the term in teaching creative non-fiction writing classes when she asked her students to explore and write about lesser-known biblical characters, "producing what she called midrash—commentary and insight into an individual based on the culture and history of that individual" (e-mail communication). L'Engle's written work employs an imaginative interaction between a reader, a scriptural text, a question or a gap, and possible answers to the question: "The gap itself is a complex concept, which essentially means any place in the text that requires the intervention of the reader to make sense of the story" (Boyarin 130).

In this essay, I contend that, viewed through the lens of midrash, L'Engle is creatively wrestling with how to faithfully read the Bible in order to better comprehend the character of God and to find ways to navigate gender trouble in the texts. L'Engle does this through reimagining biblical narratives and characters.

This essay is broken into three main sections. First, I will review, chronologically and briefly, all of L'Engle's biblical reimaginings, providing an orientation to this aspect of her writings. Second, I will then focus the discussion on *Many Waters* and her *Genesis Trilogy*, particularly *Sold into Egypt*, as they best illustrate L'Engle's working out her themes of the character of God and gender. Finally, I will discuss how these themes illustrate the fourth aspect of the midrash definition in giving voice to those whose voices are either not preserved in the story or come through in highly selective and filtered ways—women and God. Thus, L'Engle's understanding of biblical authority and how to best approach the Scriptures is related to the midrashic concept of giving voice to the voices that reside in the cracks and fissures in the written narratives.

Overview of L'Engle's Biblical Reimaginings

The retelling of biblical stories seems to have come to L'Engle from an early age and permeates two decades of her most prolific writing and publishing. L'Engle wrote a biblical reimagining story in her young adulthood, which was published as one of the creative retellings in the first of the *Genesis Trilogy*. Between 1967 and 1989, she published eight books[4] that are either completely biblical reimaginings or that include biblical fiction.

1. *The Journey with Jonah*

Published in 1967, *The Journey with Jonah* is L'Engle's only published play for children, with pen-and-ink illustrations by Leonard Everett Fisher. Like much of L'Engle's work, much of the writing seems to be pitched at the biblically literate. The play was first written for and then performed by the elementary school pupils at St. Hilda's and St. Hugh's School in New York City, where L'Engle taught.

The play follows the narrative of the prophetic book of Jonah closely, though the play features Jonah interacting with a cast of animals but no humans. The theological question addressed is that of the universal mercy of God, and the relationship between God and God's people and those deemed "gentiles." Jonah complains to a silent, unresponsive God, "I hardly think it is suitable for you to be so gracious" (50). The turtle character seems to speak on behalf of God and explains that judgment is easy, but "compassion takes eternity" (54). In *The Journey with Jonah*, God is full of mercy and hospitality to those deemed outsiders by religious insiders.

2. *Dance in the Desert*

Her young children's storybook, *Dance in the Desert*, was published in 1969, and illustrated in full color by Symeon Shimin. It tells of an unnamed family crossing the desert to Egypt. To a biblically literate reader, the family is intended to be Mary, Joseph, and a toddler Jesus. This story fills in cracks in the New Testament canon, as the flight to Egypt periscope in Matthew's Gospel is told in summary—they went to Egypt, and then they returned to Israel. This story gives us a glimpse in this gap as the family travels with a merchant's caravan. As the travelers rest around a fire after the day's travel, a host of animals comes to the edge of the caravan's party to dance with the toddler, who is never named as Jesus. The mother and the father, also never named, seem to know the animals will not harm their son. All the creatures, both mythological and non-mythological, do obeisance to the child, and some allow him to pet them. In *Dance in the Desert*, the toddler Jesus is already fully God and loving ruler of the animals. The story ends with Jesus asleep in his mother's arms, giving us indications of L'Engle's high view of the Incarnation and Christology.

3. *Ladder of Angels*

In 1979, L'Engle published *Ladder of Angels*, which is a combination of visual midrash from children paired with L'Engle's written retellings of sixty-one Old Testament Bible stories. L'Engle introduces the book with a midrashic statement, "[The children's] utterly unjaded interpretations of the old Bible stories should help us all to see them anew" (6), which provides a frame for reading the book. The children's illustrations seem to be the focal point, and the majority of the stories are simple paraphrases. In a few stories, L'Engle's rhetorical questions provide the most innovation in her interaction with the biblical texts, centered on the theme of the character of God in regard to suffering and judgment. The first-person monologue from Isaac offers up harrowing questions such as "How can you [Abraham] worship a Lord who wants your child?" (32), while the story about Jacob's dream (which inspires the title and the cover art) reflects on the complicated relationship between God and God's children. She writes, "[W]hoever touches God bears the wound and can be recognized by it, forever. How many of God's people bear the wound?" (35). This is a God who wounds, even as this God restores.

4. *The Sphinx at Dawn*

This small book, published in 1982, accomplishes a huge amount of midrashic innovation, expanding our sparse knowledge of Jesus's childhood. The two short stories envision Jesus' childhood in Egypt, with a dozen wood engravings by Vivian Berger. Like *Dance in the Desert*, neither story identifies Jesus and his parents with their English names. The first story, "Pakko's Camel," calls Jesus by the nickname, "Yos," shortened from Yehoshuah, while the second story, "The Sphinx at Dawn," calls him a child or boy. In both stories, the love and grace of the child Jesus triumph over the murderous intentions of the sphinx and the greed and selfishness of an Egyptian bully.

In *The Sphinx at Dawn*, L'Engle offers readers a Jesus who is self-emptying, a loving friend and savior, a model of one obedient to the Word of God and the Spirit of God, a Jesus who is both the Word of God and recounts the words of God. L'Engle doesn't delve into didactic preaching, as she tends to do in the *Genesis Trilogy* and *Many Waters*, but gives complexity to theological reflection on the nature of Jesus Christ. Jesus knows more than he should (quotes Shakespeare) and can do more than a normal child (raise a boy from the dead, converse with camels and unicorns). However, Jesus is not all-knowing in these stories, most notably regarding his future role as savior of the world. While stylistically and artistically pitched to middle readers, the content seems written for theologically astute (Christian) readers. Both stories investigate the incarnation and Christology and touch upon miracles, history, time and space, forgiveness, and sin.

5. *And It Was Good: Reflections on Beginnings* (Volume 1 in the *Genesis Trilogy*)

Only a year after *The Sphinx at Dawn* was published, L'Engle published the first of the *Genesis Trilogy*, *And It Was Good*. The *Genesis Trilogy* is difficult to classify, as it is mainly non-fiction, but still does include some short fiction biblical reimaginings; yet, in some ways, the trilogy is the most midrashic, as midrash seamlessly transitions between commentary and narrative expansions of the Torah.

Concentrated on the early stories of Genesis (creation to Abraham, Sarah, and Hagar), *And It Was Good* also engages with topics as varied as creation and prayer, atomic bombs and care for creation, the Word of God and literalism, evolution and creationism, the problem of evil and free will, open theism,[5] and Christian universalism.[6] A half dozen reimaginings of only two to three lines are scattered through the non-fiction narrative, with two full short stories, "The First Birth" and "The Wages of Innocence," which address the birth of Cain and the death of Abel. The second story, told in the first-person from Cain's perspective, complicates our conception of Cain, as L'Engle both sticks with some familiar tropes in the Cain/Abel story but also overturns expectations. Her presentation of Cain is of a hurting, confused, and self-centered youth who is wowed by the tempter, in contrast to Abel, who is a simple, joyful boy who understands the worship of God. In *And It Was Good*, the main theme of note, while not worked out in the biblical reimagining stories but in the non-fiction narrative, is that of the name of God. This concept will be addressed in greater detail below in the sections on *Many Waters* and the third volume of the *Genesis Trilogy*, but L'Engle introduces it in *And It Was Good*. L'Engle explains she prefers to call God El or el[7] "rather than using the masculine or feminine pronoun, because the name el lifts the Creator beyond all our sexisms and chauvinisms and anthropomorphisms" (25). However, Hebrew grammar only includes masculine and feminine words, thus El *does* have masculine gender in the original Hebrew. Thus the genderlessness of the name or word El for an English reader would not necessarily be present for a reader who speaks or reads Hebrew, although a native Hebrew speaker would not equate grammatical gender with biological gender.[8] Yet L'Engle is striving to expand her own and her readers' conception of the nature of God.

6. *A Stone for a Pillow: Journeys with Jacob* (Volume 2 in the *Genesis Trilogy*)

In 1986, L'Engle published the second volume in the *Genesis Trilogy*, *A Stone for a Pillow: Journeys with Jacob*, which does not include any sustained biblical reimaginings. However, she does more fully explain her understanding of Scripture, a theme that will be addressed in my conclusion. This book spends much time on the theme of the character and name of God, again discussing how to wrestle with the apparent masculinity of the god she sees interacting with the early patriarchs. However, she falls into a traditional dualism, calling intellectual knowledge "masculine" as contrasted to feminine "wisdom," even as she proposes a need for revision in language about God to include "feminine wisdom" (109). Like much of her work, she connects devotional reflection on the Torah with current events, such as atomic war and American nationalism.

Close Analysis of Doctrines of God and Gender in Two Works

The final two biblical reimaginings will be discussed in much greater detail in order to investigate two major themes of the character of God and gender.

7. Many Waters

Published the same year as *Stone for a Pillow* (1986), *Many Waters*, a young adult novel, appears to provide a way forward for the namelessness of women in the Bible. This Noah story (Genesis 6–8) gives names and identities to Noah's wife, his three daughters-in-law, his two daughters and one other teenage girl.[9] The 15-year-old Murry twins, Sandy and Dennys, who appear in other books of the *Time Quintet,* accidently time travel to the Ancient Near East, where they meet Noah's family months before the flood destroys nearly all human, animal, and plant life.

DOCTRINE OF GOD

The first major theological theme is the nature and character of God, who she calls "El" (and is never referred to with an English gendered pronoun[10]) and is described as a "Voice" that Noah and his father, Lamech,[11] can hear. El gives instructions but not explanations and is often not *understood* even by those who can *hear* El. As the rains begin and Grandfather Lamech is close to death, he says, "El's words are strange words. I don't understand. I don't understand the thoughts of El" (223). A short time later, Lamech has again heard from El about the coming judgment: "All will not be lost [...] El has repented [...] Noah will be spared. Noah and his family" (234–35). Multiple characters discuss that "El is a great mystery" (249). Sandy says that he doesn't like El if El won't protect Yalith (the youngest daughter of Noah and

Matred) from drowning (308). However, El can be trusted, the narrative tells us, because El tells the seraphim[12] to bring Yalith to El, just like her forebear Enoch. But even as El protects Yalith, the seraphim explain, "There is no need to understand" (335). As in the opening poem on the Annunciation, the narrative seems to say that acceptance, not understanding, is the way to receive the painful details of the story.

Other characters hear messages from the stars, which seem to come from El, but not directly. The messages the stars give are ones of peace and hope, in spite of the coming judgment. The stars communicate to Yalith, "Fear not" (312). In the face of the impending doom and loss of life, Oholibamah, the wise, good wife of Japheth says, "I trust the stars. I trust El. I trust that all this will be for good" (329). The stars also chime at Dennys: "*Do not seek to comprehend. All shall be well. Wait. Patience. Wait. You do not always have to do something. Wait*" (318). Some readers might pick up on the allusion to Julian of Norwich: "All shall be well." L'Engle comes back to this idea several times (directly quoted here in *Many Waters* and in *Walking on Water* and conceptually important in much of her work). "All shall be well" seems to be how she approaches the difficult lacunae in Scripture, perhaps especially in relation to the silence of God.

The good angels, called seraphim, and fallen angels, called nephilim (Genesis 6.4[13]), also offer ways to comprehend God in *Many Waters*. Both groups refer to El as "the One" and are not all knowing in spite of their greater knowledge. The seraphim explain their relinquishing of powers in order to stay with humans on earth as having "*accepted being chosen*" rather than "we have chosen" or "been chosen" (192–93 italics mine). This seems to be hinting at L'Engle's view of freedom of will and predestination—a both-and, rather than an either-or. Similarly, one seraph asks if El sent the twins to help Noah and his father reunite, and another seraph explains a both-and understanding of God's will—El did not *send* them, but *neither* did El *prevent* their coming. L'Engle seems to ascribe to a form of open theism where God does not pre-ordain the future, but is open to how humans will shape it. The seraphs explain, "the pattern is not set. It is fluid, and constantly changing. But it will be worked out in beauty in the end" (346). It seems El can be trusted to care for those who love El. However, it is less clear if El is directly causing the flood to bring about judgment; if the flood is a part of the birthing of the young planet; or if El only directly intervenes to preserve Noah's family. Thus, the narrative could be saying indirectly that the mercy and salvation of God does not seem to extend to those who reject God. Readers are not given much opportunity to process and reflect on the death of the masses, but are more encouraged to rejoice in Yalith's salvation (assumption) and the twins getting back to their "normal" 20th century world unharmed. Yet, the title, *Many Waters*, indicates how readers are to understand the events of the novel—

"Many waters cannot quench love, neither can floods drown it" (*New Revised Standard Version* Song of Solomon 8.7). God is a God of mercy and love, which cannot be overwhelmed by destruction and death.[14]

Theology of Gender

The second overarching theological theme in *Many Waters* is gender, which veers into the heavy-handed. The explicit messages about the marginalization and silencing of women in the Torah seem so forceful they appear to come from outside the characters (from the author or at minimum from the omniscient narrator). The main characters, Sandy and Dennys, loudly complain about the patriarchal nature of the Old Testament and emphasize that the women in the Noah story are real people with real names and identities. The tone is so strong it reads, at times, like narrator or authorial intrusion, especially because the twins remember only the barest of details about the biblical flood story. As the twins work to recall the Sunday school story, Dennys muses:

> "I don't think Oholibamah, Elisheba, or Anah are called by name in the story. Matred isn't either.... Nor Yalith."
> "It was a very patriarchal society," Sandy said. "I do remember that."
> "Meg would call it chauvinistic," Dennys said. "Whoever wrote the Bible was a man. Men."
> "I thought it was supposed to be God. Wasn't that what we were taught in Sunday school?"
> "...The Bible was set down by lots of people over lots of years. Centuries. It's supposed to be the Word of God, not written by God" [189–90].

Here we see L'Engle's characters muse about the patriarchal nature of the Bible and the missing names of women, providing us clues to L'Engle's own way of dealing with tensions in the text. She seems to differentiate between God, God's Word, and the male authors that recorded, to the best of their ability and cultural constraints, the message of God. Later Dennys gets quite upset about the lack of women's names in the story he remembers from Sunday school. He says it's a "stupid" and "chauvinist" story, because only the males have names, but he now knows the women as "real people with names" (317). He explains the lack of women's names in his Sunday school account as the authors only seeing things from their own perspective and using people. The ubiquitous "they" think that women don't matter, Dennys says. The twins, and also the seraphim, though less overtly, affirm that women do matter and their names do exist and matter.

L'Engle names her women characters after some named women characters in the Hebrew Bible. Matred, Noah's wife, is the name of the mother-in-law of a king in Genesis 36.39 and means "pushing forward." The three wives of Shem, Ham, and Japheth all have biblical Hebrew names as well.

Oholibamah and Elisheba (the positively characterized daughters-in-law) mean respectively, "tent of the high place" (one of Esau's wives in Genesis 36) and "God is my oath" (Aaron's wife in Exodus 6). Noah's penultimate daughter, Mahlah, has the same name as one of the daughters of Zelophehad, who Moses allows to keep her father's inheritance (Numbers 26–27, 36; Joshua 17). Mahlah and Anah's names do not have particularly positive meanings like the three positively portrayed women characters listed above, but are biblical names. Interestingly, Yalith, the most central female character, does not have a name referenced in the Hebrew Bible. However, Yalith seems to be an allusion to and modification on Lilith, a female demon briefly mentioned in Isaiah 34.14, but whose extra-biblical presence is vast and diverse, beginning as a Babylonian demon, reappearing in medieval Jewish mythology as Adam's first (and disobedient) wife (Gaines).[15] Lilith means "of the night," and thus Yalith means "of Yahweh." Thus, while Yalith's name is not biblical in origin, L'Engle is attributing great importance to her name by connected it with the God of the Old Testament. L'Engle's narrator restores individual personhood to unnamed women in the Noah story and also reminds readers that not all women in the biblical narratives were nameless.

However, while women are present and named, they are not as complex as the male characters. All the female characters fit into one of the classical feminine tropes: virgin, whore, or mother. The only female characters who survive the flood are all mothers (or soon-to-be mothers). None of the female characters experience real change, where four male characters experience some growth—the twins, Noah, and Lamech. However, Yalith is a central character beloved by the twins (and the seraphim) who still listens to the stars that share messages from El, so the narrative goes to great lengths to save her. While the advances of a nephil briefly tempt Yalith, she does not seem to be at real risk of falling from her virginity. However, this incident could also be read as making Yalith a real human, not only an otherworldly virgin, perhaps subverting the presentation of the virgin trope. Yet, Yalith wholeheartedly trusts her father, the seraphim, and the stars, which radiate messages of wait, have patience, and do not fear. In the end, a seraph transports Yalith directly to the Presence, creating a female counterpart to her ancestor Enoch (Genesis 5.24) and also a forerunner of the Roman Catholic and Orthodox understanding of the Assumption of Mary. While Yalith has been awakened to her romantic and sexual attraction to the twins, she remains a virgin and is told she will find the transport to El a "rapturous experience" (335). The description of Yalith's translation to El's Presence does seem to be intentionally erotic, perhaps as a nod to mystics like St. Teresa of Avila, whose union with God is both romantic and erotic.

The narrative seems to say that judgment is acceptable for those who "naturally" fit into the role of whore. The narrative punishes the explicit "whore" character, Tiglah, who has a (sexual) relationship with one of the nephilim and who also tempts the twins to experience sexual awakening. Mahlah, Tiglah's friend and Yalith's sister, also has a sexual relationship with a nephil and marries him, then delivers a half-human, half-nephil baby. She is not presented as negatively as Tiglah, but neither is she presented in a wholly positive light. After she gives birth to her baby, the narrator comments she loves her baby, so perhaps Mahlah is L'Engle's attempt to upset the virgin/whore dichotomy, as she becomes a mother. Although the reader does not see the fate of Tiglah and Mahlah, it is assumed that they perish in the flood. And despite their proto-feminist discourse, Sandy and Dennys don't seem concerned about stereotyping Tiglah, the "whore" character. In their last encounter with Tiglah, Sandy and Dennys are remarkably dismissive in the face of knowing she is soon to drown: "Thanks for nothing," Sandy says to her, echoed by Dennys's "Ditto" (342). Readers, too, might receive an implicit message that the death of the wicked does not demand mourning.

However, the implicit messages complicate the commitment to whole personhood for nameless and silent female characters in the Old Testament. The narrative mentions, without any commentary, that Noah and Matred wanted a fourth son, not a fourth daughter. Both the seraphim and nephilim are presented as "brothers," though some of the their proper names are female angel or demon names. Additionally, when Sandy assumes a griffin is male, a seraph emphatically corrects him: "*She* is half lion, half eagle" (171).

Yet *Many Waters* does offer female readers a way to see themselves in the biblical narrative. Yalith is not allowed to enter the ark, but she is transported to El like her ancestor Enoch, because of her godliness and obedience to El. In addition to Yalith, Oholibamah hears messages from the stars, which communicate peace and love on El's behalf. Overall, *Many Waters* consigns sexism and lack of women's personhood to the patriarchal biblical authors, not God/El. Dennys says to a seraph, "I'm not a bit interested in rewriting the Bible" (116). We could read this ironically—as it comes in the midst of a biblical retelling story—but L'Engle adds a complex layer to readers' understanding of gender and Scripture. And perhaps we could propose that L'Engle does not rewrite, but simply reimagines—and reimagines in order to give women and girls place, name, identity, and voice. She enables readers to see some of the women who were active participants of the Noah story.

8. *Sold into Egypt: Joseph's Journey into Human Being* (Volume 3 of *Genesis Trilogy*)

L'Engle's last biblical reimagining was published in 1989, twenty-two years after the publication of her first biblical retelling. *Sold into Egypt* is structurally the best executed of the *Genesis Trilogy* with twelve chapters for the twelve tribes of Israel and a biblical reimagining at the end of each chapter, including five women: Dinah, Bilhah (Jacob's concubine, handmaid of Rachel, Rachel's half-sister), Gad's wife (unnamed), Potiphar's wife (unnamed), and Asenath, Joseph's Egyptian wife. L'Engle's present-day reflection is concentrated on death, both of her husband and also a few close friends. Again she touches on her usual topics of literalism and evolution, pollution and atomic warfare, but also spends more time on resurrection, death, and grieving. Similar to *Many Waters*, two primary themes emerge around the character of God and gender. However, unlike *Many Waters*, the themes are inseparably woven together in *Sold into Egypt*.

In this work, even L'Engle's biblical reimaginings from the perspectives of men pay greater attention to women. For example, Reuben's chapter focuses on the love of women—how his baby sister Dinah loved him, how his father Jacob did not love his mother Leah, how he loved and was loved by Bilhah, his father's concubine. Reuben's monologue also explains Dinah's story (rape by Shechem) as one of mutual love and not rape. Judah's monologue recounts the "trouble" women and their goddesses have brought him and his sons, presenting women as a dialogic binary of love and trouble. Potiphar's wife gives a short monologue at the end of the Dan chapter, which complicates the character of Potiphar's wife, with her recounting of marital rape by her husband Potiphar, followed by a mutual relationship with one of her male servants, and thus frustration that Joseph would not return her interests. However, this agentic and self-actualized unnamed woman is also portrayed as a sex-obsessed, petty, vindictive person who does not regret that her actions lead to Joseph's imprisonment. In the non-fiction narrative, L'Engle calls her "one of the nastiest women one could imagine" (105). Thus, we can see that L'Engle does not only portray women in a positive light, but that sometimes giving voice to women portrays them in negative and still stereotyped ways while at the same time revealing motivations for their behavior (such as the portrayal discussed above of the "whore" type in *Many Waters* or providing insights into Cain's murder of his brother).

Bilhah, Reuben's lover, speaks her own monologue, where she contrasts her goddess with the god of Jacob, who, in her mind, "is a man, rough and wild" (53). She says it is folly for a woman to try to be a man and emphasizes the goodness of being a woman. Bilhah sees "it is the calling of women to give" in contrast to men who believe it is their right to take (55). As the chapters end only on the retelling monologues, it is difficult to surmise if L'Engle-the-author agrees with Bilhah's perspective on the essential nature of womanhood and the masculine nature of Jacob's god. Perhaps L'Engle is reminding readers that more emphasis needs to be placed on feminine images of God (such as Personified Wisdom in Proverbs; maternal images in Isaiah) to understand the god-beyond-gender.

In *Stone for a Pillow*, L'Engle hints at Dinah's story being not one of rape, but of mutual love. In the monologue for the Levi chapter in *Sold into Egypt*, she allows Dinah to tell her own story. Anachronistically Dinah quotes from the prayer, "Blessed art thou, O Lord, who has not made me a woman."[16] Dinah notes that no one asked for her perspective about her encounter with Shechem. She extends Bilhah's musing on the masculinity of God and says she wants no part of her brothers' and father's god if he demanded the murder of Shechem. She sees in her father's god a bloody god "as far back as I can remember," recounting the almost-sacrifice of Isaac (73). She wonders if Shechem's gods are less bloody, even as they might have been helpless in protecting the life of her loved Shechem. Gad's (unnamed) wife also reflects on the nature of Jacob's family god and her own worship of an unnamed moon goddess. Asher, one of Jacob's sons, reflects on the wives' worship of their own goddesses and wonders if this angers God. L'Engle leaves the questions hanging, not returning to answer them in the non-fiction sections.

Asenath, Joseph's wife, also questions monotheism and the relationship between the god of Joseph and her Egyptian gods and the significance of her father, a priest of an Egyptian god, giving her in marriage to a man who worshiped a different god. Asenath wonders if her god and Joseph's god are the same god, and "is there a God whose mercy is over all?" (181). In the last monologue, Joseph reflects on a conversation with his father-in-law, the high priest. As they discuss dreams and the future, Joseph understands that the high priest is given insight that does not contradict the plan of God. Joseph sees the difference in their gods is that the God of Joseph's fathers walks with his people and is with them. This God-with-us cares for God's people. Yet all of the women who are featured in the reimaginings except for Asenath seem to think the God of Jacob is a god for men and that women necessarily worship a different goddess or multiple goddesses, which proves problematic for Jewish or Christian women readers. The men too seem to agree with this division.

In her non-fiction passages, L'Engle reflects on the nature and character of God, working out the conflicting perspectives she finds in the Old Testament portrayal of God. She muses that God, El, seems to be almost two separate gods, a "tribal masculine god" and the "Maker of the Universe, Creator of the Stars, All in All, the God of Love who still lights our hearts" (58). L'Engle implies that the patriarchs—and subsequent generations—misunderstand God, but that the God of Love is present in Scripture and should be more emphasized.[17] L'Engle concludes with a call to forgiveness and invitation to come home to God, that all works together for good (again alluding to Julian of Norwich and Romans 8.28) and the love of God. L'Engle ends, not with commentary on the masculine god of Genesis, but the God of mercy. Her final lines of biblical retelling, and final lines of the book, are the monologue of Joseph, bringing together all of her reflections on the character of God and how God's children are to relate to one another:

> When my brothers threw me into the pit, God was there, in the pit with me. [...] If my heart is cold towards my brothers, does not that also chill the heart of God? The sun god looks down but is not part of the lives of those who worship the burning light. But my God—how can we bear a God who cares? [...] Oh, my brothers, because God is with us, how can I turn away from you without turning away from God? [...] And now my brothers have come, oh my brothers, and now that I love them, and they are freed to love me, joy will come again, and laughter. And I will praise God [234–235].

L'Engle does not engage with the implication that the God of Jacob and Joseph is only a god for men, but rather leaves us with this portrayal of God as one who cares and brings the estranged together. L'Engle is not constrained by an idealization of Enlightenment reason and internal consistency, allowing God to simply be a paradox.

Conclusion

In a chronological overview, we see that L'Engle's early reimaginings start to engage with the nature of God as revealed in the person of Jesus Christ. Through narrative expansion of Jesus's childhood, she engages in a midrash of the Incarnation and Christology. Beginning with *The Journey with Jonah*, we see midrash addressing the doctrine of God and the welcome of the stranger, which continues in *Ladder of Angels*, the *Genesis Trilogy*, and *Many Waters*. Her concern with women as an excluded and marginalized Other emerges in the intersection between her emerging doctrine of God and welcome for the Other. Thus, we can begin to see a development and even progression in L'Engle's engagement with her own theological musings, the biblical texts, and her context including a dialogue with emerging feminist theology, the Women's Movement, and secular feminism.

Concerns for the voices and perspectives of women in the Hebrew Bible do emerge, even as L'Engle seems to struggle with how to enable these female characters to be worshippers of God. *Many Waters* offers us women characters who worship, know, love, and are loved by God (El). However, while *Sold into Egypt* presents women in their own voices, they do not worship the same god worshipped by the patriarchs and in fact do not see this god as a god for them. Thus, we must complicate the glowing assessment of some of L'Engle's friends, who write, "No writer of the twentieth century better defines what it means to be a Christian artist than Madeleine L'Engle" (Miller 197). L'Engle herself decried being labeled as a Christian artist, and this statement is additionally problematic when looking primarily at the fictionalized characters in L'Engle's biblical retellings. Her fictional biblical women characters in the *Genesis Trilogy* seem to fall, perhaps unconsciously, toward post–Christian feminist theology that focuses so heavily on "patriarchal erasure" (Daly 23) that it is difficult to find a way for women to worship God, who often appears patriarchal or androcentric. And while L'Engle did write "openly and joyfully in response to the biblical story" as Katherine Paterson describes (99), we cannot assess her biblical retellings as purely feminist as some devotees of L'Engle might wish to do. For example, Carole Chase says the naturalness and grace of L'Engle's stories "may have disguised the feminist affirmations that are laced throughout her writing" (137). Chase unwittingly equates feminism with a lack of naturalness or grace and then argues that L'Engle's biblical stories "allow her to present a feminist perspective of Scripture." However, her definition of this feminist perspective is simply giving voice to the women without analyzing the content of L'Engle's stories (145). Some might consider this a sufficient feminist perspective, but theology is clearly important to L'Engle, and thus we must investigate the *theological* ramifications of how she gives voice to women. Readers striving to reconcile themselves with a patriarchal Bible may struggle to see L'Engle's presentation of women stereotyped as outsiders to God's family, or only saved through the flood as mothers (or assumed to God because of an otherworldly nature).[18]

Perhaps we can find a way forward both in the concept of midrash which acknowledges the paradox in the scriptural texts, and also L'Engle's own reflections on the living nature of the Bible, which "urges us to go beyond its pages, not to stop with what we have read" (*Stone* 63). She acknowledges her struggle with the Bible, citing as problematic the raped and murdered woman in Judges, the blighted fig tree, and the pervasive violence. She reaches far in her critique of wooden and frozen interpretations: "Limited literalism," she muses, "is one of Satan's cleverest devices" (*Stone* 81), which may cause us to miss the truth of the biblical narratives. She cites Karl Barth's oft-repeated line about taking the Bible so seriously that it can't be taken literally. Perhaps *Stone for a Pillow* needed to function as somewhat of a defense of *Many Waters*, the only full-length biblical reimagining novel, which took some liberties with the biblical Noah story. She asks how to read the Bible "creatively and not destructively?" and answers that she accepts it "as it is" with a desire to be open to the "deeply mythic quality" (*Stone* 66). In *Stone for a Pillow*, she explains,

> The mythic interpretation is not a facile, shallow one, but an attempt to move into the deep and dazzling darkness of that truth which the fragile human mind cannot exhaustively comprehend, but can only glimpse with occasional flashes of glory [...] The mythic world makes enormous demands of us, and that may be why it is so often shunned [80].

Thus, we can find places in L'Engle's biblical reimaginings that provide glimpses of glory. L'Engle toward the end of her publishing of biblical retellings strives to present a God beyond masculine gender. Other aspects of L'Engle's biblical retellings show an active working out and struggle to find women's voices in the midst of what L'Engle comes to understand as a patriarchal text, written by men, for men, about men, looking at God who is seen through male eyes—and is at times even seen to be a male god. L'Engle does "repopulate the ancient landscape" with women (Cohick 325), yet her biblical retellings do not present many women who worship the God of the patriarchs. However, she expands her notion of the character and nature of God to be that which welcomes the stranger and the outsider—even women.

And this view of God—an expansive, welcoming, God-of-love-for-all that runs throughout all her biblical reimaginings—also gave her difficulty with some Christian readers who thought her view of God was too expansive, bordering on universalistic. Looking at her biblical reimaginings, it seems that God is always a God of love, but also a God who saves those who turn to God in humility, belief, and repentance. The salvific work of Jesus Christ is only addressed in two of the biblical reimaginings and only appears prophetically in a few of the Old Testament reimaginings. From her nonfiction writing, the person of Jesus Christ does seem central to salvation, though in her biblical fiction she does also seem to open the possibly of salvation for all people, through the mercy and love of God.

Like midrash, which does not fit neatly into binaries of fiction and nonfiction, scripture and commentary, L'Engle resists categorization on multiple accounts, not least of all theology. Thus, I propose she is working out her faith in a similar vein to Anselm's famous dictum of "faith seeking understanding"—she is actively doing theology by telling stories, listening to Scripture and speaking back into its cracks and gaps, both filling in gaps and creating new fissures that she does not fill but allows her readers to experience. Thus, I wish to close the discussion with L'Engle's own words on how she interacts with Scripture. In *And It Was Good*, L'Engle writes,

> ...I remember that people were then, as now, struggling with finite minds to comprehend an infinite God. Anything we can say about God is going to be inadequate, a groping for truths beyond our limited capacities. And (paradox again) I believe in the Bible as the living Word of God. But this faith involves an acceptance that the Bible is not static; that at different times the living Word can speak in different ways to different ears, and that even the Bible itself can never fully express or manifest the glory of the Creator [166].

NOTES

1. "Biblical reimagining" is a term I coined to emphasize the creative, imaginative possibility of retelling biblical stories. Biblical reimagining, like midrash, fills in gaps and expands on the sparse biblical narrative, often giving voice, agency, and personhood to marginalized characters in the original biblical record.

2. I am not the first to call L'Engle's biblical retellings "midrash." In the intro-

duction of *And It Was Good*, Luci Shaw, her long-time friend, occasional co-author, and often editor, alludes to the concept—that L'Engle provides new insights into the character and person of God. Carole Chase also uses the term midrash; however, I did not discover Chase's use of the term until late into the writing of this chapter. I also disagree with Chase's completely positive assessment of L'Engle's midrash as "feminist perspective" (145). Chase does not critically assess L'Engle's feminism, but rather takes it as a matter of course. Additionally, Luci Shaw confirmed that L'Engle herself called commentary and insights into lesser-known characters "midrash" (Shaw 2016).

3. This essay does not have the space or the ability to properly situate midrash in dialogue with Talmud (Mishnah and Gemara); thus, the use of midrash is to be understood as a *literary analytic lens* to better appreciate L'Engle's biblical reimaginings, rather than an exact and technical comparison. I do not assume that L'Engle had knowledge of the "rules" of midrashic methodology, but rather she adopted the gestalt idea of midrash to write her biblical retellings. I wish to apologize for but acknowledge that "the classification of a text as midrash has become a fashionable trend" as per Strack and Stemberger (258). I chose the term midrash rather than biblical exegesis because while exegesis does describe midrash, midrash often is narrative and presents answers through new imaginative stories, while our common understanding of exegesis is that it is explanatory but not narrative.

4. Some of L'Engle's poetry could be considered "biblical reimagining," but this chapter will only address the narrative biblical retellings, rather than poetic ones, for simplicity's sake. Readers interested are encouraged to read *The Weather of the Heart*, which includes a number of biblical poems.

5. Open theism is the theological concept that God does not know the future or has not dictated or mandated the future, thus leaving the universe open to multiple future possibilities. Historic orthodox Christianity has repudiated open theism following Thomas Aquinas, who postulated that God is omniscient, or all knowing, and thus must know all possible outcomes and thus the future outcome that will occur. Open theists do assert that God knows all possibilities but not what will occur, because God has left that "open" for humans to shape. The topic has garnered much recent conversation in evangelical and post-evangelical theology.

6. Christian universalism is slightly different from universalism, as the centrality of the person of Jesus Christ is still present in Christian universalism—all will be saved through Jesus Christ, though how that occurs is a mystery—versus general universalism that says Jesus Christ is not central or necessary to universal salvation. I read L'Engle as a Christian universalist, not a general universalist.

7. YHWH is the most common name in the Old Testament, followed by the appellative Elohim. Far behind in frequency are Adonay and El, which is also an appellative, but is one of the Old Testament names for God (Feldmeier and Spieckermann, 22–23).

8. Thanks to Claudia Mazur, MFA, for this insight, who explained that a Hebrew-speaking reader of L'Engle would know that in Hebrew El is gendered grammatically masculine even though L'Engle uses it as an non-gendered English noun and pronoun substitute for both God and He/he (where He would refer to God). Thank you also to the book's editor Suzanne Bray, who further explained to me how a speaker of a gendered language (like French or Hebrew) might interact with another gendered language in comparison to a speaker of a non-gendered language (like English).

9. The biblical text offers names for Noah and his sons, Shem, Ham, Japheth, while Noah's wife and daughters-in-law are unnamed. L'Engle names the woman—

Noah's wife is Matred; Shem's wife is Elisheba; Anah is Ham's wife; and Oholibamah is married to Japheth. Noah's family in *Many Waters* also includes two married daughters, who barely appear, and two unmarried daughters, Mahlah, who becomes the wife of a nephil, and Yalith, whom the twins end up both loving.

10. See footnote 8 on the grammatical gender of the Hebrew.

11. Lamech means "despair."

12. In the Bible, seraphim are only referenced in Isaiah 6.2-4, but later Christian theology on angels placing the seraphim as the highest level of angels that worship God. In Hebrew, the "im" ending indicates that seraphim are male.

13. It is unsure if "sons of God" in Genesis 6.2 is a description of the nephilim referenced in 6.4, or if nephilim are the offspring of the sons of God and human women. In Numbers 13.33, the nephilim are "giants." L'Engle's is well within accepted Christian theology presenting the nephilim as the "brother" angels of the seraphim, but who have turned their backs on worship of El.

14. Thanks to Dr. Denise Crews for reminding me to look at the title again as indication of L'Engle's understanding of the God of *Many Waters*.

15. Lilith is left as a proper name in some English Bible translations (*New Revised Standard Version* and *Common English Version*) and is translated as "screech owl" (*King James Version*) or "night creatures" (*New International Version*) and comes from the root word for "night." Biblical commentators are also split between considering Lilith a demon (Brueggemann) or simply a frightening night creature (Childs). Many feminists, including feminist theologians, have reclaimed Lilith as a "heroine" (Plaskow 31).

16. This often quoted prayer is included in a Jewish prayer book, which was compiled after the destruction of the Temple in 70 C.E.; thus, L'Engle is playing with time here, as this prayer would likely have been unknown to Dinah, several thousand years earlier.

17. These insights sit comfortably within liberal theology, but are more difficult for conservative or evangelical Christians to come to terms with. It is common knowledge that L'Engle received much criticism from some sectors of conservative or evangelical Christianity, and she comments on how upset she is by that "slander" (*Sold Into Egypt*, 105), followed by her own criticism of both the left (the "undisciplined lust" of "sexual revolution," 135) and the right (Moral Majority, racism).

18. Perhaps this is an unconscious reference to the difficult passage in 1 Timothy 2.15 (*King James Version*): "Notwithstanding she shall be saved in childbearing, if they continue in faith and charity and holiness with sobriety."

Works Cited

Boyarin, Daniel. "Review: Midrash in Parables." *AJS Review*, Vol. 20, No. 1 (1995): 123–138. Web.

Brueggemann, Walter. *Isaiah 1–39*. Westminster Bible Companion. Louisville, KY: Westminster John Knox Press, 1998. Print.

Chase, Carole F. *Suncatcher: A Study of Madeleine L'Engle and Her Writing*. 2nd Ed. Philadelphia: Innisfree Press, 1998. Print.

Childs, Brevard S. *Isaiah*. The Old Testament Library. Louisville, KY: Westminster John Knox Press, 2001. Print.

Cohick, Lynn. *Women in the World of the Earliest Christians: Illuminating Ancient Ways of Life*. Grand Rapids: Baker Academic, 2009. Print.

Daly, Mary. *Gyn/ecology, the Metaethics of Radical Feminism*. Boston: Beacon Press, 1978. Print.

Epstein, I. Foreword. *Midrash Rabbah*. Ed. H. Freedman and Maurice Simon. Trans. H. Freedman. Vol. 1. New York: Soncino Press, 1983. Print.
Feldmeier, Reinhard, and Hermannn Spieckhermann. *God of the Living: A Biblical Theology*. Trans. Mark E. Biddle. Waco, TX: Baylor University Press, 2011. Print.
Gaines, Janet Howe. "Lilith: Seductress, Heroine or Murderer?" *Biblical Archaeology Society* 17, no. 5 (2001). Print.
Ginzberg, Louis. *The Legend of the Jews*. Trans. Henrietta Szold. Vol. 1. Philadelphia: Jewish Publication Society of America, 1909. Print.
Kalmin, Richard. "The Use of Midrash for Social History." *Current Trends in the Study of Midrash*. Ed. Carol Bakhos. Vol. 106: Supplements to *The Journal for the Study of Judaism*. Boston: Brill, 2006. 133–159. Print.
L'Engle, Madeleine. *And It Was Good: Reflections on Beginnings*. Wheaton, IL: Shaw, 1983. Print.
_____. *Dance in the Desert*. New York: Farrar, Straus, and Giroux, 1969. Print.
_____. *Journey with Jonah*. New York: Sunburst Book; Farrar, Straus, and Giroux, 1967. Print.
_____. *Ladder of Angels: Stories from the Bible Illustrated by Children of the World*. San Francisco: Harper and Row, 1979. Print.
_____. *Many Waters*. New York: Farrar, Straus, and Giroux, 1986. Print.
_____. *Sold into Egypt: Joseph's Journey into Human Being*. Wheaton, IL: Shaw, 1989. Print.
_____. *A Stone for a Pillow: Journeys with Jacob*. Wheaton, IL: Shaw, 1986. Print.
_____. *The Weather of the Heart: Poems*. Wheaton, IL: Shaw, 1978. Print.
Miller, Calvin. "In Favor of God." *The Swiftly Tilting Worlds of Madeleine L'Engle: Essays in Her Honor*. Ed. Luci Shaw. Wheaton, IL: Shaw, 1998. 197–204. Print.
Paterson, Katherine. "Taking the Bible Seriously." *The Swiftly Tilting Worlds of Madeleine L'Engle: Essays in Her Honor*. Ed. Luci Shaw. Wheaton, IL: Shaw, 1998. 85–102. Print.
Plaskow, Judith. *The Coming of Lilith: Essays on Feminism, Judaism, and Sexual Ethics, 1972–2003*. Boston: Beacon Press, 2005. Print.
Shaw, Luci. "Introduction." *And It Was Good: Reflections on Beginnings*. Wheaton, IL: Shaw, 1983.
_____. "Re: L'Engle, Midrash and You." Message to the author. 7 March 2016. E-mail.
Strack, Hermann L., and Gunter Stemberger. *Introduction to the Talmud and Midrash*. Trans. Markus Bockmuehl. Edinburgh: T&T Clark, 1991. Print.

"And what should I do in Illyria?"[1]
Discovering the American South and Its Gods in Madeleine L'Engle's The Other Side of the Sun

SUZANNE BRAY

When commenting on the Anglican author Madeleine L'Engle's novel *The Other Side of the Sun*, which takes place in the American South at the beginning of the 20th century, the American academic Donald R. Hettinga declares: "For a Christian writer not named O'Connor to place an empirically educated character in such a setting in a novel published by a secular publishing house a handful of years after a national magazine told popular culture that God was dead takes a bit of chutzpa" (173).

Nevertheless, Madeleine L'Engle was quite up to the task. Born and raised until the age of twelve in New York, with a father from the North and a mother best described as a Southern gentlewoman (Franklin) from Jacksonville, Florida, where the vast majority of her relatives lived, Madeleine L'Engle Camp, to give her birth name, knew the South well, but always "as an outsider" (Avent 30). From her earliest childhood she regularly visited her grandmother and numerous cousins, most of whom were typical southerners. In addition, Madeleine's mother regularly told stories taken from their family history to her only daughter who was fascinated by the adventures of her foremothers. Later on, the writer was to take her great-grandmother, Madeleine L'Engle's, name. This formidable lady, "whom the family generally referred to as Mado" (Rosenberg 13) and who had lived for several years at the court of Spain where her father was the American ambassador, had been a close friend of Eugénie de Montijo, Napoleon III's future wife.

In 1933, when Madeleine was fifteen years old, her family settled in Jacksonville after having spent a few years in Europe. She was sent to a boarding school in Charleston. Although Madeleine found Florida "stultifying and surreal" (Zarin 63), to her great surprise "she adored Ashley Hall" (Zarin 63), her high school in Charleston. She loved "the family [she] found there" (*Rock* 46) and, in that friendly community, she started to be reconciled to the South. However, holiday times were difficult for her and, according to her second cousin Mary, she "was completely out of place at that time and in that part of the world" (Avent 30), where all the girls her age were coming out into society and looking for an eligible husband. Madeleine, on the other hand, was preparing to go to college and become a professional writer. According to Nancy Bruce, who knew Madeleine in her youth, part of the problem came from the very nature of southern society: "Jacksonville [...] was a very class-conscious place, and of course it was segregated. As young people, we were all so used to segregation that I don't think we gave it any thought at the time" (36). For Madeleine, most at home in New York, France or Switzerland, adapting to this traditional lifestyle was not easy.

In 1945, after the publication of her first novel, *The Small Rain*, which was moderately successful, L'Engle decided to write a story set in the South. The result, *Ilsa* (1946), which tells the story of a Southern Belle and her very difficult life from the point of view of one of the men who loves her, had just one print run and is very difficult to find today. The novel did not sell particularly well and the L'Engle is said to have been dissatisfied with the book, perhaps at least partly because Ilsa "lacks the positive themes of family, love, faith, and overcoming adversity that are so prevalent in L'Engle's later novels" ("Ilsa (novel)"). She waited another twenty-five years before returning to the South for a full-length novel. In 1971, she was already famous, especially for her children's books like her classic *A Wrinkle in Time* (1962), and this time, L'Engle decided not to rely on her personal memories, but did "a good bit of research" (*Great-Grandmother* 193), both historical and in her own family, before starting to write *The Other Side of the Sun*, a work which Carole Chase describes as a tale "about Southern pride and prejudice" (Chase 34). L'Engle herself saw the novel as an attempt to play with the Southern Gothic genre with its big, decayed and near derelict houses, eerie, oppressive atmospheres and eccentric, often frightening characters. Yet, unlike many works in this tradition, l'Engle has a clear and Christian message of hope. In a writers' workshop in 1983, she claimed: "In *The Other Side of the Sun*, what I tried to do was to take the traditional Gothic form and give it theological depth" (*Herself* 213).

This novel, inspired by various stories of L'Engle's southern ancestors (*Rock* 92), presents a 19-year-old, very innocent, British woman, Stella, shortly after her marriage to a Southern gentleman. She arrives in the South to stay with her husband's family while he is absent on a secret diplomatic mission "with no preconceptions" (*Other Side* 31) and without knowing anything at all about the region. She therefore has to learn about her husband's family, culture and lifestyle in his absence. To start with she feels like "a stranger in an alien land" (33) at Illyria, the huge rural family mansion. During a conversation with the only person she can fully understand, Ron, a black doctor who was trained in England, she adapts part of Viola's first speech in Shakespeare's *Twelfth Night*. Ron understands her allusion and continues the dialogue:

- What country, friends, is this?
- This is Illyria, Lady.
- And what should I do in Illyria?

Throughout the novel, in which Stella is both the narrator and the main character, this question is explored, charting the difficult road to understanding a civilisation very different from the one Stella had known when living in England with her atheist, rationalist and academic father. She has to remind herself many times that she is no longer in "rational, reasonable Oxford" (*Other Side* 70). Stella is helped in her discoveries by her husband's elderly great-aunts, Olivia and Mary Desborough (Des), who are from the same generation as Mado, L'Engle's great-grandmother. Mado herself appears in the novel, slightly transformed into a Frenchwoman who moved to the American South on her marriage, but still has the same character, "a merry person, full of vitality" (*Rock* 91), and is supported by the same strong faith. The character Mado is already dead when Stella arrives in America, but the young bride gets to know her via her diaries. The other dominant personality in the story, Honoria, resembles the African princess, forcibly married to a slave trader, who was a close friend of Mado's real life mother-in-law, Susan Philippa Fatio (Greatie), "in a day when such a friendship was unheard of" (*Great-Grandmother* 187). Her discovery of the tensions between different racial groups in the South is particularly difficult for Stella, who "had never even seen a Negro before [she] came to Illyria" (*Other Side* 231). She cannot accept that she should not make friends with Ron, the only other educated person of her age in the area, and tells him: "I'm sorry. It's out of context" (255). This friendship, considered by much of the white population to be unnatural, will cost Ron his life.

Madeleine L'Engle's mother, born in 1881, described her youth as a period haunted by the civil war "with the memory bitter indeed" (*Great-Grandmother* 157). She also said that it was not possible for the generations born after World War I "to understand the social barriers which existed after the war" (203) in the South. This is the tense period that Stella has to discover and, through her, the reader. Donald Hettinga presents the world of the novel in the following terms:

> An isolated coastal community in the southern United States is as alien to most contemporary readers as it was to [Stella]. It is alien in part because of the social setting, a time and place in which the wounds of the civil war were still festering, a world in which African-American vigilante riders coursed the night in unhappy mimicry of white-hooded Ku Klux Klan riders [173].

However, it is above all the spiritual atmosphere which surprises the young atheist Stella. Not just the omnipresence of the Christian religion, practised with varying degrees of sincerity, but also the haunted landscape "in which voodoo haunts the swamps that surround the Christian community" (Hettinga 173) and where "a parasol-bearing Anglican white woman will drive her buggy into the scrub to consult a black fortune-teller she considers less than human" (173). Faced with this complex world, Stella has to adapt to survive and this necessary adaptation includes making a decision for or against the values of the community her husband belongs to. She has to be converted, for if she does not choose wholeheartedly to serve the Good, she will automatically open the door to the powers of Evil. As Donald Hettinga remarks, "even though she never prays the sinner's prayer" (172), Stella comes to a place where she is able to believe, to act by faith and to cast Evil far from herself.

In *The Other Side of the Sun*, L'Engle portrays a society haunted by Christ and his angels, but equally by the powers of darkness; a world where the happiness of all the characters depends on the result of a spiritual battle which has been going on for generations and is still far from any kind of victory. The author uses images and symbols of Christ to frame her universe. On the first page of the first section when Stella returns to Illyria with her grandson and tells him about the traumatic events in her youth, the reader meets a pelican who dives into the water before flying back up into the sky (*Other Side* 9). In the final paragraph of the novel, when an elderly Stella leaves Illyria for the last time, the pelican reappears, dives and flies back up again (352). In Christian symbolism, the pelican represents "Jesus, our redeemer who gave his life for our redemption" (Saunders). Pelicans symbolising Christ can be found in numerous literary and theological texts, including the 25th canto of Dante's *Paradiso*, the writings of St. Basil (one of Madeleine L'Engle's favorite authors), and even Shakespeare's *Hamlet* (Act IV, scene V). In L'Engle's novel, the appearance of pelicans evokes the benevolent presence of Christ within the community. The dolphins in the ocean near Illyria convey the same message. In Christian symbolism, the dolphin is seen as "light-bearer, representing Christ" ("Dolphin") or sometimes the Christian who follows Him. To accentuate their importance, Des informs Stella that "dolphins and pelicans belong to Illyria" while the "sharks and buzzards [belong] to [...] all the hate and anger left by the war" (*Other Side* 92). This interpretation is confirmed during the final conflict when Honoria calls on the Heavens for help. She drives away the buzzards and asks the pelicans to come and fight with the Christian community. Her prayer is answered.

The spiritual atmosphere of *The Other Side of the Sun* also comes from the angels, which Stella encounters first of all in Mado's diaries and which reappear at keys moments in the novel. As Harry Morgan observes, "these angelic figures are omnipresent" (147) in L'Engle's children's books and particularly in the fantasy novels. However, the angels in *The Other Side of the Sun* do not resemble those which we find elsewhere in her work. In the Time series, for example, the angels are definite characters, just as much as the humans; they have names, they talk and they act. On the other hand, the angels in Illyria are little more than an invisible, barely tangible presence. Mado sees them as guardian angels who, according to the former pope Benedict XVI, are pure spirits who "bring us great help and consolation: they walk at our side and protect us in all circumstances, they defend us from danger, and to them we can turn at any moment" (Benedict Forum). In the novel, after Mado's death, Clive and Honoria "keep the angels close. They won't let them go far from Illyria" (*Other Side* 268) and keep their ears open for any message the angels may bring.

In the introduction, there is no doubt that the elderly Stella is a Christian believer and that she feels the need to know what Illyria's guardian angels think of her plans. At the end of the novel, she concludes that the angels "go with people rather than places" (352) and decides to trust them to watch over her grandson and his family even if Illyria is sold. The elderly Stella's faith is alluded to at various moments in the narrative where she, as narrator, temporarily steps out of the plot to comment on the action. For example, this occurs when the wind at Illyria reminds her that "the wind of the Spirit" (51) always blows in the same place. However, when she first arrives, Stella knows neither angels nor the Spirit, but her pilgrimage to faith has already started. Shortly before she leaves England, her father dies and this sad event makes her question the things she had always believed before: "My father didn't [...] believe in the things the Church teaches. And I just took it for granted that he was right. Until his death, then [...] it didn't make sense, the idea that my father was not, that death had stopped his being" (273).

In spite of Stella's lack of faith, she discovers much later that her arrival was perceived by the community of believers in Illyria as an answer to Honoria's prayers asking God for help in their troubles. All the members of this community except Terry, Stella's husband, and Ron, whose faith is fragile and whose situation is dangerous, are either very old or mentally backward. Only James, Olivia, Des, Honoria, Clive and Saintie, three white and three black friends, all over seventy-five years old, and the twins Willy and Harry, the "holy fools" (*Great-Grandmother* 194), are fully committed to the fight against the powers of Evil. They need reinforcements. Several years previously, these people, together with Mado and her husband, had belonged to an experimental community called Nyssa, after St. Gregory of Nyssa, one of the first Christian leaders to openly oppose slavery.[2] He was also, together with his brother St. Basil and his sister St. Macrina, one of Madeleine L'Engle's favorite heroes and role models. In the novel, James, Des and Olivia's cousin, inherited the property which would become Nyssa, and promptly freed all the slaves working there, inviting those who wished to join him and his friends and relatives as free members of his new community. The black children received a good education there. Every morning and evening all the members gathered together for prayer and worship (*Other Side* 139). For Des, they were "one family, white and black" (48) and, as Clive, Honoria's husband, informs Stella, life at Nyssa for the former slaves was nothing like the life other black people were living elsewhere at the time: "Slaves didn't have no names, excepting what their masters give them [...] like a horse or a dog [...] but that's not the way it was at Nyssa and I was born at Nyssa. I always knowed who I am" (109).

Confident in his own identity and fully accepting the Faith he was raised in, Clive becomes a mature believer and knows his Bible well. In the novel, he only quotes from it on rare occasions, but L'Engle almost always describes him holding a Bible in his hand, "turning it in his dark fingers, as though seeking strength" (110), in order to remind the reader of the source of his goodness and that of his wife. However, the happiness and racial harmony which reign at Nyssa attract the hatred and suspicion of many in the white population for, according to Mado: "Nyssa is in the world and worldly people always want to destroy those whose true home is in heaven" (139). In the end Nyssa is burned to the ground and the community members have to find shelter elsewhere, many of them in Illyria. Stella learns that for most of the population, like Uncle Hoadley, "Nyssa is gone" (44), but for the former community members, Nyssa was more than a place, it was state of mind which still lives on in Illyria. Before the final conflict, Clive calls on "all of us who were Nyssa and who are Illyria" (319), in spite of their obvious weakness, to commit themselves to fighting a spiritual battle.

Finding herself in this foreign spiritual atmosphere, linked to a past she never knew, Stella gradually opens up to her surroundings. Her husband has told her to trust Clive and Honoria and she loves them at once, but she hears many things she doesn't understand, like prayer. Mado, the foreign bride who had come to this corner of the American South before her, wrote about guardian angels in her diaries, a concept which, for Stella "were not part of [her] father's cosmology" (72). In addition, the aunts quote from the Bible and the spiritual classics, expecting everyone to recognise the words, but Stella has to admit that she "knows Plato lots better" (75). At the same time, she becomes aware of the darkness which also haunts the South.

The evil threatening Illyria is embodied in the Zenumin family and their pagan religious practices. They frighten Stella who, like her creator, has been since her early childhood, "terrified of witches, with an instinctive fear of those who want to exercise controlling power over others" (*Rock* 249). The Hebrew word transcribed as *zenunim*[3] means debauchery or adultery and there may be a link between the Zenumins in the novel and Eisheth Zenunim, the angel of prostitution in Jewish mythology, who is one of the wicked angel Sammael's four evil companions and who devours the souls of the damned. Grandmother Zenumin, scary and voracious at the same time, attempts to read the lines on Stella's hand and threatens to magically kill her unborn child. She terrifies Stella when she declares that she intends to sacrifice five rams, five male goats, five lambs and a newborn baby to her dark gods. Belle Zenumin, the grandmother's adulterous but vulnerable daughter, scratches Stella's face and pulls her hair. She accuses the British woman of having stolen her son, Ron, and declares that her mother would not hesitate to use voodoo against Stella. Tron, Belle's other son, has links with the mysterious and frightening horsemen, both white and black, who ride up and down the beaches at night. In addition, Ron, the only Zenumin on the side of the angels, tells Stella how Honoria's son Jimmy was lynched by a group of white horsemen who resemble the Ku Klux Klan. Profoundly disturbed by these events, Stella wonders why her father had not "taught her about the real world" (*Other Side* 87), as his rationalist philosophy seems more and more inadequate faced with the challenges she encounters in her new home.

But it is not only the evil in the world that pushes Stella towards the Faith. L'Engle indicates she that she is also attracted by the believers she meets, with all their doubts, fears and questions. The great-aunts, Honoria and Clive quickly become her friends, but it is James and his faith that impress her the most at first. Never having gone to church before, Stella does not really want to go to the Sunday service, but she is agreeably surprised by the experience: "Cousin James read the office of Morning Prayer with authority and courtesy, and I was not embarrassed. I felt that even my father, who found all churches a blasphemy, all prayer a self-indulgence, would not have been offended. What Cousin James was doing was wholly real" (161). At James's house, Stella is equally impressed by the love shown to his sister Xenia, obliged to stay permanently in bed as the result of a heart attack. Everyone talks to her and shakes her hand. Miss Harris reads to her from a variety of books and Saintie, a former slave, reads her passages from the Bible every evening.

Mado's diaries, her joy in life and her faith in the protection of her guardian angel, even in the hardest moments, also give Stella an example to follow. Mado's humility enables Stella to realise that innocence may even "be a form of sin" (86). This realisation motivates her to ask Clive to teach her what the Bible says (174). Equally, Mado helps Stella to understand that God's love is urging her to take sides in the battle against the powers of darkness which surround her (141) ; a point of view which the young British woman is obliged to take seriously considering the great similarities between her situation and that which had confronted Mado two generations earlier. In the same ways, the prayers of the community members, the simple ones pronounced by the twins or Honoria's passionate entreaties, Clive's prophetic words and even Olivia's obvious spiritual struggles help Stella along her own personal path to faith. Olivia explains that, in the South, you do not "have much trouble believing in the devil," but wish that "believing in God were that easy" (201), a feeling that Stella comes to understand with no trouble at all. In her own words, Stella "did not know how to pray" (206) and "do[es]n't know God" (292), but, as she watches the others pray, she begins to learn.

Nevertheless, all those who claim to believe in Christ and serve his church do not give the same impression. Irene, who is very active in her parish in Jefferson, is also very superstitious. She regularly consults her horoscope, asks the Zenumin women to read her palm, tries to steal consecrated wafers for voodoo rites and seeks guidance in her Bible by opening it at random, closing her eyes and stabbing the page with a pin. Her husband, Hoadley, despite his Christian commitment, "plans a mass kidnapping to ship black citizens to Africa on a flotilla of white-owned pleasure craft" (Hettinga 173). Cousin Sarah Renier and her three sisters, whose social life is centred on the local church, are "acid and bitter" and do "not have a kind word to say for anybody" (*Other Side* 232). Stella has to distinguish between the members of her new family in order to work out who is really serving the Good

In the end it is Ron, the only character to have received an education like Stella's, who shows her the strength of the spiritual forces around Illyria, for he accepts them in spite of himself. Ron says he does "not have the spiritual sophistication to believe in a God of love." He recognises that neither his mother's harmful, occult powers nor Honoria's spiritual gifts were "included in [his] education" (129). However, he is incapable of rejecting them and finally admits he is "trapped by those angels" (268) of Mado's, who prevent him from doing anything except follow the Good, even if he must die in doing it.

Just before the final conflict, Stella prays her first prayer, crying to a God she does not yet know and in whom she only half believes: "God, be! Please be" (269). Shortly afterwards, Clive places a small metal cross in front of her and, even if the gesture is not explicit, the reader is led to believe that she picks it up. Her spirit continues to seek the reality of prayer.

When the time comes to fight, Stella and her friends have to face the forces of Evil head on. Grandmother Zenumin and her grandson, Tron, threaten to kill the child in Stella's womb and try to make her take part in a satanic ritual. At long last, surrounded by the faith of the community she loves, Stella manages to take the step of faith she needs to save herself and throws the grandmother's voodoo doll into the fire. The scene is extremely frightening and the horror of all the Zenumins' small, cruel gods is effectively evoked. Stella feels as if she is suffocating and "has death in the pit of [her] stomach," her "nostrils filled with the stench of decay" as if she is being "sucked into a vast drooling mouth of evil" (337). Finally, drawing her strength from the faith that gives her strength every day, Honoria acts out the part of the prophet Elijah before Queen Jezebel and the prophets of Baal (1 Kings, ch. 18). She condemns Evil and drives out the darkness. As Stella sees it depart, she is able at last to believe that the God she has heard so much about may eventually win the cosmic conflict.

As Stella's spiritual pilgrimage is presented here, it would be possible to suspect that the whole novel must be full of spiritual conversations and biblical quotations, but this is not the case. The plot is fast-moving and full of suspense. The reader is drawn in, with Stella, to an exotic and somewhat frightening world. In addition, the fact that L'Engle uses a narrator who knows nothing of the customs and beliefs of the country she encounters makes it possible to maintain a certain neutrality and to avoid religious didacticism. As Flannery O'Connor declares: "The real novelist, the one with an instinct for what he is about, knows that he cannot approach the infinite directly, that he must penetrate the natural human world as it is" (163). L'Engle always respects this principle and her novel is profoundly realistic. For Carole Chase, "the horror and stupidity of racism in the Old South are clearly spelled out" (132) in the plot and all the characters suffer from problems which could have been avoided with a minimum of common sense and good will on both sides. It is in this world of prejudice, violence and human weakness that highly fallible people try to live out their fragile faith.

The final message of the novel is neither exotic not supernatural, even if L'Engle gives the impression that one may need divine assistance to live it out. The Zenumins are wrong because they "don't love [...] They bow down and they kiss Hate and they worship" (*Other Side* 151). The nightriders too, both black and white, represent "darkness and hate [...] darkness [that] is not a color. It's a choking of the soul" (225). On the other hand, the Nyssa/Illyria people love. The twins hold Stella and Ron in their "circle of love" (263). Clive shows Stella that the cross is a symbol of love and tells her that love is the only method that God has given to men to help them live happy and fulfilled lives and there "ain't no other way" (328). Love is therefore Stella's vocation in Illyria and what she should do there.

Notes

1. Quotation from William Shakespeare, *Twelfth Night*, Act I, Scene II and Madeleine L'Engle, *The Other Side of the Sun* (1971), Greenwich, CT: Fawcett Crest, 1972, p.53.

2. See Gregory of Nyssa, *Homilies on Ecclesiastes*, 4. The three dolphins in L'Engle's novel *The Arm of the Starfish* are called Gregory, Basil and Macrina.

3. It is possible that Madeleine L'Engle made a mistake and got the m and the n the wrong way round.

Works Cited

Avent, Mary L'Engle "Sister." *Listening for Madeleine: A Portrait of Madeleine L'Engle in Many Voices*. Ed. Leonard S. Marcus. New York: Farrar, Straus and Giroux, 2012. 27–34. Print.

Bruce, Nancy. "Madeleine in the Making." *Listening for Madeleine: A Portrait of Madeleine L'Engle in Many Voices*. Ed. Leonard S. Marcus. New York: Farrar, Straus and Giroux, 2012. 35–38. Print.

Chase, Carole. *Suncatcher*. Philadelphia: Innisfree Press, 1995. Print.

"The Dolphin in Christian Symbolism." *The American Ecclesiastical Review*, 1890. Web.

Franklin, Hugh. "Madeleine L'Engle." *The Horn Book Magazine* (August 1963). Web.

Gregory of Nyssa. *Homilies on Ecclesiastes* 4. Web.

Hettinga, Donald R. "A Great Cloud of Witnesses." *The Swiftly Tilting Worlds of Madeleine L'Engle*. Ed. Luci Shaw. Wheaton, IL: Harold Shaw Publishers, 1998. Print.

"Ilsa (novel)." *Absolute Astronomy*. Web.

L'Engle, Madeleine. *Herself: Reflections on a Writing Life*. Colorado Springs: Shaw Books, 2001. Print.

_____. *Ilsa*. New York: The Vanguard Press, 1946. Print.

_____. *The Other Side of the Sun* (1971). Greenwich, CT: Fawcett Crest, 1972. Print.

_____. *The Rock That Is Higher*. Wheaton, IL: Harold Shaw Publishers, 1993. Print.

_____. *The Summer of the Great-Grandmother*. New York: Farrar, Straus and Giroux, 1974. Print.

Morgan, Harry. "Mythopoétique de l'ange dans les littératures dessinées et le roman pour la jeunesse dans l'aire culturelle nord-américaine." *Cahiers Robinson* 26 (2010): 147–158. Print.

O'Connor, Flannery. *Mystery and Manners*. New York: Farrar, Straus and Giroux, 1969. Print.

Rosenberg, Aaron. *Madeleine L'Engle*. New York: Rosen, 2006. Print.

Saunders, Rev. William. "The Symbolism of the Pelican." *Arlington Catholic Herald* (2003). Web.

Zarin, Cynthia. "The Storyteller." *The New Yorker* (12 April 2004): 60–67. Print.

Selected Works

Works by Madeleine L'Engle

BOOKS FOR CHILDREN
(mainly for the age group 8 to 13)

The Anti-Muffins (1980).
Dance in the Desert (1969).
Ladder of Angels: Stories from the Bible Illustrated by the Children of the World (1979).
Meet the Austins (1960).
The Other Dog (2001).
The Sphinx at Dawn (1989).
The Twenty-Four Days Before Christmas (1984).
A Wind in the Door (1973).
A Wrinkle in Time (1962).

NOVELS FOR YOUNG ADULTS
(mainly for the age group 12 to 18)

An Acceptable Time (1989).
And Both Were Young (1949)—principally for girls.
The Arm of the Starfish (1965).
Camilla Dickinson (1951)—later published as Camilla, principally for girls.
Dragons in the Waters (1976).
A House Like a Lotus (1984)—principally for girls.
The Joys of Love (2008)—principally for girls.
Many Waters (1986).
The Moon by Night (1963)—principally for girls.
Prelude (1968).
A Ring of Endless Light (1980)—principally for girls.
A Swiftly Tilting Planet (1978).
Troubling a Star (1994).
The Young Unicorns (1968).

NOVELS FOR ADULTS

Certain Women (1992).
Ilsa (1946).
A Live Coal in the Sea (1996).
The Love Letters (1966).
The Other Side of the Sun (1971).
A Severed Wasp (1982).
The Small Rain (1945).
A Winter's Love (1957).

SHORT STORIES

Many of these stories have been published in several magazines and anthologies. Only the first publication is indicated here.

"The Birthday." *The Smith College Monthly* (April 1941).
"Evening of a Governess." *The Tanager* (February 1945).
"A Full House: An Austin Family Story." *Wintersong: Christmas Readings.* By Madeleine L'Engle and Luci Shaw. Wheaton, IL: Harold Shaw, 1996.
"Intergalatic P.S. 3." (1970). First published as a pamphlet.
"Madame." *The Dude* (1957).
"The Mountains Shall Stand Forever."

Selected Works

Opinion: The Literary Section of the Smith College Weekly (April 1940).
"Night at the Fair." *The Smith College Monthly* (December 1940).
"The One Hundred and First Miracle." *Nine Visions: A Book of Fantasies.* Edited by Andrea LaSonde Melrose. New York: Seabury Press, 1983.
"Please Wear Your Rubbers." *Mademoiselle* (November 1944).
"Poor Little Saturday." *Fantastic Universe* (October 1956).
"Rob Austin and the Millennium Bug." *Second Sight: Stories for a New Millennium.* New York: Philomel, 1999.
"The Shades." *The Tanager* (December 1944)—claims to be a translation of a story written in French by Germaine Courtmont, but probably actually written by L'Engle.
"Ship's Doctor." *Opinion: The Literary Section of the Smith College Weekly* (October 1939).
"Six Good People" (originally written in 1933). *First Words: Earliest Writing from Favorite Contemporary Authors.* Edited by Paul Mandelbaum. Chapel Hill, NC: Algonquin, 1993.
"Summer Camp." *The Threshold* (August 1943).
"Transfiguration." *Stories for the Christian Year.* Edited by Eugene H. Peterson. New York: Collier, 1994.
"White in the Moon the Long Road Lies." *Opinion: The Literary Section of the Smith College Weekly* (June 1939).

Plays

18 Washington Square South: A Comedy in One Act (1944).
How Now Brown Cow (1949)—with Robert Hartung, first performed in 1945.
The Journey with Jonah (1967).

Journals/Memoirs

A Circle of Quiet (1972).
From This Day Forward: The Story of a Marriage (1988)—also published as *Two-Part Invention*.
The Irrational Season (1977).
The Summer of the Great-Grandmother (1974).

Poetry

A Cry Like a Bell (1987).
Lines Scribbled on an Envelope (1969).
The Ordering of Love (2005).
The Risk of Birth (1974).
The Weather of the Heart (1978).

Biblical Midrash
(Some of these books also appear in other categories)

Dance in the Desert (1969).
And It Was Good (1983).
The Journey with Jonah (1967).
Ladder of Angels: Stories from the Bible Illustrated by the Children of the World (1979).
Many Waters (1986).
Sold into Egypt (1989).
The Sphinx at Dawn (1989).
A Stone for a Pillow (1986).

Reflections on Life
(Faith, Art, Writing, Friendship, etc.)

Bright Evening Star: Mystery of the Incarnation (2001).
Friends for the Journey (1997), with Luci Shaw.
The Glorious Impossible (1990).
Madeleine L'Engle Herself: Reflections on a Writing Life (2001), with Carole F. Chase.
Mothers and Daughters (1997), with Maria Rooney, photographs and texts.
Mothers and Sons (1999), with Maria Rooney, photographs and texts.
My Own Small Place: Developing the Writing Life (1999).
Penguins and Golden Calves: Idols and Icons in Antarctica and Other Spiritual Places (1996).
The Rock That Is Higher: Story as Truth (1993).

Trailing Clouds of Glory: Spiritual Values in Children's Literature (1985), with Avery Brooke.
Walking on Water: Reflections on Faith and Art (1982).

PRAYERS, READINGS
AND MEDITATIONS

Anytime Prayers (1994), with Maria Rooney.
Everyday Prayers (1974).
Glimpses of Grace, with Carole F. Chase, an anthology of daily readings.
Miracle on 10th Street (1998), readings for the Christmas season.
A Prayerbook for Spiritual Friends (1999), with Luci Shaw.
Prayers for Sunday (1974).
Wintersong (1996), with Luci Shaw, readings for the Christmas season.

SELECTED ARTICLES
AND BOOK CHAPTERS

"Allegorical Fancy: Mortal Dealings with Cosmic Questions." *Christianity Today* (8 June 1979).
"Before Babel." *Horn Book* (December 1966).
"Believing Impossible Things." *Theory into Practice* (Autumn 1982).
"Bones." *Rattling Those Dry Bones: Women Changing the Church.* June Steffensen Hagen, ed. San Diego: LuraMedia, 1995.
"Childlike Wonder and the Truths of Science Fiction." *Children's Literature* (1982).
"The Danger of Wearing Glass Slippers." *Elementary English* (1964).
"Defining a Good Children's Book." *Theory into Practice* (Winter 1982), with Stephen Roxburgh, Charlotte Zolotow and Ginny Moore Cruse.
"Doubt: How Can I Question and Still Believe?" *Wrestling with Angels* (1993).
"Fantasy Is What Fantasy Does." *Children's Literature in the Classroom: Weaving Charlotte's Web.* Janet Hickman and Bernice E. Cullinan, eds. Needham Heights, MA: Christopher-Gordon, 1989.
"George MacDonald: Nourishment for a Private World." *Reality and the Vision.* Philip Yancey, ed. Dallas: Word, 1990.
"The Heroic in Literature and in Living." *The Lion and the Unicorn* (June 1989).
"The Key, the Door, the Road." *Horn Book* (1964).
"Knowing Things Ahead of Time." *Things in Heaven and Earth: Exploring the Supernatural.* Harold Fickett, ed. Brewster, MA: Paraclete, 1997.
"Light's Companion." *Parabola: Myth, Tradition, and the Search for Meaning* (Summer 1997).
"The Mysterious Appearance of Canon Tallis." *Spirit and Light: Essays in Historical Theology.* Madeleine L'Engle and William B. Green, eds. New York: Seabury Press, 1976.
"The One-Winged Chinese Bird." *Childhood Education* (1974).
"Personal Literary Statement." *The Reading Teacher* (September 1990).
"Subject to Change without Notice." *Theory into Practice* (Autumn 1982).
"Tell Me a Story." *Sharing the Journey.* Katherine Ball Ross, ed. New York: Sterling, 1997.
"What Is Real?" *Language Arts* (1978).
"What May I Expect from My Church?" *Churches on the Wrong Road.* Stanley Atkins and Theodore McConnell, eds. Chicago: Gateway Editions, 1986.

SELECTED PUBLISHED SPEECHES
AND LECTURES

Acceptance Speech upon Receiving the Margaret Edwards Award (1998).
"Are We Human?" (7 February 1988)—radio broadcast Chicago Sunday Evening Club.

"Do I Dare Disturb the Universe?" (1984)—pamphlet.
"The Expanding Universe. Newberry Acceptance Speech." *Horn Book Magazine*, vol. 39 (1963).
"Separation from the Stars" (The Fifth Archibald Yell Smith IV Lecture) and "The Rewards of Failure" (1986).

Selected Forewords, Afterwords, Prefaces and Introductions

Dates refer to the forewords, etc., not to the first publication of the book.

Anders, Isabel. Introduction to *Awaiting the Child: An Advent Journal* (2005).
Arnold, Johann Christoph. Foreword to *Be Not Afraid: Overcoming the Fear of Death* (2002).
Arnold, Johann Christoph. Foreword to *I Tell You a Mystery: Life, Death and Eternity* (1997).
Arnold, Johann Christoph. Foreword to *Seeking Peace: Notes and Conversations Along the Way* (1998).
Bernall, Misty. Foreword to *She Said Yes: The Unlikely Martyrdom of Cassie Bernall* (1999).
Butler, Francelia, and Richard Rotert. Introduction to *Triumphs of the Spirit in Children's Literature* (1986).
Ford, Paul F. Foreword to *Companion to Narnia* (1980).
Harding, Rachel. Foreword to *A Book of Condolences: Classic Letters of Bereavement* (1999).
Lewis, C.S. Foreword to *A Grief Observed* (1989).
Mandelker, Amy, and Elizabeth Powers, eds. Introduction to *Pilgrim Souls: A Collection of Spiritual Autobiographies* (1999).
Masefield, John. Afterword to *The Midnight Folk* (2000).
Rey, Margaret. Introduction to *The Complete Adventures of Curious George* (1994).
Ross, Maggie. Foreword to *The Fire of your Life: A Solitude Shared* (1983).
Roth, Nancy. Foreword to *Organic Prayer: A Spiritual Gardening Companion* (1993).
Sayers, Dorothy L. Introduction to *The Mind of the Maker* (1987).
Shaw, Luci. Foreword to *Life Path: Personal and Spiritual Growth through Journal Writing* (1991).
Vance, Barbara. Foreword to *Parenting is as Parenting Does: Getting off the Merry-Go-Round* (2006).

Works About Madeleine L'Engle

Books About Madeleine L'Engle

Anders, Isabel. *40-Day Journey with Madeleine L'Engle* (2009).
Baptiste, Tracey. *Madeleine L'Engle* (2009).
Chase, Carole F. *Suncatcher: A Study of Madeleine L'Engle and Her Writings* (1995).
Gonzales, Doreen. *Madeleine L'Engle* (1991).
Hettinga, Donald R. *Presenting Madeleine L'Engle* (1993).
Kirkpatrick, Katherine, ed. *A Circle of Friends: Remembering Madeleine L'Engle* (2009).
Marcus, Leonard S., ed. *Listening for Madeleine: A Portrait of Madeleine L'Engle in Many Voices* (2012).
McClellan, Marilyn. *Madeleine L'Engle: Banned, Challenged and Censored* (2008).
Mooney, Rodney. *Madeleine L'Engle and Sacred Idleness* (2010).
Rosenberg, Aaron. *Madeleine L'Engle* (2006).
Shaw, Luci, ed. *The Swiftly Tilting Worlds of Madeleine L'Engle* (1998).

Books About Madeleine L'Engle and Others

Hein, Rolland. *Christian Mythmakers: C.S. Lewis, Madeleine L'Engle, J.R.R. Tolkien, George MacDonald, G.K. Chesterton & Others* (1998).
Oziewic, Marek. *One Earth, One People: The Mythopoeic Fantasy Series of Ursula Le Guin, Lloyd Alexander, Madeleine L'Engle and Orson Scott Card* (2008).

Book Chapters

Bloom, Harold. "Madeleine L'Engle." *Women Writers of Children's Literature* (1997).
Filmer-Davies, Kath. "Children from Dysfunctional Families: Instruments of Mythic Healing." *Fantasy Fiction and Welsh Myth* (1996).
DeRusha, Michelle. "Madeleine L'Engle: Writing Toward the Why." *50 Women Every Christian Should Know* (2014).
Hosier, Helen Kooiman. "Madeleine L'Engle." *100 Christian Women Who Changed the Twentieth Century* (2000).
Schmidt, Richard H. "Madeleine L'Engle: Teller of Tales." *Glorious Companions: Five Centuries of Anglican Spirituality* (2002).
Townsend, John Rowe. "Madeleine L'Engle." *A Sense of Story: Essays on Contemporary Children's Writers* (1971).

Critical Articles

Alexander, Jonathan. "Late L'Engle: The Wrinkles of Time, Redeemed." *Los Angeles Review of Books* (16 August 2015).
Avakian, Tracey. "The Wildness of Christianity: The Legacy of Madeleine L'Engle." *Commonweal* (26 October 2007).
Bray, Suzanne. "Disperser l'antique terreur : le Mal et comment le vaincre dans la trilogie du temps de Madeleine L'Engle." *Cahiers Robinson* (2015)—about overcoming evil in the Time trilogy.
Bray, Suzanne. "'Et que pourrais-je faire en Illyrie?' : La découverte du Sud et de ses dieux dans *The Other Side of the Sun* de Madeleine L'Engle." *Mélanges de Science Religieuse* (July–September 2014).
Bray, Suzanne. "Transforming Memories: Madeleine L'Engle's Recreation of Her Childhood Experiences in France and Switzerland." In Marcel Arbeit and Roman Trušník (ed.). *A View from Elsewhere* (2014).
Fisher, Leona W. "Mystical Fantasy for Children: Silence and Community." *The Lion and the Unicorn* vol. 14 (1990).
Forbes, Cheryl. "Supernatural Sagas of Good and Evil: The Foolish Things of Madeleine L'Engle." *Christianity Today* (8 June 1979).
Glass, Rona. "*A Wrinkle in Time* and *The High King*: Two Couples, Two Perspectives." *Children's Literature Association Quarterly* (Fall 1981).
Henneberger, Melinda. "I Dare You: Madeleine L'Engle on God, *The Da Vinci Code* and Aging Well." *Newsweek* (7 May 2004).
Maloney, Jennifer. "A New Wrinkle in Time." *Wall Street Journal* (16 April 2015).
Miller, Meghan. "Alike and Equal Are Not the Same Thing at All (Or: Remembering *A Wrinkle in Time*)." *Forever Young Adult*. 18 Jan. 2012.
Morgan, Harry. "Mythopoétique de l'ange dans les littératures dessinées et le roman pour la jeunesse dans l'aire culturelle nord-américaine." *Cahiers Robinson* (2010)—about angels in L'Engle's work.
Oziewicz, Marek. "The Time Quartet as Madeleine L'Engle's Theology." *Journal of the Fantastic in the Arts* 17.3 (2006).
Patterson, Nancy-Lou. "Angel and Psy-

chopomp in Madeleine L'Engle's 'Wind' Trilogy." *Children's Literature in Education* (Winter 1983).

Paul, Pamela. "*A Wrinkle in Time* and Its Sci-Fi Heroine." *New York Times.* 27 January 2012.

Scaperlanda, María Ruiz. "Madeleine L'Engle: An Epic in Time." *St. Anthony Messenger* (June 2000).

Schneebaum, Katherine. "Finding a Happy Medium: The Design for Womanhood in *A Wrinkle in Time*." *The Lion and the Unicorn* (December 1990).

Smedman, M. Sarah. "The 'Terrible Journey' Past *Dragons in the Waters* to *A House Like a Lotus*: Faces of Love in the Fiction of Madeleine L'Engle." *Science Fiction for Young Readers* (1993).

Steem, Cara Joy. "Listening as Heroic Action in L'Engle's *A Swiftly Tilting Planet*." *Mythlore* (Fall/Winter 2013).

Thomas, Sally. "Fantasy and Faith." *First Things* (November 2007).

Thomas, Trudelle H. "Spiritual Practices Children Understand: An Analysis of Madeleine L'Engle's Fantasy, *A Wind in the Door*." *International Journal of Children's Spirituality* vol. 13 (2008).

Warner, Mary. "Teaching the Madeleine L'Engle Tetralogy: Using Allegory and Fantasy as Antidote to Violence." *ERIC* (1999).

Wood, Naomi. "Introduction: Children's Literature and Religion." *Children's Literature Association Quarterly* (Spring 1999).

Zarin, Cynthia. "The Storyteller: Fact, Fiction, and the Books of Madeleine L'Engle." *The New Yorker* (12 April 2004).

SELECTED INTERVIEWS

Braver, Barabara Leix. "Becoming More Human: An Interview with Madeleine L'Engle." *Christian Century* (20 November 1985).

Hearne, Betsy. "A Mind in Motion: A Few Moments with Madeleine L'Engle." *School Library Journal* (June 1998).

Rausen, Ruth. "An Interview with Madeleine L'Engle." *Children's Literature in Education* vol. 19 (1975).

Risher, Dee Dee. "Listening to the Story: A Conversation with Madeleine L'Engle." *The Other Side Online* (March-April 1998).

Voss, Janice. Interview by Jacki Lyden. *National Public Radio.* 8 Sept 2007.

Webb, Heather. "A Conversation with Madeleine L'Engle." *Mars Hill Review* (Winter/Spring 1996).

Wintle, Justin. "Madeleine L'Engle." *The Pied Pipers: Interviews with Influential Creators of Children's Literature.* Edited by Justin Wintle and Emma Fisher (1974).

ACADEMIC DISSERTATIONS/THESES

Hilder, Monika. "Educating the Moral Imagination: The Fantasy Literature of George MacDonald, C.S. Lewis, and Madeleine L'Engle." Simon Fraser University (2003).

About the Contributors

Suzanne Bray is a professor of British literature and civilization at Lille Catholic University in France. She specializes in the history of religious ideas, mainly in 20th century Britain and, in particular, in the interaction between theology and popular literature.

Sophie Dillinger teaches English at a high school in northern France. Her thesis for an MA in English literature at Lille Catholic University included work on "Women and Salvation in the Fantasy Novels of George MacDonald."

Carol S. Franko is an associate professor of English at Kansas State University where she teaches science fiction, fable and fantasy, utopian/dystopian fiction, and British literature. She has published on early 20th century and contemporary science fiction, utopias and dystopias, and fantasy.

Chantel Lavoie teaches in the department of English at the Royal Military College of Canada. She is the author of *Collecting Women: Poetry and Lives 1700–1780* (2009) and articles on Harry Potter, Gregor the Overlander, and boys in early children's literature.

Anne-Frédérique Mochel-Caballero has a Ph.D. in English literature. She teaches at the University of Picardie Jules Verne (France). She is a C.S. Lewis specialist and has published *L'Évangile selon C. S. Lewis* (*The Gospel According to C.S. Lewis*) (2011).

Gregory G. Pepetone is a professor of music and interdisciplinary studies at Georgia College & State University. He is the author of *Gothic Perspectives on the American Experience* (2003) and *Hogwarts and All: Gothic Perspectives on Children's Literature* (2012).

Gérald Préher is an associate professor of American literature at Lille Catholic University in the north of France. He specializes in the literature of the American South and the American short story. He has published extensively on Walker Percy, Elizabeth Spencer, Richard Ford, Reynolds Price and Shirley Ann Grau.

Naomi Wood is a professor of English at Kansas State University, where she teaches courses in children's and young adult literature, the history of childhood, and the

Victorian novel. She has published on Victorian and contemporary fantasists and is particularly interested in literary metaphysics.

Emily Louise Zimbrick-Rogers received a masters of divinity at Princeton Theological Seminary, an MFA in creative writing and a certificate in women's studies from Old Dominion University, and a BA in English from Wheaton College.

Index

Alps 3, 28–29, 35–36
Anglicanism 2, 34–35, 111, 134, 178
Antarctica 67, 75, 80–82, 87 131
Antisemitism 26, 33
Ashley Hall (Charleston) 16, 179
Auster, Paul 4

Bach, Johann Sebastian 112–17, 130, 135–36, 142; *St. Matthew Passion* 115
Barnett, Bion, Jr. (uncle) 18–19, 27, 33
Barnett, Bion Hall (grandfather) 27
Barnett, Charles (Charlot) 27
Barnett, Madeleine Hall (mother) 15
Barnett, William (uncle) 27
Barrie, James 121; *Peter Pan* 121
Barth, Karl 173
Benedict XVI (Pope) 182
Bernstein, Leonard 6, 33, 113, 131
Blake, William 117, 125, 128
Bolivar, Simon 24
Brent-Dyer, Elinor M. 32
Brittany 27–28, 30
Brontë, Charlotte 75, 78, 114, 119, 129; *Jane Eyre* 75–76, 78, 84, 119; *Villette* 129
Brown, Thomas E. 72, 74, 87

Camp, Charles Wadsworth (father) 4, 27–28, 35
Cathedral of St John the Divine 4, 7, 9–15
Central Park 4–5, 8, 10
Chamonix 29, 34–35
Charleston (South Carolina) 15–16, 23, 149, 179
Charvot, Yvonne (aunt) 27, 36
Châtelard School (Montreux) 29, 32, 36
Chesterton, G.K. 94, 106, 127–28, 132
Chopin, Frédéric 112–15, 117, 129
Civil War 17, 19, 21–24, 96, 130, 153, 180–81
Coleridge, Samuel Taylor 93, 95, 100, 106, 118
Collins, Suzanne 49, 64; *Gregor the Overlander* 64; *The Hunger Games* 43, 49

Community of the Holy Spirit 7, 36
Crosswicks 3, 69

Dante Alighieri 101, 122, 181; *The Divine Comedy* 122, 181
Darwin, Charles 95
The Day After (film) 60
The Diary of Anne Frank 68, 116
Dickens, Charles 92, 93, 119; *A Christmas Carol* 119; *Hard Times* 92
Donne, John 76–77

Eddington, Arthur 134–135
Einstein, Albert 72–74, 87, 93, 99, 123–24, 134–35, 140, 142
Elijah (prophet) 186

Fatio, Francis 21
Faulkner, William 150, 152–54, 157; *Absalom, Absalom!* 153; *As I Lay Dying* 152; "Dry September" 152
Florida 5, 15–17, 22, 24, 26–27, 29, 149–51, 178–79
France 5, 18–19, 27–31, 35, 127, 149, 179
Franklin, Hugh (husband) 6–7, 18, 69, 87
Franklin, Josephine (daughter) 6
Friedan, Betty 142
Frozen (film) 43

Gaboriau, Emile 34
Genesis (Bible) 2, 53–54, 62–63, 96, 99, 160–173, 176
Georgia 19, 26
Goshen (Connecticut) 6
Gothic (art or literature) 11, 22, 80, 112, 119, 123, 126, 129, 135, 179
Greenwich Village 5, 9, 15

Heinlein, Robert 70
Hildevert of Lavardin 72

Index

Housman, A.E. 151–152; *A Shropshire Lad* 151
Huxley, Thomas 122–23

Jacksonville (Florida) 5, 15–18, 22, 26, 178–79
Jeans, James 135
Jones, Alan (son-in-law) 7
Jones Voiklis, Charlotte (grand-daughter) 69, 87
Jung, C.G. 119

Kipling, Rudyard 70; *The Jungle Book* 70

Lee, Robert E. 23
Le Gallienne, Eva 6
Le Guin, Ursula K. 48, 63
L'Engle, Aunt Nadia 18
L'Engle, Madeleine (Mado) 16, 22, 178, 180
L'Engle, Madeleine (author): *An Acceptable Time* 51, 64, 90, 92–94, 96–99, 101, 103–3, 107, 123, 130, 146; *And Both Were Young* 28–34, 36; *And It Was Good* 164, 174–75; "The Birthday" 8; *Bright Evening Star* 34; *Camilla* (novel) 3, 9, 10; *Camilla Dickinson* (film) 10; *Certain Women* 6, 12, 14–15; *A Circle of Quiet* 33, 40; *Dance in the Desert* 162–63; *Dragons in the Waters* 16, 23–25; *18 Washington Square South* 6; "Evening of a Governess" 5, 8; *From This Day Forward* 4–6, 8, 15; *Genesis Trilogy* 2, 161–64, 169, 172–73; "George MacDonald: Nourishment for a Private World" 90, 98, 100–1, 103; "The Heroic" 90, 94, 94, 96, 101–2; *A House Like a Lotus* 16, 25; *Ilsa* 16–19, 21, 149, 156, 158, 179; *The Irrational Season* 160; *The Journey with Jonah* 162, 172; *Ladder of Angels* 163, 172; *A Live Coal in the Sea* 16, 26; *Many Waters* 2, 51–64, 90, 94, 96, 97, 99–102, 105–6, 161, 163–67, 169–70, 172–73; *Meet the Austins* 63–70, 78, 84–85, 87; *The Moon by Night* 65, 68, 76, 87, 113, 116, 119, 131; "The Mountains Shall Stand Forever" 30–31; "Night at the Fair" 29–30; *The Other Side of the Sun* 2, 16, 22, 25–26, 130, 150, 179–86; "Please Wear Your Rubbers" 8; "Poor Little Saturday" 16, 19, 21, 149; *A Ring of Endless Light* 65–68, 7–75, 78, 83–87; *The Rock That Is Higher* 49; *A Severed Wasp* 6, 9–10, 13, 26, 29–30; *The Small Rain* 6, 14, 17, 28–33, 179; *Sold into Egypt* 161, 169–172; *The Sphinx at Dawn* 163–64; *A Stone for a Pillow* 164–65, 171, 173; *The Summer of the Great-Grandmother* 28; *A Swiftly Tilting Planet* 43, 63–64, 80, 86, 90, 96, 99, 102, 104, 114, 121–22, 130, 144–46; "Transfiguration" 8–9; *Troubling a Star* 65–68, 74–75, 79–81, 83–87, 124, 131; *Walking on Water* 114, 124, 166; *The Weather of the Heart* 160, 175; "White in the Moon, the Long Road Lies" 16–17, 149–158;

A Wind in the Door 55, 90–93, 95, 105, 114, 121–23, 133, 138, 140–41, 143–45; *A Winter's Love* 29, 33–35; *A Wrinkle in Time* 1–2, 40–48, 52, 64, 66, 69, 77, 83, 90, 93–94, 98, 103, 114, 122, 126, 128, 133, 135, 143–45, 179; *The Young Unicorns* 10–11, 13, 15, 65, 86–87, 102
L'Engle, Susan Fatio 16, 22, 180
L'Engle, William 21, 23
Lewis, C.S. 2, 47, 49, 95, 106, 133–147; *The Chronicles of Narnia* 49, 133, 135, 136, 138–39, 146; "De descriptione temporum" 135; *The Discarded Image* 135; *The Last Battle* 136; *The Lion, the Witch and the Wardrobe* 139, 143; *The Magician's Nephew* 136, 139; *Out of the Silent Planet* 133, 145; *Perelandra* 136, 139, 146; *Prince Caspian* 136, 139; *The Silver Chair* 139; *That Hideous Strength* 137; *The Voyage of the Dawn Treader* 136, 139
Lovecraft, H.P. 140

MacDonald, George 2, 90–106; *At the Back of the North Wind* 95–97, 103, 105–8; "Fantastic Imagination" 94, 100; *Lilith* 91–93, 95, 101, 103–6, 168, 176; "On Polish" 100; *Paul Faber: Surgeon* 101; *Phantastes* 91, 94–95, 97, 103, 105; *The Princess and Curdie* 91, 101–2, 108; *The Princess and the Goblin* 91, 94; *Unspoken Sermons* 100–7
Metropolitan Museum of Art 4, 7, 10
Meyer, Stephenie: *Twilight* 43, 48
Midrash 2, 160–174
Montgomery, L.M. 4, 87, 174
Moore, Bishop Paul 11
Moore, Cornelia Duryée 10, 14–15
Mozart, Wolfgang Amadeus 80, 112–13, 115, 117, 130, 135

New York 3–15, 27–28, 31, 33, 35–36, 74, 81, 86–87, 179
Novalis 114, 119, 124, 127–29

O'Connor, Flannery 77, 186

Paris 19, 27, 30–34, 117
Poe, Edgar Allan 129
Proust, Marcel 31

Romanticism 2, 111–31, 135
Rowling, J.K. 44, 48; *Harry Potter* 44, 48–49
Roy, Léna (grand-daughter) 7, 69, 87

St. Augustine 101, 116
St. Basil 181, 183, 187
St. Gregory of Nyssa 183, 187
St. Hilda and St. Hugh's Episcopal School 7, 162
Salinger, J.D. 9; *Catcher in the Rye* 9
Schumann, Robert 113–15, 117, 119–20, 129–30

Shakespeare, William 79–82, 87, 114, 142, 163, 180–81; *Hamlet* 19, 80, 123, 181; *Twelfth Night* 180, 186
Smith College 5, 16, 142, 149, 151
South Carolina 15, 25–27, 149
Staten Island ferry 5, 10
Stravinsky, Igor 112–13, 117, 129
Switzerland 27–33, 35, 98, 149, 179

Temple, Archbishop William 125
Thompson, Francis 80
Tolkien, J.R.R. 95, 100, 120–21, 130; "On Fairy Stories" 95

Vaughan, Henry 75
Venezuela 24–25

Wagner, Richard 112, 114–15, 117–18, 129–30, 135
Wallis, Jim 11, 130–31
Warburg, April 5
Washington Square 6, 10, 13–14
Welty, Eudora 149, 151–52; *One Writer's Beginnings* 152
West, Canon Edward Nason 11, 108
White, E.B. 70; *Charlotte's Web* 70–71, 73, 80
White, Gilbert 27, 30, 33
Wilkerson, David 11; *The Cross and the Switchblade* 11
Wolfe, Thomas 152, 154
Woolson, Constance Fenimore 149, 151
Wordsworth, William 93, 104, 117–18